Women in the British Army

'In the twenty-first century, the British armed forces continue to be anxious about deploying women in combat roles. Lucy Noakes tells us why. It is an invaluable guide to the trials and tribulations of military women during the two world wars. It is a riveting story from start to finish — a story for our time.'

Joanna Bourke, *Birkbeck College, London*

From Boadicea to Joan of Arc, through wars of occupation and resistance, to civil wars and world wars, women have been active participants in warfare at many different points in history and in many different situations. However, women's presence in the forces has consistently been viewed as problematic and in this fascinating, timely and engaging study Lucy Noakes examines women's role in the army, and female military organisations, during the First and Second World Wars, as well as during peacetime and the interwar and postwar periods.

Providing a unique examination of women's struggle for acceptance by the British army, Noakes argues that women in uniform during the first half of the twentieth century challenged traditional notions of gender and threatened to destabilise clear-cut notions of identity by unsettling the masculine territory of warfare. Noakes also examines the tensions that arose as the army attempted to reconcile its need for female labour with the desire to ensure that the military remained a male preserve.

Drawing on a range of archival sources, including previously unpublished letters and diaries, official documents, newspapers and magazines, *Women in the British Army* uncovers the gendered discourses of the army to reveal that it was a key site in the formation of male and female identities.

Lucy Noakes is Senior Lecturer in the School of Creative Arts, Film and Media at the University of Portsmouth. She is author of *War and the British: Gender and National Identity, 1939–1991* (1998).

Women's and Gender History
General Editor
June Purvis
Professor of Sociology, University of Portsmouth

Sylvia Pankhurst
Sexual politics and political activism
Barbara Winslow

Votes for women
June Purvis and Sandra Holton

Women's history
Britain 1850–1945
June Purvis (ed.)

The women's suffrage movement
A reference guide, 1866–1928
Elizabeth Crawford

Women in Teacher Training Colleges, 1900–1960
A culture of femininity
Elizabeth Edwards

Women, work and sexual politics in eighteenth-century England
Bridget Hill

Women workers and gender identities, 1835–1913
The cotton and metal industries in England
Carol E. Morgan

Women and work in Britain since 1840
Gerry Holloway

Outspoken women
British women writing about sex, 1870–1969, An anthology
Lesley A. Hall

Women's History, Britain 1700–1850
An introduction
Hannah Barker and Elaine Chalus

The Women's suffrage movement in Britain and Ireland
A regional survey
Elizabeth Crawford

Students: A gendered history
Carol Dyhouse

Women in the British Army
War and the gentle sex, 1907–1948

Lucy Noakes

Routledge
Taylor & Francis Group

LONDON AND NEW YORK

First published 2006
by Routledge
2 Park Square, Milton Park, Abingdon, Oxon OX14 4RN

Simultaneously published in the USA and Canada
by Routledge
270 Madison Ave, New York, NY 10016

Routledge is an imprint of the Taylor & Francis Group

© 2006 Lucy Noakes

Typeset in Garamond by
Newgen Imaging Systems (P) Ltd, Chennai, India
Printed and bound in Great Britain by
The Cromwell Press, Trowbridge, Wiltshire

British Library Cataloguing in Publication Data
A catalogue record for this book is available from the British Library

Library of Congress Cataloging in Publication Data
Noakes, Lucy.
    Women in the British Army: war and the gentle sex,
1907–1948 / Lucy Noakes.
        p. cm. – (Women's and gender history)
    Includes bibliographical references and index.
        1. Great Britain. Army – Women. 2. Women soldiers –
Great Britain – History – 20th century. I. Title. II. Series.

    UB419.G7N63 2006
    355.0082'0941–dc22   2005024945

ISBN10: 0–415–39057–5 (pbk)
ISBN10: 0–415–39056–7 (hbk)
ISBN10: 0–203–08832–8 (ebk)

ISBN13: 978–0–415–39057–6 (pbk)
ISBN13: 978–0–415–39056–9 (hbk)
ISBN13: 978–0–203–08832–6 (ebk)

Contents

Acknowledgements

Over the course of researching and writing this book I have incurred many debts: to colleagues in academia, to the staff of the archives and libraries used, to the bodies which have provided financial support, to my editors at Routledge and last but not least, to friends and family.

I would first like to thank the institutions that have bestowed the financial support which has enabled this work. Southampton Institute provided me with a sabbatical to carry out some of the initial research whilst the University of Portsmouth and the Arts and Humanities Research Council supported me with a year's sabbatical which ensured the book's completion. The Centre for International and European Studies Research at the University of Portsmouth was a generous provider of funds for research trips to archives and libraries, as well as providing travel grants for conference attendance. Colleagues at both Southampton Institute and the University of Portsmouth provided a supportive and stimulating environment in which to carry out the research.

The field of war and gender remains a fascinating area in which to work, and this book has benefited from the expertise and generosity of colleagues working in this areas. Joanna Bourke, Susan Grayzel and Penny Summerfield have offered ongoing support and encouragement, which has been greatly appreciated. The ideas and arguments within this book have also been shaped by the comments of audiences and panel members at a number of seminars and conferences, especially members of the 'Women on the Borders' strand at the Popular Culture Association 2004 Annual Conference in San Antonio and members of the History Faculties at the University of Sussex and at McQuarie University, Sydney, in particular Mary Spongberg.

Staff at the British Library, the Mass-Observation material at the University of Sussex, National Archives, the National Army Museum, the Women's Library and above all the Imperial War Museum were extremely helpful and I would like to thank the Trustees of the Mass-Observation Archive at the University of Sussex, Dorothy Sheridan at the Mass-Observation Archive and Mary Wilkinson and Michael Moody at the Imperial War Museum. Philippa Grand at Routledge has been a helpful and encouraging editor, and I greatly appreciate her ongoing support of this project. June Purvis has been both a sympathetic series editor and a good colleague.

No book is written in a vacuum and I am grateful to friends and family for their support. Hannah, Calum and Skye have been a welcome distraction as well as an inspiration, and Martin Evans a supportive partner. Catherine Barry and Clive Myrie were great hosts in the United States as well as good friends. I would also like to thank Sue Bruley, Sara-Jane Finlay, Sue Harper, Trixie Lauterwasser, Marisa Linton, Paul Marchbank and Catherine Moriarty. This book is dedicated with love to my parents, Brenda and Ken Noakes.

Lucy Noakes
Brighton, 2005

Preface

Women have long played a vital role in the armed forces. At the beginning of the twenty-first century women have worked in, and alongside, the combatant forces of many nations: as camp followers in the European armies of the eighteenth and nineteenth centuries, as nurses and first aid personnel, in revolutionary movements as partisans and guerrillas and as support staff in modern-day armies. However, whenever women have moved into new roles in the armed forces, this movement has been accompanied by outcry and protest. Women, it has been claimed, would undermine the morale of the male soldiers, they would be physically and psychologically too weak to undertake the work that was demanded of them, their gender would preclude them from developing the team spirit and identity so necessary to the successful prosecution of warfare. War has long been seen as a fundamentally male sphere of interest, and combat the most masculine of all aspects of war.

In the British army today, approximately 70 per cent of all posts are open to women, with the exception of front-line combat roles. The decision to expand the positions open to women from 40 per cent to 70 per cent was taken in 1998, and was followed by a comprehensive review of gender roles in the British military. *Women in the Armed Forces*, the result of this review, was published by the Ministry of Defence in 2002, and upheld the ban on women serving in front-line combat roles within the army, although women could serve on fighting ships with the navy, and pilot fighter aircraft with the Air Force. The Report surveyed women's physical and psychological effectiveness in combat roles and concluded that although a small number of women were capable of reaching the required levels physical fitness, strength and endurance demanded of combat troops, the exclusion of women from front-line positions should be maintained. Despite experiments which demonstrated that mixed gender groups operated at least as effectively as single gender groups, the impact of including women in mixed gender combat groups was given as the prime reason for excluding women from these positions.[1] The Report concluded that 'the impact of women would ... involve a risk with no gains in terms of combat effectiveness' and that therefore combat positions should remain open to men alone.[2] The current exclusion of women from front-line combat roles in the British army is justified by a 'Catch 22' argument – the true impact on combat effectiveness and unit cohesion of using mixed gender groups in front-line combat can only be discovered by their use in warfare, but because there is a chance that this impact may be detrimental, the experiment cannot be undertaken.

Alongside the official reasoning which excludes women from combat positions, other, more invidious beliefs and attitudes act to limit women's position in the armed forces and to exclude them from the sense of group identity so important to successful military organisations. The British army remains a deeply conservative institution in which levels of sexual harassment and bullying remain high and in which the promotion of a 'macho' culture amongst recruits operates as a means of lessening individuality and building a sense of group culture in which traits such as sensitivity, understanding and compassion are routinely denigrated in favour of the unquestioning obedience and aggression believed to be essential to combat effectiveness.[3] To a large extent, this identity is based around a sense of masculinity which defines itself against femininity, and unofficial army culture appears to actively encourage sexist and homophobic attitudes. For example, *The Army Rumour Service*, the unofficial website of the British Army, currently includes numerous discussion strands which assume the male, heterosexual nature of readers and participants, such as 'Reader's Wives', which discusses the physical attributes of soldiers' wives and partners and strands ridiculing the sexual attractiveness of female soldiers.[4] Given this misogynistic environment, it is perhaps not surprising that women currently only make up just over 8 per cent of the British armed forces.[5] Although the Ministry of Defence, and the current British government, emphasise their commitment to equal opportunities for minorities within the British armed forces, and are actively attempting to recruit from non-traditional groups such as women as a means of making up a shortfall in recruitment numbers, attitudes amongst members of the army reflect an institutional culture which actively excludes and ridicules these minorities.

In this culture, women who work in positions closest to combat, and traditionally associated with masculinity, are often those singled out for abuse and ridicule. Well-known cases in the United States, such as the Tailhook scandal of 1991, following which the US government investigated charges of sexual misconduct amongst naval officers at an annual convention, the attempts to exclude women from the Citadel, an elite military training college in South Carolina, and ongoing allegations of sexual abuse and harassment of women at West Point Military Academy, demonstrate the extent of sexism within military cultures. When women attempt to enter the military, especially either as officers, in control of men, or in positions close to combat, they threaten to undermine the hegemonic masculinity of the organisation. The female combatant, and the female officer, in charge of men, is seen as transgressive and 'unnatural'; woman out of place.

The masculine nature of warfare is emphasised in times of war, when the role and status of front-line combat troops is highlighted. For the most part, female soldiers were notable by their absence in coverage of the 2003 invasion and subsequent occupation of Iraq, with embedded journalists often emphasising the role of the combat troops they were placed with. The two main exceptions to the absence of women soldiers in coverage of the war and occupation both served to demonstrate the ongoing belief that women do not belong in a combat zone. The extensive media coverage of the rescue of Private Jessica Lynch by United States special forces from her hospital bed emphasised her femininity, youth and fragility. Lynch went on to become an icon for Americans who supported the war; a young, pretty, vulnerable woman who went to fight for democracy in Iraq. However, her capture and subsequent rescue by male special forces demonstrated her inherent unsuitability for active military service. While the case of Jessica Lynch was intended to reassure the public that, in a hugely unpopular war, soldiers on 'our' side were acting in an honourable and heroic manner, the later coverage given to the abuse of Iraqi prisoners in Abu Ghraib jail illustrated the disjuncture between civil and military codes of behaviour in wartime. Coverage of Abu Ghraib emphasised the role of Private Lyndy England in the abuse and of army reserve Brigadier-General Janis Karpinski, the officer in charge of the jail and the only woman commander in the war zone. Both England, captured posing next to humiliated, naked, blindfolded Iraqi men, and Karpinski, whose regime allowed the abuse, were seen to have abandoned their femininity by their actions. The particular focus on England's role in the actual abuse demonstrates the continuity of beliefs that femininity endows women with nurturing, gentle qualities. Whilst examples of atrocities in warfare may be decried by civil society, there exists an unspoken recognition that they will sometimes occur, that they can be an unwelcome side effect of the encouragement of an aggressive, macho masculine identity amongst combat troops. When such behaviour is indulged in by women, it is seen as unnatural, unexpected and somehow worse than comparable male behaviour.

This book charts women's struggle for acceptance by the British army, and the army's concurrent struggle to find a balance between its need for women's labour and its desire to preserve the army, especially its fighting units, as a male preserve. As this prologue has shown, despite the social and cultural developments in Britain over the past decades, and the organisational changes within the British armed forces, the army remains an institution which chooses to largely define itself along gendered lines. Leaving aside the question of whether unconditional acceptance of women as soldiers by such an institution is ever possible, or indeed desirable, the continuity of the belief that combat is, by nature, a male occupation, is remarkable. Although the period that this book covers ends in 1948, almost sixty years ago, and although the Ministry of Defence, and the British armed forces, now identify themselves as 'equal opportunities employers', the continuities between the attitudes to military women in the period surveyed, and attitudes today, are striking. Women in the British army remain a marginalised group, excluded not only from combat positions but often from the masculine culture which dominates in the organisation. In today's army, continuity and conservatism continue to dominate modernisation and change in the military's attitude to its women.

1 Introduction

Gendering war

In May 2002, Captain Phillipa Tattersall became the first woman to complete the notoriously gruelling nine-week long training course necessary to become a member of the prestigious Royal Marines Commandos. The course, which has a 55 per cent drop out rate amongst its predominantly male participants, is widely recognised as one of the most demanding military training courses in the world. In order to pass the course, Captain Tattersall had to complete a 30 mile 'yomp' across Dartmoor in under eight hours, carrying a 35 lb pack and assault rifle, scale a 30 foot wall and sprint 217 yards whilst carrying a fellow trainee in a fireman's lift. Nevertheless, despite her achievement, she can only serve with the Commandos in a support role as the army still forbids women from serving in combat positions. The argument most often made to support the exclusion of women from front-line positions is that of physical strength, particularly the comparative upper body strength of men and women. As Captain Tattersall had proved herself to be as strong as, and stronger than, most men, her exclusion from combat had to be justified on different grounds. Major General Julian Thompson, a former commander of the Royal Marines Commandos, argued that 'women would be a disruptive influence on the team', thus encapsulating the belief that not only is combat a 'naturally' male occupation but that the presence of women threatens the masculine cohesion and efficiency of combat units.[1] As this introductory chapter will show, women in the military, particularly women in combat positions, or close to combat positions, have long been seen as problematic. From Boadicea to Joan of Arc, through wars of occupation and resistance, to civil wars and world wars, women have been active participants in warfare at many different points in history and in many different situations. However, the combatant woman appears again and again as, at best, an ambiguous figure and at worst as an object of hate.

Women in the military threaten to destabilise clear-cut ideas about gender by occupying the very male territory of warfare. These women have often been punished, both in myth and in reality. Boadicea, martial Queen of the Iceni who led her people against the Roman conquerors in the first-century AD, was, we are told, flogged and saw her daughters raped before poisoning herself rather than face further humiliation. Tales of the mythical Amazons tell again and again of their defeat and military and sexual subjugation by the forces of ancient Greece. Joan of Arc, having led the French forces to victory, was burnt at the stake for heresy. The term 'camp follower', used to describe the women who followed and provided services for the standing armies of eighteenth and nineteenth-century Europe, rapidly became an epithet for prostitute. Moving into the twentieth century, Klaus Thewelweit described in detail the fantasies of murdering 'Red' revolutionary women of the Freikorps, the proto-fascist armies which roamed Germany following the First World War.[2] A common nickname for the Auxiliary Territorial Service (ATS), the women's section of the army during the Second World War, was 'the groundsheets of the army' reflecting widely held beliefs about the prevalence of promiscuity amongst the largely working-class service. The underlying antagonism towards women in military uniform continued after the war: Joe, the narrator and hero of Braine's 1957 novel *Room at the Top* described a direct hit on a Women's Auxiliary Air Force (WAAF) mess room as 'simply a mess to be cleared up'.[3] In the late twentieth century, 24 female American soldiers reported that they had been sexually assaulted by their male comrades during the Gulf war.[4] Again and again, women who step outside the bounds of femininity to become active participants in warfare are punished by rape, defeat, humiliation and death. This introductory chapter explores some of the ways in which combat has been designated as a male activity, examining images of femininity and masculinity in warfare.

Wartime is a period in which the contours of gender roles can be seen extremely clearly. Men go away to fight; women remain at home. The image of the waiting woman is one which spans the centuries from the Lady of Shalot of Arthurian legend to the First World War posters telling men that 'Women of Britain Say Go!' to the campaign to 'Tie a yellow ribbon' for the US troops of the 1991 Gulf War and the 2003 Iraq War. However, in the two total wars of the twentieth century and in the more recent wars in Vietnam and Iraq, women have taken a more active role, working in uniform to provide the support services so vital to the successful maintenance of the military. At times, women have also taken part in combat. Although numerically insignificant, these women have a symbolic importance, both to those arguing for an expanded role for women in the military and to the nations for which they fought. The role of women combatants in Russia is probably the best known. During the First World War, the Russian Women's Battalion of Death fought in battle against German soldiers and in the Second World War the Soviet Union deployed women in combat, most notably as fighter pilots and snipers. Maria Botchkareva, the Commander of the Women's Battalion of Death claimed in her autobiography to have joined the army in 1915 as a foot soldier and combatant, on the special authority of the Tsar. In this rather self-serving memoir Botchkareva portrays her time in the ordinary army as a combination of masculine combat, fighting and bayoneting German soldiers, and female caring, rescuing over 50 men from no-man's-land following her first battle.[5] Botchkareva the female soldier also became a symbol of Russian resistance to German aggression, a position she drew upon in her creation of the Battalion of Death, formed primarily to shame Russian soldiers, increasingly deserting the Front during the 1917 Revolution, into military action. In her recruiting speech, Botchkareva encouraged potential recruits to set 'an example of self sacrifice' so that 'you men will realise your duty'.[6] Imagined less as an effective military unit than as a propagandist tool with which to lead men back into war and away from Bolshevism, 250 women from the Battalion of Death fought in the last Russian offensive, of whom 6 were killed and 30 wounded, before being disbanded by the Soviets.[7]

The Englishwoman Flora Sandes fought with the Serbian Army in the same war, a position she fell into almost by accident, having originally worked as a nurse in a military hospital in Valjero. When she returned from sick leave in England to find that the hospital was now behind enemy lines, she joined the Second Serbian infantry as a field hospital worker on the Serbian Army's long and arduous retreat through the mountains of Serbia and Albania. Accidentally falling behind her Unit whilst riding with a Captain Stayodinovitch, Sandes was enrolled as a soldier with one of the Units protecting the retreat from the rear, taking part in battle and eventually being promoted to Sergeant-Major. Sandes was awarded the King George Star, Serbia's highest military award, for her service, and after being wounded and declared unfit for military service, returned to Britain to raise funds for the Serbian cause.[8] Constance Marciewicz, a nationalist and suffragist, was Second in Command of 100 men at St Stephen's Green in the doomed Dublin Easter Rising of 1916 and was briefly sentenced to death by the British government for her part in the rebellion. However, these women are exceptions, either eulogised as extraordinary individuals as in the case of Botchkareva, Sandes and Marciewicz or ignored and warned not to 'speak of the services you have rendered' in the case of Soviet airwomen. Indeed, it seems that these women have been eulogised precisely because they *are* unusual. Established gender roles can survive the actions of a small number of individuals who are determined to break with convention virtually unscathed; it is when large numbers of people act in ways which have the potential to transgress social boundaries, as when women are drawn into the military in large numbers, that these roles are challenged.

The symbolic importance of the masculine nature of warfare can be seen in the organisation of militaries and in the status of their members. Within all militaries, the combatant man has the highest symbolic status; although in reality he may be the youngest, least educated and from the lowest social class of the army's recruits, and thus the most 'disposable' of its members, it is the combatant who is remembered on war memorials and eulogised in poetry, prose and film. Many militaries have also worked hard at separating these combatant men from their support services, especially when these are composed of, or include, women. In the First World War and well into the Second, British women worked with and alongside the military, not within it, as they were enrolled for service, not enlisted as men were. The American

Army resisted the idea of utilising women's labour during the First World War, and the Women's Army Auxiliary Corps, formed in 1942, was primarily employed in communications and clerical work, and kept well away from combat. While camp followers were sometimes described as 'belonging to the army', and could at times be subject to military discipline their status was very different from that of the soldiers, and they were often perceived by civilian society as an embodiment of immoral behaviour and a potential threat to military morale.[9] The role of militarised women, from the camp followers of the eighteenth century onwards, has been secondary to that of the militarised man, the fighter. Although the work of these support workers is vital to the logistical function, and therefore the success of an army, it is of far lower status than that of the combatant man. Combat remains an essentially male role, and even though the numbers of men who will actually take part in close physical combat are small, and diminish ever further as wars become more and more a triumph of technology, all men are potential combatants, and, as De Groot argues 'all men enjoy the status which combat accords'.[10] The overwhelming absence of women from combat thus serves to reinforce the gender divisions which exist in peacetime society.

Margaret and Patrice Higonnet have described the pattern of gender roles visible in wartime as a 'double helix, with its structure of two intertwined strands'.[11] Within the double helix, they argue, the female strand is both opposed and subordinate to the male. Whenever the female strand moves, the male strand moves in tandem to maintain its position of superiority. In the First and Second World Wars, women moved forward to take up male roles, but men moved forward into the higher status role of combatant. Although women were working in large numbers outside the home in occupations previously only undertaken by men, gender relations remained essentially unchanged. In this game of follow my leader, both genders move forwards, with women always remaining one step behind men: only those killed in combat are considered worthy of war memorials and commemoration on national days of remembrance. The maintenance of gender roles in wartime means that the society that is being fought for can be represented as essentially stable, despite the enormous social, familial and economic shifts that war can bring about. When men return from battle, women will return to the home, as was overwhelmingly the experience in Britain following both of the twentieth century's total wars. Women in uniform, even if not actual combatants, challenge this established pattern of gender roles; when men are working alongside women in the forces, they cannot be told that they are fighting to defend women and the home. The female soldier is both a necessary feature of British society in total war and a threat to social stability and the existing order.

The link between masculinity and soldiering can be seen throughout the centuries. Indeed, it is a relationship which is often valorised and exalted. As a counterpart to this glorified military masculinity, femininity has long been linked with peace and with pacifism. This gendering of warfare can be seen in one of the most ancient stories of war *The Iliad*, where Hector, anticipating his death in battle with Achilles, tells his wife Andromanche to

> Go home, attend to your own handiwork
> At loom and spindle
> As for the war, that is for men.[12]

The Iliad was read by Simone Weil, writing from occupied France during the Second World War, as a hymn to male force, as it valorises the male soldier and accepts death and destruction as an inevitable aspect of war.[13] Throughout the books women remain within the city walls fulfilling the role of the 'waiting woman' so familiar from later wars:

> Now when Hector reached the Scaean Gates
> Daughters and wives of Trojans rushed to greet him
> With questions about friends, sons, husbands, brothers.[14]

Women of the Iliad were the opposite of the fighting men: their femininity has to be protected, but it is also dangerous, threatening to weaken the resolve of the men and sap their strength. As Helenus Priamides warns Hector,

> Here make our troops hold fast, before the gate
> Or back again they go, pell mell into the arms of women-
> A great day for our enemies[15]

This representation of women as non-combatants, as needing the protection of men, can be seen again during mediaeval and early modern modern periods. When, under the feudal system, noblemen went away to fulfil their duty to fight for the King, women stayed behind to defend their family's property. During the religious wars of seventeenth-century Europe, undefeated cities were often represented in contemporary verse and print as virginal women. When Lutheran Magdeburg fell to Catholic forces in 1631, celebratory verse proclaimed: 'Praise God in all eternity, Magdeburg is quenched and its virginity is no more.'[16] This military penetration of a virginal city was matched by the rape of the city's female citizens; an all too common expression of the city's subjugation, seen again in the Bosnian War of the early 1990s.[17] German women who 'surrendered' to soldiers too willingly were believed to have dishonoured their community and were often expelled from the city as a means of purifying it and maintaining civil order. Women represented continuity and the maintenance of the social order. Their role in wartime was to symbolise the society for which the men were fighting.

As the city states and autonomous regions of the early modern period developed into the nation-states of the modern world, this gendered division of warfare was codified into state policy. Despite the large numbers of women who acted as camp followers during the Napoleonic wars of the eighteenth and nineteenth centuries, providing essential support services to the large armies of the period, war was clearly seen as the concern of men. Only men were enlisted or conscripted to fight for their country, and the male soldier came to occupy an almost sacred space within the concept of the nation. Heinrich Von Trietschke, Bismark's publicist and disciple, and Chair of History at Berlin University between 1874 and 1896, conducted a lecture series each year on the 'virility of war' in which he described war as manly and peace as effeminate. He argued that 'it is war that turns a people into a nation ... The men of action are the real heroes of history ... The features of history are virile, unsuited to sentimental or feminine natures'.[18] These sentiments, which place war as the great driving force of history, and men at the centre of wars, can also be found in the prose and poetry of Victorian Britain, in which soldiers and schoolboys alike were urged to 'Play up! Play up! And play the game'[19] and the 'correct' approach to warfare was characterised by Tennyson's Light Brigade:

> Their's not to reason why
> Their's but to do and die[20]

War was a man's duty, and to die for one's country was 'the ultimate sacrifice'.

This glorification of warfare as the supreme fulfilment of men wasn't really challenged until the mechanised slaughter of the First World War. In Brooke's poem *1914*, where the soldiers setting off for war

> Leave the sick hearts that honour could not move
> And half-men, and their dirty songs and dreary
> And all the little emptiness of love.[21]

defined a man, separating him from the non-combatant 'half-men' and women. It was not only the Romantics who glorified war, looking backwards to find stories of gallant men riding out to defend the honour of noble women. The Futurists, who by their very name, scorned the past, also glorified both war and masculinity. Marrinetti, in his *Manifesto of Futurism* wrote that:

> We want to hymn the spirit of the man at the wheel, who hurls the lance of his spirit across the earth ... we will glorify war — the world's only hygiene — militarism, patriotism, the destructive gesture of freedom bringers, beautiful ideas worth dying for, and scorn for women.[22]

Proto-fascists, romantics, nationalistic historians, early modern legislators and pamphleteers and ancient Greek storytellers — all were agreed on one principle: war was man's business.

This principle has been reinforced by the work of many military historians, much of which has tended to reinforce the gendered divisions of warfare. The respected military historian John Keegan, Professor of History at Sandhurst Military Academy, summarised his beliefs about women and war in *A History of Warfare*:

> Half of human nature – the female half – is in any case highly ambivalent about warmaking. Women may be both the cause or the pretext of warmaking . . . and can be the instigators of violence . . . they can also be remarkably hard hearted mothers of warriors, some apparently preferring the pain of bereavement to the shame of accepting the homeward return of a coward. Women can, moreover, be positively messianic war leaders . . . Warfare is, nevertheless, the one human activity from which women, with the most insignificant exceptions, have always and everywhere stood apart. Women look to men to protect them from danger, and bitterly reproach them when they fail as defenders . . . Women, however, do not fight. They rarely fight among themselves and they never, in any military service, fight men. If warfare is as old as history and as universal as mankind, we must now enter the supremely important limitation that it is an entirely masculine activity.[23]

Keegan is correct in his assertion that combatant women form only the most 'insignificant exceptions' to the general rule that combat is a male affair, although wrong to state that women 'never . . . fight men' as the experience of Russian women in both world wars illustrates. However, his argument appears to be underpinned by a belief in an essential, natural division between the martial man and the peace-making woman. In Keegan's overview of warfare, women may instigate wars, become great war leaders, or follow men into battle to help the wounded and support the survivors. Their main role, however, is, as bystander to war, the civilian which the soldier fights to defend.

John Laffin, the prolific and popular author on issues of war and warfare almost exactly echoes Keegan in his approach to women and war. Whilst women are noticeable by their absence from the vast majority of his books, the 1967 *Women in Battle* provides an overview of the various individual women and small groups of women who have taken part in warfare over the ages. In a survey which takes in not just Countess Marciewicz, Flora Sandes and Maria Botchkareva, but lesser known examples of female combatants, such as the 'Amazon Corps' of Dahomey, West Africa during the nineteenth century, who both acted as the palace guard and took part in combat, Laffin argues that 'it is clear women have the intelligence and discipline to be efficient soldiers . . . women . . . have exhibited qualities of leadership which men would like to believe are a masculine monopoly'.[24] However, despite this acknowledgement of women's potential as soldiers, Laffin firmly believes that war is a man's business, concluding his book with the claim that:

> I admire women soldiers and I like to see the neat, trim yet feminine uniform which the services of most countries now provide for their she soldiers...But...a woman's place should be in the bed and not the battlefield, in crinoline or terylene rather than in battledress, wheeling a pram rather than driving a tank. Further, it should be the natural function of women to stop men from fighting rather than aiding and abetting them in pursuing it. One of the great inducements to the end of a war is the intense desire of men to return home to women and bed. If a man is to have women at war with him, if he is to think of women as comrades in arms rather than as mistresses on mattresses, that inducement disappears.[25]

Although expressed in somewhat more colourful language than Keegan, the conclusion is the same: women do not belong in the military. On the contrary, Laffin states that woman's 'natural function' is to stop men from fighting, arguing that women belong in the home, not in the military. Both Keegan and Laffin position women as the opposite to the combatant man, regarding militarised women as not only unusual, but also deeply unnatural. This conviction may account for the absence of any discussion of, or reference to, women as participants in warfare in not only Keegan and Laffin's work but in the majority of military histories.[26]

Military histories such as these tend to emphasise combat and the role of the combatant, a position echoed in many other attempts to represent and understand war. The dominance of military history as a means of approaching and understanding warfare meant that histories of war tended to be dominated by studies of battlefield tactics and political strategies. Martin Gilbert's authoritative histories of both the First and Second World Wars, for example, combine political and military history in their descriptions of the conflicts, and pay only passing attention to the social and cultural impact of the conflicts.[27] As battles are generally fought by, and high politics overwhelmingly determined by, men, any female perspective on war is largely absent from these histories. The same pattern can be seen in many literary studies of war. For example, Paul Fussell's *The Bloody Game: An Anthology of Modern War* includes only 6 women authors amongst its collection of 97 first hand observations of war.[28] Similarly, the edited collection *The War Decade. An Anthology of the 1940s* has 17 pieces of poetry and prose written by women amongst its 309 pieces.[29] As Margaret Higonnet has argued, much writing on war continues to privilege the experience of the combatant, reflecting his special status in society as one who will fight, kill and perhaps die for his nation's interests and beliefs.[30] Samuel Hynes' *The Soldiers' Tale: Bearing Witness to Modern War* supports this status in its claim that combatants have been transformed through an experience which 'isolates them from other men – cuts off the men who fought from older and younger men who did not share that shaping experience'.[31] We could add to this that the experience of combat, both actual and as a potential, acts to divide men from women.

However in modern warfare, combat is increasingly difficult to define and is experienced in its traditional form, as close combat on a battlefield, by very few. Is the soldier programming the computer which will send a missile to its target and kill the enemy a combatant? Should combat be defined as only attempting to kill or otherwise disable the enemy, both of which can now be achieved at some distance, or should we use a narrower definition, one which assumes close physical contact? New military technologies further work to break down the distinction between combatant and non-combatant, so central to military organisation in the past, by ensuring that soldiers working far behind the front lines can be the targets for bombs and missiles. In the Gulf War of 1991, female soldiers undertook a wide variety of roles officially designated non-combatant: driving trucks which supplied men in the front line, radar and radio operation, cooking, cleaning and working as clerks. Despite the traditionally feminine nature of most of these occupations, it proved impossible to maintain the distinction between combatant and non-combatant, both because the ground war moved so rapidly and because of the use of missiles to target army bases behind the lines. Eleven non-combatant servicewomen died in the war.[32] By March 2003 sixteen US servicewomen had died during the later war and subsequent occupation of Iraq, again despite being designated non-combatant.[33] Modern warfare, with its rapidly moving, and often difficult to identify, front lines, and use of long range weaponry, blurs the line not just between combatant and non-combatant troops but between military and civilian. Civilian populations can also, at times, be thought of as combatants: the population of the blitzed cities of Britain in the Second World War were described by the US reporter Quentin Reynolds as 'good soldiers' in his commentary for the 1941 documentary film 'Britain Can Take It'. Nevertheless, despite the haziness of the boundary between combatant and non-combatant, military histories have continued to emphasise the traditional form of combat, involving relatively close physical proximity between opponents, and hence the almost exclusively male nature of battle.

Perhaps the key difference between male and female troops, and between the military and the civilian populations, is that male soldiers are the designated killers of the enemy. Whilst men and women, soldier and civilian, can all die in warfare, it is overwhelmingly only the male soldier who acts as a combatant. Governments and militaries have again and again attempted to define the female role in the military in ways which exclude women from this role. In Britain in the Second World War members of the ATS undertook almost every role on the anti-aircraft sites: they could plot directions, operate searchlights, load the shells into the guns, but not fire them at the enemy aircraft. Female members of the Home Guard in the same war were enrolled rather than enlisted and were not permitted to train with arms. The Vietnam War saw North Vietnamese women mobilised for a wide variety of roles within the People's Liberation Army, often armed with rifles, but it nevertheless remained 'general policy to discourage active combat for women'.[34] The Israel Defence Force, often cited as an example of a gender integrated military, assigns women to combat units but excludes them from the vast majority of combat roles there, with women overwhelmingly working in traditionally female occupations, forming 68 per cent of the total staff in Human Resources and 83.3 per cent of the Israeli Defence Force's Education Department.[35] With very, very few exceptions, the position of combatant remains exclusively male in the majority of the world's militaries and guerrilla movements. As women are killed in warfare, this exclusion from combat roles would seem to have little to do with a desire to protect women from the horrors of combat. Rather the taboo on female combatants reflects widely held ideas about women as killers. The binary distinction between the female life-giver and the male life-taker has been so widely naturalised that when women *do* kill, they are often seen as more ferocious and more dangerous than men. The poet Rudyard Kipling warned British soldiers serving in India and Afghanistan that 'the female of the species is more deadly than the male' whilst in the Spanish Civil War women were believed to show greater cruelty to prisoners than men.[36] The female soldiers of Dahomey in West Africa during the nineteenth century apparently had 'a reputation for cruelty' whilst Stanley Kubrick's 1987 film *Full Metal Jacket* depicted a lone female sniper laying waste an entire United States' Army Unit.[37] In British popular culture the image of the 'Moors Murderer', Myra Hindley, became an icon of evil in a way which her partner and the principal instigator of the killings, Ian Brady, never did. Whilst combat and killing are widely viewed as 'natural' aspects of masculinity, albeit ones which have to be tightly controlled by laws and socially shared mores, female killers step outside the accepted bounds of femininity and, unless killing to defend their children and thus following a maternal instinct, are demonised for acting 'unnaturally'.

In addition, the armed female soldier threatens the long established linkage between masculinity and the military. By feminising the combat role, the female soldier would devalue it, undermining both the status of the role and men's access to it. As Joanna Bourke has argued 'combat was the ultimate signifier of manliness: women would symbolically castrate the armed forces'.[38] This, however, has never been a line of argument articulated by male military leaders, who have argued instead that female combatants would undermine morale, as soldiers quarrelled over them and sought to defend them in combat because their weaker physiques would make them easy targets for the enemy. Although recent years have seen an expanding role for women in the armed forces of most industrialised nations, the combat taboo has largely been maintained. Amongst NATO members Canada has opened up the highest proportion of combat roles to women, but the perceived feminisation of the military by significant numbers of soldiers and officers led to an increase in reports of rape and sexual harassment by servicewomen.[39] France employs women in a range of positions which could be designated combatant, yet stated in a 1994 NATO policy document that 'a woman's role is to give life and not death. For this reason it is not desirable for mothers to take direct part in battle.'[40] In 1997 the British government allowed servicewomen to take up a greater range of positions than ever before but maintained the fighting forces of both infantry and tank regiments as male-only institutions. With the post Cold War forces needing fewer recruits, many of those that do join are more likely to be trained in highly skilled, technical positions. When they fight, more and more of the fighting is done with new weaponry and new technology, much of which needs less muscle power than the old, and some of which further alleviates the need for close physical contact between opposing troops, although as the Iraq War and occupation have shown, this remains an important aspect of ground warfare for the infantry. All of these changes are acting to increase both the numbers of, and the positions available to, women, yet gender divisions remain drawn along lines which define men as combatants, women as non-combatants.

Although even the most cursory survey of warfare would illustrate that both states and guerrilla movements draw women into combat positions when it is deemed absolutely necessary, the same study would show that, at war's end, women overwhelmingly return to a more traditional role. There certainly was a determined attempt to reinstate peacetime gender roles following the end of both world wars. In Britain, legislation was introduced which encouraged women back into the home and into traditional spheres of female employment. Following the First World War French women were dismissed from the 'men's work' they had been engaged in during the war, and attempts to introduce female suffrage were rejected by Senate. Towards the end of the Second World War in the Soviet Union gender distinctions were reinforced by a new pro-natalist family code, which made divorce more difficult to obtain, and, in an echo of the family policies of Nazi Germany, awarded motherhood medals to women with five or more children. Women who had served with the military found themselves the subject of scandalised gossip and rumour, in which they were widely seen as sexualised 'camp followers'. Vera Malakhova, a physician decorated for her service with the Red Army, recalled that 'I didn't like to show myself (with my medals) because many people thought I was some kind of front-line "W" (whore).'[41] Women drawn into guerrilla movements in later wars also often found themselves back in the home at the war's end. Following the Franco-Algerian War, Algerian women were excluded from both the armed forces and the political decision-making process. The Sandinista government of Nicaragua, having utilised women during the war against the American equipped Contra forces, introduced a male-only conscription policy, and, although women continued to form 20 per cent of the Nicaraguan Army, very few were deployed close to combat zones.[42] Even the actions of the small numbers of women whose combat role has been celebrated have to be contained. When the Soviets disbanded the Women's Battalion of Death in 1917 they were 'ordered home and told to put on female attire'.[43] In his introduction to Flora Sandes' autobiography, the Serbian Minister of Foreign Affairs emphasised that 'she only took to a rifle when there was no more nursing to be done'.[44] Following the establishment of a Free State in the South of Ireland, the Irish President, Eamon de Valera, who had fought alongside Constance Markievicz in Dublin, called for women to return to their homes and families. Although armies may draw on women's labour when necessary, and on occasion use them in a combat role, militaries remain overwhelmingly male organisations, with the highest status occupations within them generally only being open to men. Whilst women have historically always occupied a variety of different roles in wartime, the figure of the female soldier has been marginal to both the militaries that fight wars and to our memory of these wars.

If a reliance on military history for one's knowledge of warfare would do much to convince the reader that war was 'an entirely masculine activity', much feminist analysis of war would only serve to strengthen this belief.[45] The division between male and female, combatant and non-combatant, expressed by Keegan and Laffin has been echoed by many feminist writers and activists. Within much feminist criticism, and feminist histories of warfare, there has been very little acknowledgement of women working within the armed forces; instead, theorists working within this paradigm have often concentrated on women's role in national and international peace movements, and the ways in which women have been victims of male violence in wartime.[46] Women in the armed forces have been viewed at best with ambivalence as feminists have focused on oppositional movements and the lives of women who have resisted patriarchal authority. Military women, working within an organisation which has long been an important symbol of male authority, have largely been absent from these feminist histories. This echoes the long-standing linkage between feminism and pacifism, seen in the actions of female Quakers of the seventeenth century who expressed their commitment to peace and in the actions of nineteenth-century women who worked to relieve suffering during the Franco-Prussian and Crimean wars. Many female pacifists of the First World War saw links between femininity and a desire for peace, the United States Women's Peace Party claiming in 1915 that, 'as women, we are especially the custodians of the life of the ages',[47] whilst in Britain Catherine Marshall wrote that 'I believe that women...are much more likely than men to find some other way of settling international disputes than by an appeal to force, partly because that is an appeal which is not open to them.'[48]

Peace campaigns provided an opportunity for women to work in the sphere of public politics. The Women's Peace Conference in the Hague in 1915, which called for universal disarmament, and the 1919 conference in Zurich which founded the Women's International League for Peace and Freedom were the first campaigns to formally link pacifism with femininity. During the inter-war years the British Women's Co-operative Guild were active pacifists, organising a 'white poppy' campaign in memory of *all* those killed and injured in warfare, combatants and civilians alike. The best known of the pacifist groups at work in this time was Canon Dick Sheppard's Peace Pledge Union, which was able to claim over 100,000 members by 1939. The author Vera Brittain, who was to become a life long pacifist following the death of three of the men she loved, her fiancée, brother and close friend, in the First World War, was a leading organiser and propagandist for the Peace Pledge Union. This was the largest organisation in Britain through which women could work for peace, and women consistently made up one-third of its membership. By the beginning of the Second World War 43,000 women had signed the Union's postcards renouncing war, even though the organisation had only begun to approach them as signatories in 1936.[49] Although the Second World War was to severely weaken both the European and American Peace movements, women's role as pacifists was becoming accepted and established on both sides of the Atlantic.

Perhaps the best known of the many feminist theorists to connect war with patriarchy was Virginia Woolf. In *Three Guineas*, published in 1938 as an answer to her nephew Julian Bell who had written to Woolf, who opposed his participation in the Spanish Civil War, to ask 'how are we to prevent war?' Woolf wrote:

> if you insist on fighting to protect me, or 'our' country, let it be understood, soberly and rationally between us, that you are fighting to gratify a sex instinct which I cannot share; to procure benefits which I have not shared and probably will not share...As a woman I have no country...as a woman, my country is the whole world.[50]

Woolf emphasised the links that she saw between the participation of men in war, and the male dominated nature of inter-war British society, where men held all the positions of power, not just in the military, but in the professions, in the City and in government. She distanced women from war, denying its status as an act which functioned primarily to 'protect' women and children and claiming it as a male pursuit which, in its defence of nationhood and the status quo, was of little or no benefit to women. Women, Woolf argued, stood outside this 'man's world' of patriotism, nationalism and war.

These thoughts were echoed nearly fifty years later in the campaigns of the early 1980s against the renewed arms race and the alarming spread of short-range nuclear missiles in Europe. These campaigns found their most potent voice in the women's peace camps, such as the camp established outside the US Airforce Base at Greenham Common in Berkshire. The Greenham Camp opposed a life-giving and vibrant femininity to a bleak and militarised masculinity. Outside the Airforce Base women expressed their opposition to nuclear war by pinning family snaps, children's drawing, clothing and nappies to the perimeter fence whilst inside men guarded weapons of mass destruction. The camp was an attempt to move away from the sense of inadequacy and powerlessness that many felt when confronted by these weapons, expressed by Women Oppose the Nuclear Threat in 1980 as a feeling that 'many of us see war as a male activity...over which we have no control'.[51] Some women associated with the peace movement argued that the proliferation of nuclear missiles was intricately linked with masculinity. 'Take the toys from the boys' was a popular slogan of the time, articulating a connection between masculinity and aggression that some radical feminists believed was innate. Andrea Dworkin, for example, has contended that 'Male aggression is rapacious...men create wars'.[52] Thus, radical feminist theory of the late twentieth century reproduced the gendered divisions that have appeared in writing on warfare throughout the ages.

Another strand of feminist thought has taken a very different approach to the question of women and war, rejecting the idea that women are inherently more peaceful than men. Liberal feminists, particularly those working within the paradigm of US feminist criticism, have often emphasised the 'equal rights issue', discussing the battle for equal terms of service and equal treatment by the military that female soldiers have often had to fight. Within this tradition, female soldiers have been represented as symbols of the struggle for equal rights; women working within the definitively male world of the armed forces, overturning stereotypes and proving women's ability to undertake the same duties as the male soldiers.[53] From this perspective, the marginalisation of women within the military mirrors women's marginalisation within civil society and the historical exclusion of women from high status professional positions. Liberal equal rights feminism advocates the incorporation of women into the armed forces under the same conditions as men, subject to conscription and undertaking a combat role alongside male soldiers.[54] The assimilation of women into the forces, it is argued, will not only transform the military, turning it into a more democratic and egalitarian organisation, but will also assist in the transformation of the wider, civil, society. This argument is based on the conviction that women will only achieve full citizenship alongside men once they have attained equal treatment within the military. In the Gulf War of 1991, described by one author as 'a big victory for liberal feminism', the US forces employed nearly 40,000 women and the United Kingdom approximately 1,000.[55] As described earlier, although these women were officially excluded from combat roles, they participated in all other facets of military activity and, despite initial concerns, the public largely appeared to accept the inevitable death and capture of some servicewomen. Following the war, the US military continued with its policy of integrating women into the forces and opening up a wider range of positions for them, begun in the 1970s following the end of conscription after the Vietnam War. Britain went on to abolish the Women's Royal Army Corps in 1992, incorporating women into the male army. The public's acceptance of women in a war zone, and the moves by the British and US military to allow women an expanded role in the forces led one commentator to claim in 1993 that 'the army of the future will be female to a greater extent than ever before', continuing, 'the end of the decade will see Western militaries open all roles – including infantry, artillery and tanks – to suitably qualified women'.[56]

However, examples of the military drawing on women's labour, and opening up a wider range of positions within the military to women, have rarely been matched by a concurrent shift in women's status within the wider civil society. The impact of war upon gender roles has been widely discussed and researched by historians interested in both questions of masculinity and femininity and in the wider effect that war has upon social change. Within the British context the central strand in this debate has been the thesis that war helps to modernise society. Proponents of this argument, most notably Arthur Marwick, have pointed to the widespread changes in women's lives during the two total wars of the twentieth century and, whilst not arguing that war itself brings about social change, have contended that total war has tended to accelerate existing trends.[57] The extension of the franchise to most British women in 1918, for example, has been widely interpreted as a reward for women's part in the war effort. Working in the auxiliary forces, as well as on the land, in the factories and in the hospitals, war ensured that women could no longer be seen as the domesticated creatures of the home of the Victorian period. They had served their country in wartime and thus earned the right to direct political representation. The two World Wars have also been understood as modernising women's lives in less tangible and quantifiable ways. War work in both wars provided women with increased access to public, previously male, spaces as women moved out of the 'traditional' areas of female employment into a variety of occupations which were previously the domain of men. Female appearance changed as the practical demands of war work combined with fabric shortages to replace pre-war frills and flounces with more practical and austere skirts and sometimes trousers. Women's figures changed as they discovered that the hard physical work and better diets of wartime led to weight gain and muscular development. With many men away in the forces, women at home took over all aspects of home management, including those which had traditionally been seen as falling within the male sphere, such as child discipline and household repairs. Most difficult to assess, but vividly represented in many of the diaries and autobiographies of women who lived through both wars, is the increased confidence felt by many of them. However, the expansion of feminist histories from the 1970s onwards saw a new and more critical approach to this modernisation thesis. Looking at the specific circumstances of women's war work, and the employment patterns of women following both wars, Gail Braybon and Penny Summerfield argued that any wartime changes in gender roles were short lived, curtailed by the continued existence of pre-war ideas about masculinity and femininity.[58] Female liberation, they argued, was just 'for the duration', and the cessation of hostilities also signalled the end of women's progress into the wider, male sphere of activity.

Nevertheless, although women may have returned to the constraints of a traditional femininity at wars' end, the impact of wartime changes was felt far beyond the immediate postwar periods. Their wartime experiences continued to resonate in their lives, with many women remembering these periods as times of relative personal autonomy. Penny Summerfield has described how a talk she gave to an adult education group on women's factory work during the Second World War, in which she argued that 'the war did little to alter women's position', was greeted with annoyance by two women in the audience, who recalled their wartime lives quite differently, emphasising 'their sense of the war as a special and different period in their lives'.[59] Summerfield's eventual response was to examine the disparity between the feminist emphasis on the temporary nature of wartime changes for women and these women's sense that it had been a period of personal emancipation. She found that for many women the social, economic and cultural changes of wartime had an important influence on their lives. Although the majority of women may have returned to a traditionally feminine role in the immediate aftermath of war, their war work, and the wider example of women undertaking new roles and responsibilities more usually associated with men continued to shape their lives and their sense of their own capabilities. Although the state may have acted to return gender roles to their pre-war status quo as soon as possible, the wartime challenge to this status quo could not be entirely avoided.

Women in military uniform provide a very visible challenge to existing gender roles, not just in wartime but also, when they become permanent members of the military, in peacetime. As Martin Shaw has commented, 'warfare has been defined in most societies as a male prerogative, and warlikeness as an attribute of masculinity.'[60] As the distinctive character of the armed forces has historically emphasised its masculine nature, any move to increase the numbers of women in the military, or the range of roles available to these women, is inherently problematic, questioning a fundamental aspect of the military's identity. The incorporation of women into the armed forces reflects an underlying tension in the military's relationship with civil society. The military analyst Christopher Dandeker has argued that the military has to be both culturally distinct from civil society, providing a space where the violent actions rejected by civil law are not only condoned but often encouraged, and also has to reflect the mores and values of the society which the armed forces serve and defend.[61] This tension can be seen in the debates which have accompanied the military's resistance to changing attitudes to minority populations, resulting in, for example, its institutional unwillingness to oppose discrimination against gay men and lesbians within the forces, which exists alongside attempts to open up the military to these same groups.[62] Thus the military has to reflect shifts in the social category of gender, perhaps by admitting women into the forces, or by extending the roles available to them there, whilst at the same time maintaining its status as an organisation separate and distinct from civil society. This entry of women into the military threatens to destabilise not only the civil–military nexus but also existing paradigms of masculinity and femininity.

The aim of this book is to examine the ways in which the British army drew on women's labour in an increasingly official capacity during the first half of the twentieth century, exploring the relationship between the military's need for women workers and the concurrent attempts to both maintain the masculine nature of the services and the traditional discourses of masculinity and femininity in civilian life. The book traces both the changes and the continuity in the treatment of female soldiers and the shifting ways in which they were represented. Although female participation in all three military services, as well as women's work in the farms and factories, was vital to Britain's victory in both World Wars, their involvement was by no means universally welcomed, and was indeed often marked by public derision, ridicule and anger. However, as the numbers of women in uniform increased, public reaction became more favourable and the media began to criticise 'women slackers' instead of women in uniform.[63] Attitudes to women in uniform were by no means unchanging over this period, shaped and influenced instead by factors such as feminism and the campaign for the vote, ideas about social class, conscription, the number of women in the services, women's changing public role and a widespread desire to rebuild both home and nation in peacetime. This book explores the chronological development of women's work with the military, focusing on the British Army as the largest of the services and the first to employ a women's corps.

The first chapter looks at the early history of militarised women, focusing on the formation of the First Aid Nursing Yeomanry (FANY) in 1908, the first well-known and reasonably large-scale example of a British female paramilitary organisation, whose largely upper and upper middle-class members attempted to combine the feminine vocation of nursing with the masculine discipline of soldiering. Their offers of help rejected by the War Office in the First World War, the FANY went on to work with the French and German armies. A large number of female voluntary organisations did spring up in the first years of the war however, many of them associated with the suffrage movement, and these are the subject of Chapter 2. The two organisations most closely allied with militarism, the Women's Legion and the Women's Volunteer Reserve found themselves treated very differently by both the Army and the wider public, and the chapter considers the reasoning behind this very different treatment within the framework of a discussion of contemporary understandings of gender during the war. In 1917 the War Office realised the necessity of formalising its use of female labour and formed the Women's Army Auxiliary Corps (WAAC), the focus of Chapter 3. The history of the WAAC is, in large part, a history of the Army's attempts to regulate the behaviour, appearance and activities of women whom it employed, as it attempted to utilise female labour without disturbing the masculine identity of the armed forces. At war's end, there was a concerted effort to return gender roles to more traditional terrain, with men returning from the war to their old positions and attempts to force women into the private sphere of the home and domestic work. Although peace heralded a welcome return to normality for many women, others sought to maintain the sense of personal liberation which the war had bought them. Chapter 4 explores the complicated nature of women's relationship with the military in the inter-war years, tracing the War Office's initial refusal to form a voluntary women's reserve force and the gradual realisation, as war loomed again in the 1930s, that the forces could not afford to ignore women's offers of help. The formation of the ATS in 1938 was the eventual outcome of years of campaigning by a small number of women, and Chapter 5 discusses the role of the Corps in the Second World War. This war, the 'people's war' was very different from the war of 1914–1918, marked as it was by a widely shared sense that Britain was becoming more democratic, and a shift towards the Left in British politics. However, the story of the ATS is marked by a determination to once again contain all aspects of its members' lives so that the masculine identity of the Army was not challenged. As a large and mainly working-class organisation, it was also subject to a poisonous 'whispering campaign' about the morals and behaviour of its members, similar to an earlier set of rumours about the WAAC, which brings into question the extent to which the 'democratic' nature of wartime Britain included young, working-class women. When the First World War ended the WAAC had been disbanded, reinforcing the notion that women's new role within the armed forces had been 'just for the duration'. However, in 1945 the decision was taken to maintain the ATS and in 1948, to form the Women's Royal Army Corps (WRAC) as a permanent branch of the Army. Chapter 6 examines the debates which surrounded this decision within a wider consideration of the wider pressures on women to 'return' to home and family as part of postwar reconstruction.

The first half of the century saw two total wars, the enfranchisement of women, the 'great depression' and the rapid rise of the Labour Party as a major force within British politics. It was a period of enormous change and development in all aspects of life, with new communications, new forms of housing and transport, new technologies, new areas of employment and rapidly changing relations between the social classes. In some ways it was a period of rapid change for women, with domestic service in decline, companionate marriages growing whilst the birth rate fell, the achievement of the vote and expanding opportunities for education and professional employment. It would be easy to write a narrative history of women in the British Army which mirrored this story of change and development, celebrating the gradual acceptance of women by the armed forces as symbolic of women's greater gains in society, and indeed, this is the predominant way in which their story has been told.[64] However, the history of women in the Army is far from being simply a straightforward narrative of female persistence and achievement eventually overwhelming a conservative and reactionary institution, with brave female soldiers convincing crusty old generals that they could do a job as well as a man. Although there are of course elements of this, and many examples of feminine bravery and persistence, and several crusty old generals, the history of women in the army is far more complicated. Women did not just join the forces because they were 'equal rights feminists', they had a variety of motivations, and some women held political convictions that many today would find abhorrent. Although those who formulated military policy gradually came to recognise the value of having a large body of women under its control, the maintenance of divisions between male and female soldiers remained a key concern. In a manner which mirrored patterns of change in women's wider lives in the first half of the twentieth century, the challenge to gender roles which women in uniform provided was matched by the military's determination to contain that challenge. The history of women in the British Army is as much a history of the force's determination to draw on female labour whilst resisting the 'femininization' of the military, as it is a history of women's gradual movement into a male sphere of activity.

2 Early days
Women and the armed forces before 1914

Women have long had a multitude of roles within the British Army. Long before the military officially incorporated women into its ranks, women had acted as cooks, nursemaids, cleaners and sexual partners for the men of the standing armies of modern Europe. As camp followers, these women retained their civilian status and were not officially incorporated into the army but were nonetheless essential to the successful function of the military, the range of services they provided being necessary to the maintenance of the fighting men. When the government sent troops to combat the American revolution of 1776, approximately 20,000 women accompanied the soldiers across the Atlantic.[1] Many of these women were soldiers' wives, whilst others became camp followers as a somewhat tenuous occupation. Overwhelmingly, they came from the same social background as the majority of soldiers – from the poor and the industrial working class. As Cynthia Enloe has contended, the very term 'camp follower' has connotations of both parasitism and prostitution, and their existence was regarded with a mixture of pragmatism and disdain by the upper echelons of the armed forces.[2] Whilst their services were of use to the military, their presence was tolerated, but when camp followers, often accompanied by small children and the trappings of domesticity, were felt to be damaging the operations of the army, perhaps by slowing down a long march or lengthy military campaign, they were dismissed. Thus camp followers provided services which were often vital to the army but remained marginal to its organisation. This peripheral relationship with the army provided a long lasting model of gender relations followed by the British armed forces.

However, although women's actual role within the armed forces may have been marginal and of the lowest status, this did little to prevent the romance of army life appealing to a range of women. There are numerous stories of women disguising themselves as men in order to serve with the British army, and these individual women acted as icons and sometimes role models for many others. Mary Lacey disguised herself as a man and joined the Navy in 1759, training as a ship's carpenter and working in Portsmouth's Royal Naval Dockyard when she left shipboard service. Accounts of the life of Phoebe Hessel, probably the best known woman to serve with the British armed forces, variously state that she was disguised as a boy by her soldier father and enrolled in the 5th Regiment of Foot and that she enrolled herself as an adult in order to follow her lover into the army. Mary Anne Talbot claimed to have enlisted as a footboy in the navy in the late eighteenth century. Christian Davies, describing her transition into the soldier Christopher Welsh, recalled simply cutting her hair, binding her breasts and dressing in her husband's clothes to evade detection. Believable or not, these stories and histories were a popular facet of late eighteenth- and early nineteenth-century popular culture.[3] Nonetheless, these women were only able to become heroines and icons precisely because they were the exception; military life and combat in modern Britain remained the preserve of masculinity.

Throughout the nineteenth century an acceptance of, and, increasingly, a pleasure in, military culture grew in Britain. Graham Dawson has identified a 'pleasure culture in war' developing throughout the nineteenth century, as an early mass, popular culture drew on the stories of heroic soldiers of Empire.[4] These stories were told and retold in a range of different sites, becoming a popular feature of mass entertainment from at least the middle of the nineteenth century. Battle scenes were reconstructed for popular entertainment, military parades and reviews began to take a central place in Royal and state ceremonies, and autobiographies, adventure stories, comic books and novels were assured of an audience if they focused on British military campaigns. British popular culture has a long history of glamourising and romanticising war, repeatedly representing warfare as a chivalric and heroic alternative to the mundanity of everyday life.[5] This interest in chivalry, popularised by the novels of Walter Scott, permeated through society during the nineteenth century, perpetuating a widely shared belief in the nobility of warfare. Seen most notably in the cult of 'muscular Christianity' of the British public school, chivalric, heroic acts were primarily seen as the preserve of the social elite, the valiant and brave officer class being produced by the public schools. However, the Crimean War of the 1850s and the Indian mutiny of 1857, represented in the British press and in literature and poetry such as Tennyson's *Charge of the Light Brigade* as moral as well as martial campaigns, enabled the extension of the chivalric model of warfare to the wider British army. This romanticised image of warfare, in which British soldiers were fighting on the side of God and Empire, gradually superseded the belief of the radical press and much of the working class that the army was to be distrusted as a potential instrument of social control. During the second half of the nineteenth century a popular militarism became a deeply embedded feature of British society and a key facet of a shared national culture.

The industrialisation and urbanisation of Britain was accompanied by a fear that the new working class were an immoral and potentially anarchic mass, beyond the reach of the civilising influence of either their 'social betters' or the church. With the development of a mass society came increased literacy, and religious tracts, novels, newspapers and magazines were increasingly seen as a means of reaching out to and socialising the urban working class. As Jeffrey Richards has argued, literature was seen as an especially useful tool for reaching the young:

> The aim of juvenile literature was clearly stated for a century. It was both to entertain and instruct, to inculcate approved value systems, to spread useful knowledge, to provide acceptable role models.[6]

The Education Act of 1870 further expanded the literacy rate and, by the 1880s, more than 900 juvenile titles were being published annually.[7] Action–adventure stories were widely felt to be the most appealing to a young audience, and numerous novels and stories were published which narrated the chivalric adventures of British 'christian gentlemen' in the British Empire. Alongside these however appeared a quantity of cheaply produced serial papers for working-class boys, deplored as 'penny dreadfuls' which related the often violent adventures of their heroes with little regard for chivalry or Christianity. Magazines such as *Boys of England* and *Young Men of Great Britain* provided more agreeable fare, combining their action–adventure stories with articles on self help and British history.[8] The year 1879 saw the publication by the Religious Tract Society of the first edition of the *Boy's Own Paper*. This popular magazine had the stated aim of providing 'healthy boy literature to counteract the vastly increasing circulation of illustrated and other papers and tales of a bad tendency', and combined a deeply moral tone with stories and articles focusing on British history and chivalric representations of warfare, representing the noble, Christian warrior, preferably the product of a British public school, as an ideal of masculinity.[9] The *Boy's Own Paper* rapidly became the best selling of the magazines aimed at boys, its success based on the appeal of its moral tone to parents, whilst the exciting adventure stories appealed to boys, and in 1880 it was joined by a companion paper for girls, the *Girl's Own Paper*.

Although the vast majority of the cultural products described in the previous paragraph were aimed at an overwhelmingly young, male audience, it is perhaps unsurprising that the concept of war as an escape from the constraints of everyday life should appeal to at least some Victorian and Edwardian women. The *Girl's Own Paper* reflected little of this, and whilst the *Boy's Own Paper* emphasised the physical role of British men and boys in the maintenance of a Christian nation and empire, the reader of the *Girl's Own Paper* was told again and again that 'the essence of girlhood is in spiritual qualities rather than in actions'.[10] Articles and stories in the paper focused on traditionally feminine pursuits which sat comfortably within the archetypal Victorian conception of separate spheres, with an emphasis on the reader's future role as wife, mother and homemaker. The growing influence of eugenics in the last third of the nineteenth century led to an increasing influence on women's role as the guardian of the race as eugenicists and pro-natalists argued that the high infant mortality rate in British cities was the result of physically and morally weak motherhood.[11] The recognition of adolescence as a biologically and psychologically distinct period of life, was shaped by existing beliefs about the separate roles of male and female. The highly influential *Adolescence*, a two volume tome by the American author G. Stanley Hall argued that whilst adolescence for boys was a period when the physical and mental limitations of childhood should be challenged if the boy was to grow into a flourishing specimen of manhood, adolescent girls needed to take care not to overstretch either their physical or mental ability if they were to successfully fulfil their womanly role of motherhood.[12] Once girls reached womanhood however, the discharging of their role as mothers of the empire could not be guaranteed. Women could be distracted from their role as mothers by the demands of paid work, if they were working class, or by the emergent arguments of feminists and suffragists if they were middle class. However, despite the attempts of the *Girl's Own Paper* and its ilk to guard against the appeal of alternative models of femininity, women's role was changing, and the example of the 'new woman', increasingly demanding an education and an expanded role in the public world of men, led to a gradual shift in the ideology of separate spheres.

As Carol Dyhouse has argued, the new girls' schools of the late nineteenth century, modelled on the public school for boys, provided new occupations and new role models for girls, encouraging participation in team sports and the development of intellectual abilities.[13] Even here however, an emphasis on girls' future role as mothers of the race was maintained: sporting prowess was encouraged as a means of ensuring girls' development into strong and physically competent women, able to produce equally strong progeny for the British race. Education for working-class girls focused more directly on homemaking and motherhood, as girls were provided with classes in childcare, laundry and needlework in an attempt to ensure that the skills believed necessary for motherhood, and perhaps for domestic service, which were not being passed on in the working-class home, were taught in school. However, opportunities for women were slowly expanding, and given the Victorian emphasis on the role of the morally upright British Christian warrior in the maintenance of the Empire, it should not be surprising that some women and girls imagined for themselves a role in this national culture which did not revolve around individual motherhood. Suitable women were encouraged to emigrate to the outposts of the empire, both as a means of reducing the perceived problem of 'surplus women' and as way of ensuring that the colonies were peopled with physically and morally strong Britons. The promotion of emigration received a boost following the Boer War of 1899–1902, after which women were given official encouragement to migrate to South Africa as suitable companions for British men. The journal *The Nineteenth Century* argued that

> The emigration of women to South Africa has become a question of national importance. If that country is in the future to become one of the great self-governing countries of the British Empire . . . it must be

peopled with British women as well as British men... It is women of high moral character possessed of common sense and a sound constitution who can help to build up our Empire.[14]

Whilst the Empire provided an imagined landscape in which women could fulfil their fantasies of escape, action and adventure, nearer home a small number of vocations were beginning to emerge which appeared to offer women the opportunity to develop a female counterpart to the heroic and chivalrous male warrior. The British military nurse, typified for many by Florence Nightingale's work at Scutari Hospital during the Crimean War, exemplified this female figure.

Although very few female nurses were employed by the British military prior to the Boer War, Nightingale was nonetheless an important symbolic figure, combining the feminine qualities of nurturing and caring with a more masculine capacity for action and adventure, and representing an opportunity to travel abroad and to escape the domestic confines of life in Britain. The work of Nightingale and other female carers such as Mary Seacole was popularised by W. H. Russell, the first war correspondent, reporting on the war for *The Times*. Whilst the women who travelled with Nightingale were working in an environment new to 'respectable' middle-class women, the work that they were undertaking had been performed by the camp followers of earlier years, and Nightingale was keen to avoid any association in the public mind between her small band of military nurses and the often derided camp followers. Uniform was an important means of both marking out the 'professional' nature of the work carried out by Nightingale and her nurses and a means of symbolically separating them from the public disapproval of camp followers. The nurses wore a uniform consisting of 'grey tweed wrappers, worsted jackets with caps and short woollen cloaks' accompanied by a brown scarf 'embroidered with the words Scutari Hospital'.[15] The list of regulations drawn up by Nightingale emphasised the importance she attached to these uniforms, and to the avoidance of symbols of femininity and individuality by her nurses, who were ordered 'never to wear flowers or coloured ribbons' and that 'no crinolines, polonaises, hair pads etc are to be worn on duty in the hospital'.[16] In this attempt to avoid the trappings of fashion and frivolity Nightingale recognised that the signs and symbols of femininity were widely understood to be inimical to the discipline and rigours of service life.

Following her return from the Crimea, Nightingale worked to provide nursing training for women, and in 1860 established an Army Training School for military nurses. Jane Shaw Stewart was appointed the first superintendent of a female nursing service in Woolwich in 1861 and became the first woman to receive official recognition in the British Army List. In 1866 the army agreed that female nurses could be appointed to Military General Hospitals but the Army Nursing Service did not come into official existence until 1884. Despite the formation of this new organisation, numbers of female military nurses remained small, a symbol of active femininity rather than a feasible occupation for many. Military nursing provided women with a symbolic part in 'national service'; working alongside and caring for the men of the armed forces, female nursing provided a means both acceptable and exciting for women to move onto the public stage and to take some share in the honour and approval which the Imperial nation awarded to its male combatants.

Other organisations which seemed to combine the potential for action and independence with a recognised role within the Empire were the various youth movements of the late nineteenth and early twentieth centuries. As Anne Summers has argued,

> one of the most striking features of the girls' movements which sprang up in Britain at the beginning of the century was the extent to which they adopted either the military nurse, or the first-aider, or both, as role-model for their members.[17]

The Girls' Guildry and the Girl's Life Brigade, non-conformist organisations for girls and counterparts to the Boys' Brigade and the Boys' Life Brigade, founded following the Boer War, dressed their members in quasi-military uniform and taught drill and marching alongside first aid instruction. The Church Red Cross Brigade, founded in 1901 was a female equivalent to the Anglican Church Lad's Brigade which, while they did not practise drill, again wore a uniform and trained in nursing and first aid, undertaking public first aid duties during Edward VII's funeral.[18] The best known and most popular of the youth organisations of this period was the Boy Scout movement, founded by Baden-Powell in 1909. Baden-Powell had published *Scouting for Boys* in the previous year in an attempt to encourage patriotism and oppose socialism, providing moral and physical training for the future defenders of empire. By November 1909 around 6,000 girls had formed themselves into groups of Girl Scouts, enjoying activities such as 'leaping over dykes, and crawling about in fields on hands and knees, or even on one's tummy'.[19] The first large official Boy Scouts rally, held at Crystal Palace in 1909 was attended by a group of girls in uniform, calling themselves 'Girl Scouts' and demanding to take part in the parade and inspection alongside the boys.[20] The combination of physical exercise, military training and moral leadership, which the Scouting movement offered, appeared to be attractive to girls as well as to boys. In response to this interest from girls in the scouting movement, Baden-Powell created the Girl Guides, an organisation which he hoped would provide a more appropriate and 'womanly' model of behaviour for its members.

However, it soon became apparent that the aspects of Scouting which had appealed to girls were the very activities which Baden-Powell believed to be unsuitable for them. Indeed, *Scouting for Boys* opened by arguing that 'every boy ought to learn to shoot and obey orders, else he is no more good when war breaks out than an old woman', emphasising not just a link between youth and combat but between masculinity and militarism.[21] Marching, drilling and adventure were a part of the martial life deemed both a natural aspect of masculinity and a necessary means of regulating the energies and appetites of the adolescent male which, if not so controlled, could lead to uncontrolled violence or 'unsuitable' sexual activity. Adolescent girls were believed to have no such 'energies' and thus to need less regulation. Instead, it was imperative that they did not overstrain themselves during adolescence, as this would lead to physical weakness and a potential inability to conceive and rear physically strong children. Thus, the skills of domestic science replaced those of martial training, and the animal names chosen by the girls' organisations were replaced with flower names and insignia. This attempt to feminise the movement was often unpopular amongst its young female adherents, and the biography of Baden-Powell's wife, Olave, recalled that girls who had 'revelled in their Scouting' were found to be 'rather lukewarm about being Guides', insisting on keeping the patrol cries they had developed as Owls and Foxes because, 'as they explained, Sunflowers and Pimpernels did not make any nice noises'.[22] Scouting, as designed by Baden-Powell for boys, was seen as unwomanly and unsuitable for adolescent girls, whose transition into womanhood had to be carefully monitored if they were to develop into physically and morally strong mothers. However, Baden-Powell recognised that in order to attract girls to the Girl Guides the organisation had to provide opportunities for excitement and adventure, albeit within a designated feminine sphere. In a 1909 pamphlet *Girl Guides: A Suggestion for Character Training for Girls*, Baden-Powell and his sister Agnes urged girls to:

> imagine that a battle has taken place in and around your town and village...what are you going to do? Are you going to sit down, and wring your hands, and cry? Or are you going to be plucky and go out and do something to help your brothers and fathers who are fighting and falling on your behalf?[23]

There are two important points to note about this extract. First, the girls were being urged to take an active part in the defence of the home, represented here as a town or village. Second however, the form that this action took was that of helping the male combatants, rather than taking any leading or equal role in combat. Although the suggested role for girls had expanded from the Victorian ideal of the angel in the home, they were still expected to take a supportive role in times of war or combat; working behind the lines to support the male combatants.

This suggested role for Girl Scouts can be seen as an extension of the tradition of female philanthropic work with the armed forces which had been a feature of the nineteenth century. Nightingale's hospital at Scutari and the foundation of 'Sailor's Rests' by Agnes Weston in the 1870s were early examples of this work, providing middle and upper-class women and girls with a role assisting the armed forces which avoided the derogatory associations of camp followers. Acceptance and approval of the armed forces had grown in Britain throughout the nineteenth century, and the size of the armed forces themselves had expanded, the development of the Volunteer Force, in particular, accounting for 2.7 per cent of the male population aged between 15 and 49 in 1903, with over 8 per cent of all men having undergone some form of military training.[24] The Volunteer Force, a precursor of the Territorial Force which provided part-time training for men in military service, had become popular during the invasion scare of the mid nineteenth century, when many were convinced that France, under the leadership of Louis Napoleon, was planning a full scale invasion of Britain. The regular army, overstretched and denuded by the campaigns of the Crimea and the Indian Mutiny, was numerically insufficient to provide national defence, and so the Volunteer Force recruited men to defend the nation. Although the expected invasion never came, the Volunteer Force remained a popular facet of mid and late Victorian society, its parades and shows providing an outlet for an expanding popular militarism. Volunteers did see military service, although the War Office was not keen to draw on their labour, seeing them as an amateur and inefficient auxiliary to the regular army. However, over thirty thousand volunteers saw combat during the Boer War, demonstrating the increasing importance of a reserve force to the British army in this period.[25] The increasing importance of militarism in Victorian and Edwardian society meant that the armed forces had to be rethought and reshaped, assimilated as far as possible to civilian norms of behaviour. The female influence was particularly important here, and women's philanthropic work with the armed forces can be seen as a means of 'civilising' soldiers, as well as providing an outlet for the time and talents of middle-class women.

The foundation of military leagues such as the National Service League in 1901 and the Navy League in 1895 provided further evidence of the growing linkage of patriotism and militarism in an increasingly militarised society. The National Service League, which had approximately four thousand members by 1906, campaigned for universal male military conscription along the lines of the Volunteer Force, with all young men who were not already in the armed forces undertaking a period of military training each year. The extent to which Edwardian Britain was, if not a militarised society, a society which equated patriotism with militarism, can be seen in the League's membership figures, which increased from approximately four thousand members in 1906 to 98,931 members by 1912.[26] The League had a separate women's section but did not campaign for any model of female military service. Thus the popular militarism of the Edwardian period, whilst appealing to both men and women, was based on a model of gender relations which associated militarism with masculinity.

However, this popular militarism was not only seen in aspects of public life concerned with the armed forces. Instead, a martial language infused many aspects of Edwardian society, and a system of organisation based upon that of the armed services, could be seen in many different areas of life. Many members of the National Service League were involved in the Scouting movement, strengthening the organisation's existing tendency towards militarism, reflected in the *Boy's Own Paper*'s description of Scouts as 'little soldiers'.[27] Officer Training Corps was a popular feature of male public school life, and its members were the recipients of numerous speeches by military leaders and propagandists, emphasising the importance to Britain of a militarised youth. Much Edwardian popular culture likewise reflected the increasing concern with security and defence in Britain, with a gradual shift towards regarding Germany, rather than France, as the national enemy. Militarism was not simply confined to the armed forces and proto-military organisations like the Scouts. Fiction such as 'Perils of the Motherland – A Story of the War of 1911', written by Captain Frank Shaw, an ex-officer with the Merchant marine and published in *Chums*, a magazine for boys published by the Harmsworth Press, warned of a future war which would involve the whole nation – a precursor to total war. In Shaw's story, Britain was invaded by Russia. The whole nation, regardless of class or political allegiance, united to fight the invaders, and although the first episode ended with the defeat of the British civilian defenders, the title of the sequel, 'Vengeance of the Motherland', promised the eventual victory of a united Britain.[28] The new entertainment medium of film similarly displayed a fascination with the heroics of past wars and the possibilities of a future conflict. Films such as *The Battle of Waterloo* (1913), *The Battle* (1911), which reconstructed the American Civil War and *The Sneaky Boer* and *The Call to Arms* (both 1902) pandered to the audience's fascination with combat whilst *The Airship Destroyer* (1909), *Aerial Anarchists* (1911) and *Flight of Death* (1914) represented future wars, which all involved the destruction of British towns and cities by enemy bombardment.[29] Whole nations, not just armies, would be involved in any coming war.

The language of war entered many facets of Edwardian life: eugenicist fears about the physical deterioration of the British race, heightened after the Boer War, were expressed as a concern that 'the future colonizers and soldiers' of Britain were threatened, and women were reminded that the raising of healthy sons was their imperial duty.[30] The female role in the nation and in imagined future wars was primarily that of mother, nurturer and carer, providing physically and morally strong sons for the armed forces and working as nurses and carers behind the lines, supporting the male role of combatant. Images of war, chivalry, nation and duty were so deeply intertwined within British culture that they could be drawn upon by a wide variety of organisations and interests. The suffrage campaign, alongside more overtly militaristic organisations such as the Boy Scouts and the National Service League, drew on a martial symbolism and language. Although all branches of the suffrage movement saw themselves as fighting a battle for full female citizenship, this can be seen most clearly in the activities of the radical suffragette movement. The Women's Social and Political Union (WSPU) consciously used the word 'militant', with its connotations of combat, rather than 'radical' to describe their aims and activities. Histories of the suffragette movement, written by suffragettes themselves, tended to emphasise action over debate, and individual acts of heroism over committee meetings.[31] Approximately 1,000 women and 40 men were imprisoned for law breaking activities in the name of female suffrage between 1905 and the outbreak of war in 1914, when the campaign was suspended.[32] These activities included a wide range of acts of civil disobedience: window breaking, destroying telephone and telegraph wires and the destruction of mail in post boxes were all common forms of protest, whilst perhaps the best known, Emily Davison's death under the hooves of the King's horse in the 1913 Epsom Derby, embodied notions for many of bravery and personal sacrifice, qualities closely linked with the ideal of the chivalric British soldier. The WSPU also had a form of uniform: hats, badges, brooches, scarves and sashes in the organisations' colours of purple, green and white widely used to signify membership of, or support for, the WSPU and its aims of female enfranchisement. It seems that the WSPU often celebrated and embraced notions of battle and heroism. Sylvia Pankhurst recalled how, from approximately 1907 onwards:

> The spirit of the WSPU now became more and more that of a voluntary army at war... processions and pageantry were a prominent feature of the work, and these, in their precision, their regalia, their marshals and captains, had a decided military flavour. Flora Drummond was called the General and rode at the head of processions with an officer's cap and epaulettes.[33]

The WSPU consciously represented their campaign as a war, claiming for themselves the ideals of chivalry, valour and heroism so closely linked with militarism and combat in Edwardian Britain.

Given the omnipresence of military ideals, symbols and metaphors in Edwardian life, it seems almost inevitable that the first group of women to openly adopt a military uniform and structure should be formed in this period. In 1907 Richard Haldane, the Secretary of State for War, created sweeping reforms of the army. These were embodied in the Territorial and Reserve Forces Act of that year which created a British Expeditionary Force of approximately sixteen thousand men by transforming the Volunteer Force of the Victorian era into the Territorial Force. As Summers argues, this territorial army was a 'British version of the Germanic ideal of the nation in arms' which was represented 'not as a professional force' but 'almost as an instrument of national moral regeneration'.[34] The First Aid Nursing Yeomanry (FANY), founded in the same year, attempted to combine the ideals and imagery of nursing with the sense of valour and patriotism associated with this voluntary military service. Retired Sergeant-Major Edward Baker, a veteran of the Sudan campaign of the 1890s, who launched the FANY, advertised for members in the national press, stating that it was the new organisation's 'mission' to 'tend soldiers in the field', drawing on the image of Florence Nightingale in his statement that members would 'prove ourselves worthy country-women of the first and greatest of Britain's army nurses'.[35] Baker, having first-hand experience of battle, and of the numbers of men dying of injuries which they may well have survived had adequate first aid been available, wanted to create a corps of women who could ride out onto the battle field and minister there to the wounded, staying with them until they could be collected by ambulance units which would take them to Base hospitals. Baker discussed the origins of the Corps in the organisation's gazette *Women and War* in 1910:

> During my period of service with Lord Kitchener in the Sudan campaign, where I had the misfortune to be wounded, it occurred to me that there was a missing link somewhere in the Ambulance Department, which, in spite of the changes in warfare, had not altered very materially since the days of the Crimea when Florence Nightingale and her courageous band of helpers went out to succour and save the wounded.[36]

Thus, whilst the appeal of the FANY to many of its members was undoubtedly the potential it appeared to offer for travel, action and excitement in the military sphere, Baker's initial concept of the Corps was firmly embedded within the established feminine ethos of caring for and supporting men in wartime.

Despite this, the FANY still faced some resistance from a sceptical public and army. The Corps attempted to address this by emphasising the femininity of its members, and their nursing, nurturing role, over and above the proximity to combat it was expected they would experience. Although the Corps was run on military lines, with officers, NCOs and privates, the more martial aspects of the organisation were often played down in publicity material. The same edition of *Women and War* argued that 'there has been a great deal of misconception about us from time to time' going on to underline the Corps' femininity in its claim that 'the Corps was established to point the way to all loyal and patriotic women who desire to work under the Red Cross Flag'. Indeed, the article made a direct link between nursing and female patriotism, arguing that 'the day is not far distant when every woman in Britain will belong to one or other of the movements which work under the influence of that flag'.[37] Further on in the same edition of the gazette the same issues were addressed in a more colloquial format, in an article purporting to recount a conversation in a public house entitled 'Why Private Muldoon Changed His Mind'. The working-class Muldoon began by expressing his rather traditional views about a woman's role and the perceived threat of the FANY to the male bastion of the army:

> A woman's rightful place is in the 'ome, and for women to take to drillin' an ridin' in khaki tunics means the downfall of the British Army, and if ever we 'ave to take our place to defend the honour of our beloved country, either them or me won't be there – that's all!

However, on listening to the narrator of the tale explain the FANY's role, Muldoon changed his mind, exclaiming that:

> It's 'umbled me to the dust...to think of the 'ard and unkind things wot I said before I knew what was the mission of them brave women wot 'ave enlisted in the Corps of the FANY...if she couldn't do anything to ease my pain, God knows she could put 'er arms around my neck en bid me goodbye.[38]

The juxtaposition between the appeal of the FANY to many of its members as a potential entry route to a world they perceived as active and exciting and the still dominant ideology of femininity which saw a women's key role in warfare to be comforter and carer was one which remained a central issue for the Corps and for the women's military organisations which were to follow it.

The emphasis in FANY propaganda on the femininity of the organisation, together with the class position of most of its members and its small numbers, acted to limit public disdain for the Corps. Members of the Corps were expected to be able to ride and preferably to own their own horse. Membership of the FANY was 10 shillings, plus 6 shillings per month as a subscription to the riding school. In addition to these costs, members had to provide their own uniform and first aid materials. The cost of joining the FANY, combined with the necessity for riding skills, meant that membership was effectively limited to middle and upper-class women. Flora Sandes, who went on to achieve a form of fame and notoriety for her role as a Captain and decorated combatant with the Serbian Army during the First World War, was one of the Corps' earliest members. In February 1908, the *Daily Graphic* described the impressions of a male reporter of the FANY headquarters in Old Holborn:

> On giving the password to the pretty sentinel on duty at the door, he found himself in the presence of a busy band of aristocratic amazons in arms. Their purpose was peaceful. In their picturesque uniforms, they were engaged in recruiting work. There was a constant stream of Lady callers, most of them society folk, whose patriotism had impelled them to enrol in the Corps which is being formed to enable women to help their country in wartime. Surrounded by gaily garbed sergeants and corporals, Lady Ernestine Hunt, the eldest daughter of the Marquess of Aylesbury, who looked dashing in her uniform of scarlet tunic and dark skirt, relieved with white braid, was hard at work.[39]

Although the women are described here as amazons, this is offset by the imagery of the 'pretty sentinel' at the door and the 'picturesque uniforms' of the women. The ideology of patriotism, mentioned here, offered these upper-class women a means of expanding their role in public life. As Krisztina Robert has argued in relation to women's work in the First World War, this patriotic impulse was strongly associated with the upper classes, who were seen as acting out of the selfless impulse of devotion to one's country, whilst the work of the middle and working classes was believed to be motivated by personal ambition and financial self-interest.[40] This linkage between elite social class and patriotism, together with an allusion to the difficulties of preserving traditional symbols of femininity whilst undertaking the duties associated with military service, was echoed in a poem printed in a later edition of *Women and War*:

> I wish my mother could see me now
> With a grease gun under my car
> Filling the differential
> 'Ere I start for the sea afar
> Atop a sheet of frozen iron, in cold that
> Would make you cry
> I used to be in society once
> Danced and hunted and flirted once
> Had white hands and complexion once
> Now I am FANY[41]

The FANY, providing a site through which a socially elite group of women could present themselves as patriotic and selfless, also allowed them to stake their claim to a public role in national service.

Recruits had to train in First Aid, horsemanship, veterinary work, signalling and camp cookery. The social class of the members meant that many of them had social and family links with the more elite army regiments, and in 1908 a Colonel of the Grenadier Guards, impressed by the women's horsemanship, invited them to participate in the Royal Naval and Military Tournament being held at Crystal Palace, where members of the Corps won an award for their riding.[42] Shortly after this, the Commanding Officer of the Royal Horse Guards offered his services as a Riding Officer, and the FANY began to drill at the Whitehall barracks of the Guards, known as 'the blues'. The memoirs of a Mrs Robinson, a member in 1908, help to provide some impression of the combination of training and socialising which members of the Corp took part in:

> I drilled 'B' Troop every Saturday afternoon at riding stables near St James' Park, and every Monday or Tuesday all the officers and NCOs met at the Royal Blues Barracks and were drilled by Major King or his Sergeant-Major, who spared us not!... Talking of the 'Blues' officers reminds me of how they gave us (officers and NCOs) an invitation to one of their smoking dinners in their mess... we sat, smoked and joined in the sing-song, and had a wonderful time.[43]

Small in number and socially elite, the FANY were tolerated and even welcomed by some within the armed forces as a potentially useful adjunct and support.

The origins of the FANY betray Baker's romantic conception of the Corps. Imagined by Baker as a group of ministering angels, merging the independence and taste for action of the 'new woman' with the ability to care for men seen as a central facet of femininity, the FANY were seen to combine chivalry with female compassion. The original uniform of the Corp, designed by Baker, consisted of a long dark blue skirt, a high collared scarlet tunic with white braid and a scarlet cap with a shiny black peak. This outfit was completed by black patent riding boots, white gloves, a riding crop and a first aid haversack. The Corps also had a 'mess uniform' of white muslin dress, worn with scarlet bolero and crimson sash.[44] Although the frontispiece of *Women and War* shows a uniformed woman astride a rearing horse, holding a banner aloft, members were expected to ride side-saddle. The blue and scarlet uniform, with its connotations of military history, was replaced in 1909 by a more practical, though less romantic, khaki uniform with a shorter skirt which could be buckled up to allow the wearer to ride astride, rather than side-saddle. The khaki uniform, although less glamorous than the scarlet and blue, had the symbolic advantage of visually linking the work, and potential sacrifice, of the Corps' members with that of the men in the armed forces. However, it also left the FANY open to the criticism that they were assuming a male role alongside a male uniform, as seen in the account of one group of members being mistaken for suffragettes by 'factory girls' who 'started shouting, booing, throwing things and calling "you... suffragettes"'. On seeing the Red Cross badges which the women, who were on their way home from a First Aid Class, were wearing, the girls 'melted away' with 'sudden, shame faced sorrys'.[45] It appears that the Red Cross badge, with its connotations of nursing and femininity, had the power to counteract the apparent masculinity of women appearing in public in a khaki uniform.

However, the early history of the FANY was also riven by internal strife and dissension, much of which seems to have stemmed from the dichotomy of a female organisation being led by a man. Following internal dissent regarding money raised by a charity matinee held in London, Mabel St Clair Stobart and Lady Ernestine Hunt broke away from the FANY in December 1909, taking most of its early members with them to found the Women's Sick and Wounded Convoy Corps which worked with St Clair Stobart in the Balkan Wars of 1912 and then during the First World War. The move from Baker's romantic red and blue uniform to the more serviceable khaki, combined with riding astride, appears to have coincided with the rise through the ranks of Grace Ashley-Smith and Lilian Franklin, both of whom had joined the Corps in 1909. Ashley-Smith and Franklin had less romantic notions about the identity and aims of the Corps, Ashley-Smith commenting that 'it was solely because of its title yeomanry that I had sought out this Corps'.[46] Ashley-Smith emphasised the hard work and dedication demanded of the FANY, arguing that 'it is not a corps of shirkers, but of workers... those who look upon the training of the Corps as a pleasant pastime are advised to think twice before offering themselves at headquarters as recruits', a far cry from

Baker's idealised but often impractical ideas for the organisation.[47] By 1911, Ashley-Smith and Franklin were running the Corps. Ashley-Smith's diary details her determination to restructure the organisation:

> I spent the next few months fighting for my way in the office. Soon I had all the girls in khaki astride skirts with tunics to match, and I wrote out a scheme of training based on the R.A.M.C. training manual.

As part of this re-organisation along more professional lines, Ashley-Smith felt it necessary to purge the FANY of its more frivolous members describing how she worked to

> weed out ... a soulful lady with peroxide hair, very fat and hearty, who insisted on wearing white drawers with frills under her khaki skirt. She also insisted on falling off at every parade and displaying them ... she had to go. No women's movement could have survived those frilly drawers on parade.[48]

Although still almost entirely staffed by volunteers from the upper classes the FANY became a more professional organisation under Ashley-Smith's leadership, following Royal Army Medical Corps training protocols and weekly riding drills with the Royal Hussars and the Surrey Yeomanry. However, emancipation for women was never Ashley-Smith's aim. Although she described the FANY as a 'women's movement', and despite women in uniform being mistaken for suffragettes, the FANY were never consciously a part of the feminist movement. Instead Ashley-Smith aimed for acceptance and integration into the army for her small band of women. The FANY intended to win acceptance into a conservative bastion of masculinity for a small group of socially elite women, not liberation for the many.

The organisation remained independent of and separate from the War Office and the military establishment, although it had many sponsors connected with the armed forces, numbering twenty five patrons of military and naval rank amongst its official supporters in 1909.[49] Whilst this allowed them the freedom to dress and train as they wished, it also meant that, for much of their pre-war existence, the FANY were searching for a role and for recognition. The Corps appeared at many public events: attending the Derby as first-aiders, performing a military tournament in Brighton and presenting a wreath at Buckingham Palace on the death of Edward VII in 1910, although their offer of their services at the funeral was turned down by the Metropolitan Police. In 1912 the hotly contested Home Rule Bill for Ireland was passed by the House of Commons, and, for a while, civil war in Ulster looked likely. Ashley-Smith was quick to offer the FANY's services to Edward Carson, leader of the Ulster Unionists and a patron of the Corps, prompting several Irish members, described by Ashley-Smith as 'ardent Sinn Feiners', to resign in protest.[50] According to Ashley-Smith, Carson provisionally accepted her offer and the FANY were appointed as the Ulster Ambulance. Ashley-Smith's recollections of her involvement in the Ulster crisis, with its descriptions of 'secret drill halls' and of being 'thrilled by the passwords and signs', betray her excitement at finally being involved in some form of military campaign, and demonstrate the extent to which she saw war as an opportunity to be welcomed, almost a game, rather than an experience to be avoided. Although the FANY did not travel to Ireland, and the predicted civil war did not ensue, overtaken instead by events on the continent, her action had the effect of raising the Corps' public profile, a photo in the *London Budget* describing the FANY as consisting of 'thirty five gentlewomen' who were acting as 'a women's mounted ambulance corps'.[51] As war in Europe began to seem more and more inevitable Ashley-Smith believed that the FANY would be invited to help by the War Office. When war was declared she was travelling to South Africa to visit her sister but returned to Britain on the first available ship to find that the War Office had no role for the corps. The FANY with their small membership and independence were to go on to find work autonomously in Belgium and France during the war, whilst more traditionally organised groups of women were immediately utilised by the War Office.

The Voluntary Aid Detachment (VAD) had been launched by the War Office in August 1909 as a means of recruiting both male and female volunteers to work in a medical capacity with the Territorial Force created by Haldane in 1907. The VAD, which quickly developed into a female rather than a mixed service, joined two pre-existing women's military nursing organisations: the Queen Alexander's Imperial Medical Nursing Reserve, which consisted of a few hundred nurses employed to work with the army and the Territorial Force Nursing Service. This service had been set up in July 1908, organised by Haldane's sister Elizabeth to run along similar lines to the Territorial Force itself, being organised on a County basis. Elizabeth Haldane visualised the Nursing Service as a female counterpart to the male Territorial Reserve, complementing the male 'service' of combat with the female 'service' of nursing. In an appeal for volunteers, she urged nurses to come forward for the service, declaring that 'the manhood of the country are playing up splendidly' and that it was now time 'for women – for nurses – to play their part also in the scheme of defence.[52] Nursing with the armed services provided an acceptable, and highly visible, route through which women could demonstrate their patriotism whilst enjoying some of the status associated with national service for the state.

However, the Territorial Force Nursing Service, although its members numbered approximately three thousand by 1912, was not large enough to undertake all of the medical services associated with the Territorial Force and the VAD was created in 1909 to take over some of these duties.[53] The year 1909 is significant as it was a year which saw a wave of jingoism and invasion panic, largely sparked by the popular production in London of Gerald Du Maurier's play about an imagined invasion '*An Englishman's Home*' which 'bought men and women rushing to enlist' in all the volunteer services.[54] However, despite this rush to serve, and the widespread belief in the necessity of widespread militarisation which was seen throughout the Edwardian period, women and women's organisations had to be careful to emphasise that their actions were motivated solely by patriotism, rather than by any feminist notion of equality and opportunity. An article in the St John Ambulance Brigade Journal *First Aid*, which argued that women from the Brigade could be given training in military hospitals, concluded with the statement that the idea was 'in no way connected with the Female Suffrage, for which I entertain a very strong measure of contempt'.[55] Patriotism may have been claimed by women of the upper classes, but its most successful claimants remained uniformed men.

The VAD had a complicated organisational structure. It operated on a local basis, recruiting its members via the county Territorial Force and being organised under the auspices of the Red Cross whilst its members had to possess St John Ambulance Association First Aid and Nursing Certificates. The VAD was often run at local level by 'County ladies', the social counterparts of the men who ran the county Territorial Forces, and much of the attraction of the service lay in the role it promised to give them in the defence of the country, seen in the following extract from a 1910 VAD Training Handbook from Devon which imagined a village in the aftermath of invasion:

> Let us suppose the schoolhouse, or the church, or the hall will hold forty wounded. Forty beds must be provided ... Is there anyone whose help is not required? Not one. Where is his or her place ... what does he or she do? That will be told them ... we can give the knowledge, we can provide the organisation.[56]

Thus the VAD, as well as offering its largely female members a public role, also seemed to ensure that structures of social class would be maintained in the event of war or invasion, providing upper and upper middle-class women with a female equivalent of the volunteer work of the Territorial Force. Unlike the FANY, traditional feminine domestic skills retained their importance in the training given to VADs. As well as receiving training in First Aid and nursing, VADs were expected to demonstrate competence in a range of 'housewifery', including home hygiene, darning, sewing, knitting and laundry, spending some of their training sessions sewing pillow cases and hot water bottles.[57] Although VADs would have a place in wartime, it was increasingly becoming clear that this would be a traditionally feminine place, working as flexibly as possible within the female sphere to support and care for the male combatants.

In July 1912 the War Office withdrew responsibility for Territorial Force hospitals from the Red Cross and directed that the VAD would work directly under the leadership of the Territorial Force Medical Service. This was both an attempt to simplify the complicated organisational structure of the VAD and a move to eliminate as far as possible the element of independence which the VAD still possessed. Although the VAD were clearly performing duties associated with the female sphere, they were training to perform them within the masculine sphere of warfare and combat, and thus needed to clearly come unto the control of the armed forces. As one Royal Army Medical Corps (RAMC) Officer wrote to *First Aid* in January 1913:

> When one or more VADs combine to form a temporary hospital and if the commandant of the most senior detachment is a lady, will she command any men's detachment that may be attached to her Unit? .... I do not think it would be wise for a woman to act in any capacity other than a nursing sister or matron.[58]

The War Office faced a dilemma in their attempts to make use of women's labour through the VAD: whilst it was becoming increasingly obvious that a militarised nation could make use of women as support workers and nurses, this work needed to be closely regulated in order to avoid any gender transgressions, such as women commanding men or working independently close to the front line. The War Office reforms of 1912 meant that VADs would be less independent and that members would be sent to work individually in hospitals run by the Territorial Force Medical Service. Rather than running hospitals and clearing stations independently in detachments formed of and led by women, individual women would work under the leadership of men in existing military medical organisations or in civilian hospitals. As a correspondent to *First Aid* put it in December 1913, the reforms 'put an end once and for all to the idea that women would ever be used in the field'.[59]

Unlike the FANY, the VAD received War Office funding and recognition, with at least 32,000 women serving in the organisation as military nurses during the First World War and another 11,000 working in hospital administration as General Service VADs.[60] Both the women's military organisations, such as the FANY and the VAD, together with other semi-militaristic organisations such as the Girl Guides and Boy Scouts can be seen as aspects of the increasing militarization of Edwardian Britain. However, women often struggled to find a place outside of the role of nurse and carer, which increasingly appeared to be the patriotic female equivalent of the male soldier in this militaristic and nationalistic society. The nationalism of the age was increasingly focused around the image of the chivalrous male soldier of the Victorian period and the perceived need to create a 'nation in arms' along the lines of Imperial Germany. Whilst the transformation of the Volunteer Force to the Territorial Force created by Haldane in 1907, and the expansion of the armed forces gave men a clear-cut means of expressing their patriotism and determination to defend their country from invasion, there was no such straightforward route for women. The appeal of both the FANY and the VAD to many of their members lay both in their visible expression of female patriotism and in the opportunities they appeared to offer for active, public service – a means of escape from the confines of Edwardian domesticity.

However, women attempting to undertake such work, particularly those appearing in uniform, closely associated with the valour and chivalry of the ideal male soldier, were often the subject of public derision and scorn. They were widely perceived as an aspect of the feminist movement which was seeking to play at war games, attempting to attain the status of heroic patriots alongside combatant men, but without taking a direct part in combat. Despite the appropriation of the language and symbols of service by the FANY, their appearance in public was often greeted with 'scepticism and mirth', one recruit recalling that when she appeared in full uniform for lunch at a Brighton hotel, she and her friend were placed 'behind a screen at the end of the room' escorted out through a side door to the back street.[61] The nurses of the VAD were less vulnerable to this accusation than the more militaristic FANY, as their activities were more clearly situated within the traditionally feminine sphere, but they too were often the subject of concern, their work with the military appearing to threaten the unrealistic but symbolically important gender divide between male participants and female civilians in wartime. However, although they were often associated in the public mind with the very visible campaign of the suffragettes, neither the VAD nor the FANY saw themselves as organisations concerned with feminist aspirations for an extended role for women or with the question of the suffrage. Both were essentially conservative, patriotic bodies, run and largely staffed by upper and upper middle-class women of independent means, their voluntary status largely excluding women from other social backgrounds. Women's pre-war work with the military was never seen by the majority of those involved in it as a means of liberating women as a whole; instead, the organisations acted as a structure through which a small number of women could display their patriotism and dedication to service whilst enjoying some access to the active, male world of the military. At the outbreak of war these militaristic organisations remained the preserve of small groups of often socially conservative elite women, fighting to demonstrate their individual loyalty and nationalism, rather than to prove the usefulness of women as a whole in wartime.

3 'The Women Were Marvellous'

The First World War and the
female volunteer

The call to arms in August 1914, when nearly 300,000 British men enlisted, was matched by a rush to organise for the war effort amongst upper and middle-class British women.[1] The mood of the time was caught by the young Vera Brittain, whose diary entry for 3 August, 1914, the day before war was declared in Britain read:

> Today has been far too exciting to enable me to feel at all like sleep – in fact it is one of the most thrilling I have ever lived through... That which has been so long anticipated by some and scoffed at by others has come to pass at last – Armageddon in Europe![2]

Brittain's comments reflect a relief at the end of a period of uncertainty and an exhilaration in experiencing a recognisably historic, public event. Despite her description of the inevitability of war as 'exciting' and 'thrilling', Brittain's diary entry does not unequivocally express an enthusiasm for the coming war; instead it depicts the overwhelming nature of events, a recognition of the impact of epoch changing events on individual lives, expressing a mixture of unease and exhilaration. In a similar mood, another middle-class diarist, Mrs Eustace Miles, described the outbreak of war as 'awful as it is – it is very thrilling'.[3] The ambiguous responses of these women to the declaration of hostilities were reflected both in the country as a whole, and in the suffrage movement's response to the war.

It has often been argued that a sort of 'war fever' swept across Britain in these first days, and, that although a significant number of Labour and Liberal activists campaigned and argued for peace, Rupert Brooke's claim that 'Honour has come back, as a King, to earth' encapsulated the feelings of many, and helped to explain the general mood of excitement and anticipation.[4] However, Adrian Gregory's reassessment of British war enthusiasm has demonstrated how mixed emotions and ambiguity characterised the British response to the outbreak of war, arguing that the rush to arms of early August was not a reflection of a belligerent mood amongst the British public in the days and weeks preceding war's declaration but instead the result of a mixture of early enthusiasm and a pragmatic response to the sharp rise in unemployment which accompanied the buildup to war, with male employment rates falling by 10 per cent between July and September.[5] In a nuanced account, Gregory describes in some detail the shift from an unenthusiastic but largely resigned nation before the war to a more positive public mood, in which anti-war sentiment was increasingly marginalised, arguing that the shift in public opinion was in large part attributable to the decision of Liberal politicians and influential newspaper editors to support the war.[6] Newspaper opinion varied between the poles of the moderate, pacifist tendencies of the *Manchester Guardian* and the *Daily News* and the more jingoistic, bullish opinions of the *Daily Mail* and *The Times*, which warned its readers before the outbreak of hostilities that this was a war in which 'we must fight for... civilisation',[7] setting the scene for later claims of German brutality and barbarism in occupied territories.[8] As the country moved towards war, public opinion was divided, rather than overwhelmingly supportive. However, the declaration of war was greeted by large public demonstrations of enthusiasm and national solidarity, with large demonstrations in the centre of London reported by many of the daily newspapers.[9] Despite an initial lack of enthusiasm amongst the British public for the prospect of a European conflict the actual outbreak of war simplified and clarified earlier ambiguities, perhaps offering an escape from the complexities and problems of pre-war Britain: the suffrage campaign, Home Rule in Ireland and industrial unrest.

The immediate impact of the war appeared, in many ways, to deepen the existing differences between the sexes and to lessen women's claim to the franchise; as Martin Pugh has argued the 'sex war' was overwhelmed 'by the Great War'.[10] Patriotic activity was gendered from the very beginning of the war, and activities that could be undertaken in support of war aims were shaped by gender as well as by class. For young men who wanted to be involved in the coming war the path was clear. On 6 August, parliament agreed that the Army could recruit an extra 500,000 men. Kitchener's first recruitment appeal, famously telling British men that 'Your Country Needs You' was issued the following day. One hundred thousand men were enlisted by 25 August, although initial organisational incompetence sometimes combined with a reluctance on the part of families to see men join the Army meant that many who wished to were unable to enlist at first.[11] Routes by which women could participate in the war effort were not so immediately obvious, and for many working-class women, the early impact of the war was economically disastrous. Although one of the dominant images of women in the war is of women working-in industrial and other occupations, replacing the men who had gone into uniform, the immediate impact of the war on female employment was largely negative. Large numbers of working women were made redundant in the first months of the war, as the upper classes dismissed servants, and trades, which had traditionally employed women, such as millinery and dress-making, were hit the hardest by the economic uncertainties of wartime. This contraction in the conventional areas of female employment was motivated by a desire to contribute to the war effort amongst the upper classes and expressed a willingness to cut back on the extravagances of pre-war life, described by Mrs Alec Tweedie in 1918 as a period in which 'women stopped going to tea parties and buying new hats, and boldly stepped out in men's shoes.'[12] The textile trade alone contracted by 43 per cent in the first five months of the war, and clothing manufacture, a large area of employment for women, shrank by 2 per cent, as employees were laid off or put onto shorter hours.[13] Fifty thousand women who normally undertook paid work were unemployed by March 1915, some put out of work by the activities of wealthier women who had joined the many sewing and knitting organisations that had sprung up at the beginning of the war to sew for the troops.[14]

For many of these women, joining an organisation such as Queen Mary's Needlework Guild, which was launched on 8 August 1914, or simply sewing or knitting at home, fulfilled a need to be doing something perceived as useful and active. The newspapers carried appeals for women to join sewing and knitting circles, and Queen Mary's Needlework Guild was launched on 10 August with the declaration that 'the women of England have been as deeply stirred by this war as the men ... They have not failed yet. They will not fail now.'[15] Vera Brittain, waiting for the results of her Oxford Entrance Exam, wrote on 6 August that

> Today I started the only work it seems as yet possible for women to do –
> the making of garments for soldiers. I started knitting sleeping helmets.
> As I have forgotten how to knit and was never very brilliant when I knew,
> I seem to be an object of some amusement. But even when one is not
> skilful it is better to proceed slowly than to do nothing to help.[16]

These early contributions to the war effort were not always appreciated. *The Daily Call* commented in November 1914 that 'They knit all kinds of things – describable and indescribable. It is safe to say that when "Tommy" receives many of these articles he will be at a loss to know what to do with them.'[17] However, this outbreak of sewing and knitting served the dual purpose of maintaining links between the man at the front and the woman at home, and provided women with an activity they could engage in as a useful part of the war effort, as well as perhaps offering individuals an activity which could help to distract them from personal worries about family and friends at the front. A traditionally feminine activity became imbued with patriotic overtones, and women 'who had neglected this feminine craft' were warned that they could find themselves 'humiliated and somewhat despised' if they showed no talent for sewing.[18] As activities which could be undertaken both individually and as part of a locally or nationally organised group, needlework and knitting both fitted neatly within a dominant ideology of femininity which situated women within the home and provided a means of integrating them within a public, national, war effort.

Women's role within the home, and the linkage of this home with the nation that the men in the trenches were fighting to defend, was often referred to in early press articles and propaganda. The ideology of separate spheres, which linked women with the private, the domestic world and men with the public world of politics and paid work, was utilised in early propaganda and updated to support a discourse of masculinity specific to the needs of wartime. The naturalisation of the relationship between masculinity and soldiering, and women and the domestic was shown visually in 'Women of Britain Say Go' a recruitment poster of 1915, which showed a mother and her two children inside the home, looking out on the uniformed men marching away to war (Figure 3.1).[19] This association of women with home crossed pre-war political boundaries as some leading feminists used the rhetoric of a domestic femininity to call on women's support for the war effort.

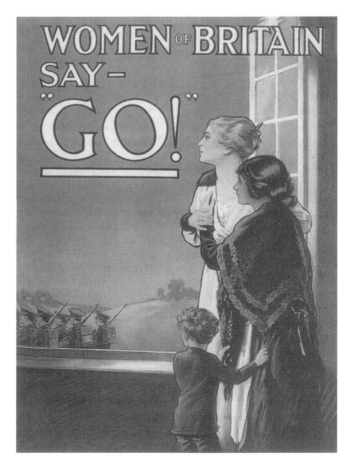

Figure 3.1 Women of Britain Say Go: British propaganda poster of the First World War by E. V. Kealey. Courtesy of the Imperial War Museum, London, PST 0313.

The invaded nation of Belgium was commonly referred to as female, and the treatment of women there, allegedly attacked in their homes by German troops, was drawn upon by Lady Frances Balfour to argue for an extended female role and the enfranchisement of women in wartime as assaults on women in Belgium showed that women could not 'be spared in modern war-fare'.[20] The alleged rape of women by German soldiers was used in British propaganda both to strengthen the linkage of women with the home and to convince women of the importance of recruiting men for the forces, one early poster asking women 'Do you realise that the safety of your home and children depends on our getting more men NOW?'[21] Millicent Garrett Fawcett of the National Union of Women's Suffrage Societies, the umbrella organisation of pre-war suffragists, called in *Contemporary Review* for women to ensure that men returning from the war 'find that women at home have been doing work no less vital for the health of the nation'.[22] A vital part of this wartime role in the home was to send the men away from it: articles inciting support for the war encouraged women with men leaving for the front to 'send them cheerfully on their way', claiming this as a 'sacred duty which England demands they should perform'.[23] The same newspaper suggested that young women should use their closest relationships with men as a means of persuading them to join up:

> Let girls refuse to be seen in the company of any young man who does not wear the khaki hallmark of manhood . . . cut the acquaintance of your sweetheart unless he is prepared to wear khaki and show that he deserves the name of a man.[24]

Similar ideas were expressed in a Parliamentary Recruiting Committee poster addressed 'To the women of Britain', arguing that 'some of your men folk are holding back on your account. Won't you prove your love for the country by persuading them to go?'[25] The *Times* published a similar appeal to its younger female readers in a letter headed 'To English Girls':

> The English girl who will not know the man – lover, brother, friend – that cannot show an overwhelming reason for not taking up arms – that girl will do her duty and will give good help to her country.[26]

Baroness Orczy, the popular author of the 'Scarlet Pimpernel' novels formed the 'Women of England Active Service League', which had as its object the recruitment of men for the forces, and whose 20,000 members pledged 'never to be seen in public with any man who, being in every way fit and free for service, has refused to respond to his country's call.'[27] Thus desirable masculinity was explicitly linked with the military, the role of women being to ensure that men were aware of this. An early poster cited earlier which began by reminding women that their safety, and that of their homes and children, depended on recruiting more men for the army continued by asking them to consider:

> When the war is over and someone asks your husband or your son what he did in the Great War, is he to hang his head because you would not let him go? Won't you help and send a man to join the Army today?[28]

Women's role in wartime appears here as that of sending men away to defend the home, and at the same time defending gender boundaries by reinforcing the relationship of women with the home and men with the military. Demands such as this bear comparison with the activities of the Order of the White Feather, launched by Admiral Penrose Fitzgerald in 1914 and which attempted to shame men into military action by encouraging women to hand out white feathers to men who were not in uniform.[29] The activities of the Order of the White Feather, sometimes mocked in the press for handing out feathers to wounded soldiers and war heroes on leave, are perhaps more expressive of the desire amongst many women to be doing something, anything, to help in the war effort, rather than as evidence of a widespread jingoism amongst the female population. The limited appeal of recruitment activities such as this can also be seen in the numbers responding to Baroness Orczy's Active Service League: although 20,000 signed her pledge, the initial appeal had been for 100,000 signatures.[30] However, if a man's 'natural' place was in the trenches, women also had their own clear-cut, 'natural' role in wartime: that of providing the raw material for the trenches.

As the men marched off to war, women were reminded of *their* corresponding duty to the nation: motherhood. In a letter to *The Times*, published less than two weeks after the start of the war Margaret Llewelyn Davies of the Women's Co-operative Guild, a leading campaigner for the endowment of motherhood, wrote that 'When the perils of war are about to be faced by the men of the nation, the vital importance of the care of motherhood is obvious.'[31] Davies seized on the rhetoric of war to promote maternity as women's work for the state and thus worthy of endowment. Writing to the *Westminster Gazette* on 26 August, 1914, she emotively contrasted the 'wreck and waste of young vigorous lives upon the field' with 'the imperative need of caring for the mothers and young children of the race'.[32] In 1915 the Women's Co-operative Guild published *Maternity*, a collection of letters from working-class mothers edited by Davies, which vividly demonstrated the hardships which many women faced when attempting to bring up families on low incomes in inadequate housing.[33] Arguing along similar lines the *Daily Mail* told women readers that 'the most important thing that women can do ... is to keep themselves and their families in the best possible state of health', whilst Austin Harrison, editor of *The English Review*, claimed early in 1915 that 'motherhood (was) the first duty of women.'[34] When women undertook paid work in wartime they were reminded that this work, whilst necessary to the war effort, was temporary and a reflection of the unusual demands of a society in total war and that when the war was over their 'vision of a dream child ... will be a reality one day'.[35] Thus, even when women worked in areas previously closed to them because of their sex, such as engineering and munitions, motherhood, women's unique contribution to the war, was raised above all other forms of female wartime service. Throughout the war, the politics of eugenics and of pro-natalism combined to produce a discourse urging women to consider their actual or potential role as mothers as of primary importance in wartime.

However, fears about the impact of 'khaki fever' on young women led to a moral panic about the numbers of illegitimate babies allegedly being born. Although it was never proven that the war had led to an increase in illegitimate births, with soldiers and sailors as the fathers, the anxiety about their possible existence was part of a wider unease about the impact of the war upon women.[36] The appeal of 'walking out' with a soldier and of being able to 'have a regimental badge to stick on the front of her jacket and a button to display' was disparagingly described as being motivated by a desire for vicarious excitement and association with the status being accorded to men in military uniform.[37] Young women collecting for various 'flag days', a common scene in wartime, were widely attacked in the press as a 'grave menace to morality', perceived as being in danger of 'falling victims to vice, sooner or later, through the freedom which the collecting box creates'.[38] The linkage of femininity in the masculine, public space of the street with prostitution, which was implied here, was widespread in wartime. George Lansbury's left-wing newspaper the *Herald* reported on an incident it dubbed 'The Cardiff Outrage', in which a military order was passed by Colonel East, Commander of the Severn Defences, enabling women whom the local police claimed were 'leading an immoral life and suffering from disease' to be imprisoned if they were found on the streets after 7 o' clock at night.[39] The parallels with the Contagious Diseases Act, which the feminist movement of the nineteenth century had fought hard to have removed from the statute books, were obvious. C. Nina Boyle, writing in the suffragette journal *The Vote* argued that prostitution was only prosecuted when it was perceived as 'inconvenient and dangerous – to men, not to girls'.[40] East, however, defended his actions to the *Herald*, arguing that he was merely interested in protecting the health of his soldiers, the nation's most valuable resource in wartime, prompting the *Herald* to comment that 'the physical and moral degradation of women does not count' with the military authorities.[41] Despite this, some elements within the feminist movement sided with the authorities and the mainstream press in their persecution of alleged or potential prostitution. Mrs Alec Tweedie, a vociferous author and organiser, called early in 1917 for martial law to be introduced to combat 'loose living among girls'.[42] Tweedie believed that 'loose women are like a plague spot' arguing a year later that 'every woman who lets herself go is as bad as a German spy and a traitor, not only to her sex, but to her country.'[43] Upper-class women organised 'Tipperary Clubs' as meeting places for working-class women away from the supposed temptations of the public house.[44] The National Vigilance Association (NVA) called for female patrols to combat the alleged threat of female immorality; work women were believed to be especially suited for because it sat comfortably within their 'sphere of influence'. From these patrols, the first women police officers emerged, patrolling the open spaces and streets of cities to monitor and control the activities of women.[45] The harassment of one group of women thus led to increased opportunities for employment and voluntary wartime activities for other groups.

Many women, however, continued to express a sense of frustration with the limited sphere of activities which were being offered to women keen to participate in the early days of the war. Although work such as sewing and knitting, sitting comfortably within the 'women's sphere', constituted much of women's early contribution to the war effort, the existing political organisations and networks associated with the pre-war suffrage campaign provided a framework for many new female activities. Numerous voluntary organisations appeared in the first months of war. *The Times* for 31 August 1914 lists twelve London-based organisations in its 'Work for Women' list, including The Women's Emergency Corps, The British Women's Patriotic League and Harvest Work for Women and the Women's Suffrage National Aid Corps.[46] Some organisations, such as the Association of Infant Consultations and Schools for Mothers were an extension of the social and philanthropic work that had been undertaken by some upper- and middle-class women before the war, while others, such as the Women's Co-operative Guild, existed to represent the interests of working-class women and their families. Organisations such as these, despite their diverse political aims, were working within a sphere of activity already becoming widely accepted as the concern of women, that of caring educating and campaigning for, mothers and children. However, many other of these wartime organisations were the result of the suffrage movement's suspension of its campaign and the enthusiasm with which many of its leaders and members threw themselves into the war effort. As the voluntary wartime organisations expanded, taking up more and more of the time and energy of middle-class committee women, the activities of the suffrage societies declined. *The Times* noted on 11 August 1914 that the Women's National Liberal Association, the National Union of Women's Suffrage Societies (NUWSS) and the Women's Freedom League were all abandoning their political campaigns and instead 'devoting themselves to helping those who suffer from the war'.[47] Within two weeks of the declaration of war, all the leading suffragist and suffragette societies had declared an end to their activities for the duration of the war, and, on 16 August, the government announced a general amnesty for militant suffragettes, releasing those who were imprisoned and dropping prosecutions of others.[48] The suffrage campaign had used the language and metaphors of war to describe its activities prior to 1914, and, when war came, it was quick to use this imagery to describe women's war work. A 1919 article, looking back on the suffrage movement's contribution to the war effort described the transition in the following terms:

> I watched the Suffrage movement through its later phases of struggle, desperation and success...the fight was largely a soldier's battle. What devotion was shown and what courage! Delicate women surrendered their health, rich ones their money. Timid ones their reserve and dislikes... when the time came, the women's army was there, fit and mobilised, to answer the call.[49]

However, this appropriation of military imagery by the women's movement was contested in some quarters. Cicely Hamilton's 1919 novel, *William – an Englishman* contrasted the masculine realities of war with the suffrage movement's readiness to adapt the language to describe its activities. Hamilton repeatedly and ironically describes the suffragette movement as 'warriors', who, whilst pacifist in their international outlook, believed they were fighting a battle at home. Describing a pre-war meeting at which Griselda, a militant suffragette and her fiancée, William, are ejected, Hamilton has Griselda tell William 'remember this is War – God knows it's horrible, but we must not shrink from it.'[50] Following their wedding, they honeymoon in the Ardennes, are caught up in the German invasion and Griselda is raped and killed, leaving William to bitterly reflect upon their ignorance of the realities of war. William returns to London, denounces his pacifist friends in the socialist movement and joins the army, albeit as a clerk, as a means of both avenging Griselda's death and of demonstrating his new loyalty to, and appreciation of, the British state. A sense of national unity in adversity, a nation united against the common, external enemy of Imperial Germany, brought together diverse groups, who had previously been fighting the British state, in a common, widely shared belief in the 'righteousness' of the Allied cause.[51]

The ambiguity and divided opinion amongst the wider British public at the outbreak of war portrayed by Gregory were mirrored in the response to war of the suffrage movement. The previously militant Women's Social and Political Union (WSPU), run somewhat autocratically by the Pankhursts, announced a suspension of its activities within days of the outbreak of war. The position of the WSPU was that suffrage for women was of no use in a beaten and subjugated Britain; the war effort therefore had to prevail over the campaign for the vote, Emmeline arguing in September 1914 that 'we are fighting for our existence as a nation and all the ideals for which our fore-fathers have fought and sacrificed in the past.'[52] Emmeline and Christabel Pankhurst dedicated their movement to recruiting men for the services and women for the factories, both emphasising the importance of women's role in the war in their campaign for women to take up war work in industries traditionally associated with male labour, and reinforcing the difference between the sexes in their crusade for men to join the forces. The Pankhursts travelled the country holding numerous recruitment rallies and meetings, the first of which was at the London Opera House on 8 September 1914.[53] A large recruitment pageant was held in London in July 1915, with Emmeline Pankhurst described in a celebratory account of women's role in the war by the American journalist Molly Potter-Daggett as 'England's most active recruiting agent'.[54] These pageants drew upon the suffrage campaign's earlier use of symbolism, *The Times* and *The Daily Chronicle* commenting on the large and colourful parade organised by the Pankhursts in which over 20,000 women marchers were divided into 125 contingents, each carrying a flag of red, white or blue, rather than the suffrage colours of purple, green and white.[55] As well as demanding work for women, the marchers carried placards which accentuated the gendered differences becoming so visible in wartime, with slogans such as 'Shells made by a wife may save a husband's life.'[56] The parades and rallies organised by the Pankhursts served both as an effective recruitment tool and as a means for women to assert their patriotism. They also functioned as a means of reminding both the government and the public of the pre-war demands of the suffragettes, Potter-Daggett describing the processions as 'the most important feminist parade that has ever appeared in any city in the world... marching straight for the goal of economic independence'.[57] In *The Times* the parading women were compared favourably with 'the men in Mufti of service age' who 'came out shamelessly' to watch them. When one man 'passed a contemptuous remark' a woman turned on him, declaring 'we're going to do our bit... Are you going to do yours?'[58] The parade was supported by the government and especially by Lloyd George, then Minister of Munitions and concerned by the shortage of male labour for the munitions industry. Questions were asked in Parliament regarding the £3000 of expenses paid by the Ministry of Munitions to the Pankhursts for the parade, illustrating the extent to which the previously militant suffragette movement used the war to shift into the mainstream of British political life.[59]

The journal of the WSPU, *The Suffragette* was replaced by *Britannia* in October 1915, which provided a platform for the Pankhurst's jingoistic views in its advocacy of military conscription and the internment of 'enemy' aliens.[60] Both Emmeline and Christabel were frequent public speakers throughout the war, and although the WSPU never renewed their direct campaign for female suffrage, they did call for equality of service and citizenship for men and women, Emmeline Pankhurst demanding 'universal obligatory national war service for men and women' in 1915.[61] At a 1918 speech to The Women's Party near the large munitions works in Woolwich, Christabel Pankhurst explicitly linked war work with citizenship, asserting that male strikers in the engineering industry 'have lost... any idea of what it is to be a British citizen' and claiming for women workers a 'determination to have a vigorous prosecution of the war'.[62] Women's role in the war was represented by the Pankhursts and their followers as both that of war worker and as that of agitator and guardian of the nation's morals and war aims,

Emmeline Pankhurst comparing men's response to recruitment campaigns unfavourably with that of women:

> Men have always told us that fighting was their business. That being so, for heaven's sake, let them go and do it. There are thousands of women ready and anxious to serve their country by filling up the ranks of the workers at home.[63]

Although the WSPU never resumed its direct demands for female suffrage, veiled threats were embedded in many of the Pankhurst's wartime pronouncements; if men did not take up their 'proper' military role, and thus show their patriotism and earn their rights as citizens, there were women at home ready to take their place in the nation's public life. The leaders of the WSPU linked themselves with the popular patriotism of the early days of the war, unequivocally abandoning calls for female suffrage and replacing them with calls for a national war service. For the Pankhursts, citizenship for both sexes became something to be earned through war service, rather than claimed as a right.

The path towards war service was less clear-cut for the democratic NUWSS. Under the leadership of Millicent Garrett Fawcett the society, which had been opposed to the war right up until its outbreak, swiftly changed its position to one of support for the war effort. Like Emmeline and Christabel Pankhurst, Fawcett shifted her position on the relationship between the sexes in wartime to embrace an ideology of separate spheres, arguing at a London meeting in October 1914 that

> While the necessary, inevitable work of men as combatants is to spread death, destruction...sorrow untold, the work of women is the exact opposite...to help, assuage, to preserve, to build up the desolate home, to bind the broken lives, to serve the state rather than destroying it.[64]

Writing in the suffrage newspaper *Common Cause* at the outbreak of war, Fawcett argued that it was the duty of the NUWSS to dedicate its considerable resources and organisational skill to the war effort:

> In the midst of this time of terrible anxiety and grief, it is some little comfort to think that our large organization, which has been completely built up during past years to promote women's suffrage, can be used now to help our country through the period of strain and sorrow.[65]

This shift in the organisation's position led to a split in the NUWSS between Fawcett and her followers, who believed the war was being fought for the democratic principles the suffragists had campaigned for and pacifist members of the Society who believed that the bonds of international sisterhood overrode national concerns. When an international peace convention was organised at The Hague in 1915 the NUWSS was riven between those who wished to attend the Conference and those who believed the Conference was a betrayal of British war aims. Several members of the executive committee resigned, and pacifist and internationalist feminists from all parts of the suffrage movement joined together to form the Women's International League for Peace and Freedom (WILPF). Together with the Women's Peace Crusade, and later, the Women's Co-operative Guild, the WILPF were part of a feminist, pacifist movement which linked female suffrage with peace, arguing that 'only free women can build the peace...themselves understanding the eternal strife engendered by domination.'[66] However, for the majority of the suffrage movement, British war aims were entwined with the rights of women, the war providing an opportunity for women to prove that they were 'every bit as ready as the men to offer themselves for service' and the WILPF remained a numerically small organisation, claiming only 2,458 members in 1916 and 3,687 by 1918.[67]

The NUWSS organised the Women's Emergency Corps (WEC) in London, which, through its London Bureau, 'chiefly acted as a clearing house for voluntary and paid labour',[68] placing 'women who are ready to respond to the urgent appeal of patriotic duty' in both traditionally feminine positions such as 'cooks, interpreters.. care of crèche, care of mothers' and in some of the new areas which were beginning to open up to women like 'motor drivers'.[69] Recruitment literature for the WEC illustrates how the NUWSS identified the cause of women with the cause of the nation, one poster, entitled 'The Call of the Country' stating that

> Women! Your country needs you. Today the country needs every woman no less than it needs every man. It is for us women to wage unremitting and strenuous war against all conditions of poverty and disease and misery that weaken the Empire at its heart. It is for us as women to fight in dead earnest against the spirit of social apathy, indifference and despair. It is for us as women to show that loyalty in each other which is manifested by comrades in the field: to stand by those who have lost their economic weapons and to save them from the defeat that comes with loss of independence. Therefore, we call to the women of the country to come and help us. Come quickly! Give of your best in the same spirit in which your brothers have answered the Nation's call.[70]

Thus, the WEC placed women's work in wartime alongside the male work of combat. Using a militarised language, they urged women to fight poverty and inequality at home with the same vigour, and sense of national duty, which men were believed to have displayed by going to war. The philanthropic and charitable work that many women of the upper and middle classes had undertaken before the war was accordingly situated as work of national importance, the female equivalent of fighting for one's nation.

Organisations such as this provided a useful resource for women who wanted to undertake war work, as they were often the only means of discovering what occupations, paid and unpaid, were needed and available. Although newspapers in the early months of the war were full of calls for women to take up war work and contribute to the war effort, there was no state-sponsored means for women to do this, and individual efforts to find work of national importance were sometimes frustrated. Even though rumours of a 'battalion of suffragettes' arriving at the British lines in France ready to fight were widely reported in the British press in 1914 and 1915, with the author and journalist Cicely Hamilton commenting that stories about the 'woman in khaki who serves at the front' were 'accepted with absolute faith in some quarters' very few British women found employment near the front lines.[71] Despite the prominence in British propaganda of Maire Chisholm and Elsie Knocker, the 'Angels of Pervyse' who nursed soldiers within range of German guns, determined efforts were made to exclude most women from service near the front lines. Offers of help from both organised groups of women and individual women alike were turned down by the War Office. At the outbreak of war Grace Ashley-Smith, by then in charge of the First Aid Nursing Yeomanry (FANY), returned from a trip to South Africa to offer the Corps' services to the War Office. This was turned down and Ashley-Smith went on to Antwerp where the FANY were given a hospital to run. When the city of Antwerp fell to German troops the FANY went on to work in Calais, working in a Belgian hospital and driving an ambulance to the Front. Eventually they were commissioned by the British Red Cross to provide transport for wounded British to Calais with Lilian Franklin running a convoy of ambulances between the Front and the port.[72] When individual women like Dr Elsie Inglis went to the War Office to offer their services as Doctors at the front, they were told that their help was not needed, and many letters were published in the newspapers from aggrieved women who had offered themselves for war work only to be turned down.[73] Individual upper-class women with a taste for adventure, such as Dr Flora Murray and Flora Sandes, found their own way to the front line where they served as doctor with the Allied forces and a nurse and soldier with the Serbian Army respectively, despite the War Office's rejection of their services. The help of other less qualified, upper-class volunteers, eager to be involved in the war effort was also turned down by the authorities as Mrs Alec Tweedie found when she wrote to Lord Kitchener, soon after war began, offering to 'enlist one hundred women, largely from her friends. They could muster at her house... drill ourselves so as to get fit for *work of any kind*'(original emphasis).[74] In the early days of the war, the only routes into war work for the majority of women sat firmly within traditional feminine spheres of activity.

In addition to directing and co-ordinating the large number of volunteers and offers of relief for refugees which flooded in during the first months of the war, the WEC also attempted to lessen the sometimes devastating impact of the war on working women. One of its earliest leaflets stated that 'what is wanted by the women of the middle and working classes is not relief but wages.'[75] The Corps helped to find work for some of the women displaced by the war; seamstresses and embroiderers, working in the industries hit hardest by the upper classes' decision to dispense with 'luxury goods', were employed making towels and sheets for Dr Flora Murray's hospital in France, as well as 'the shirts and bed jackets and apparel of every kind down to the set of baby clothes sent to the wife of a Belgian officer'.[76] Other female workers were employed making toys in WEC workrooms, including 'cunningly devised' toy trenches which were described with a retrospectively astonishing lack of irony in the *Daily Citizen* as looking 'for all the world as if they have been rained on and have become caked with the jolliest mud possible'.[77] Despite the absurdity inherent in providing toy trenches for the children of men who may well have been injured or killed in the real trenches, the workrooms were successful in their aim of finding work for women displaced by war, and the first Annual Report of the WEC stated that, of over 260 women employed, 180 had gone on to 'obtain good situations elsewhere'.[78] Groups such as the WEC were part of the expansion of voluntary organisations either run by women or in which women played a prominent role seen at the beginning of the war. The existing suffrage organisations, with their experience of mobilising and organising large numbers of women were able to draw on this knowledge to build effective structures for mobilising women's labour in wartime. However, although these organisations were widely welcomed, and praised in the press as an illustration of the nation's unity in the face of war, they remained voluntary and largely unpaid, without formal recognition or funding from the state.

The first signs of a change in official attitudes towards women's war work came in 1915, during parliamentary debates concerning the application of the proposed National Registration Bill to women.[79] In a debate which was to be echoed twenty-six years later in the dialogue about women's national service in the Second World War, politicians deliberated the extent to which women's work in wartime should be directed. Debates in parliament revolved around women's national role in wartime, with supporters of female inclusion on the Register arguing that women wanted 'to take their place with men and do what they can to serve the country'.[80] Women's role as workers in wartime was contrasted to women's role as mothers and homemakers. Opposition to women's inclusion on the Register was focused around their role as mothers, and the necessity of recognising that 'the best service (women) can do to the country in this time of war' was 'raising a healthy family', whilst the government responded defensively that they were only proposing to include women in response to women's 'almost unanimous demand . . . that they should be included'.[81] The Bill was passed, and the subsequent National Registration Act required householders to record the occupations of both men and women aged between 16 and 65. Women of the suffrage movement broadly welcomed the inclusion of women in the Act, and although relatively few women were placed in war-related employment via the Register, the National Service Department which oversaw its organisation was to provide official war-related employment for many women already active in public life such as Violet Markham, Katherine Furse and Lady Rhondda.

However, the work available through the clearing house of the WEC and later, through the National Service Department, was not enough for women who wished to 'take a more vigorous part in England's defence'.[82] Numerous uniformed, voluntary organisations for women sprang up: the Home Service Corps, the Women's Auxiliary Force and the Women's Signallers' Territorial Corps amongst them.[83] The Women's Legion and the Women's Volunteer Reserve (WVR), two linked organisations formed early in the war under the umbrella of the WEC, were the two largest voluntary organisations outside of nursing services such as the Voluntary Aid Detachment (VAD). These uniformed units aimed to provide a framework for women who wanted to take a more active role in the war than was available through the existing organisations. In December 1914 the WVR was launched at a meeting in Mansion House. Formed in response to German bombing raids on East Coast towns, in which 78 women and children were killed, the WVR was initially conceived as a response to the changing patterns of war for British people, in which 'non-combatants may suffer very severely'.[84] Attacks on the home provided an opportunity for feminist campaigners to argue that British women were now, in effect, combatants and thus had the right to defend themselves and their homes. This argument utilised very traditional images of femininity, sustaining the linkage of women with domesticity. In direct response to the raids, Eleanor Rathbone, at that time a leading member of the NUWSS, suggested the organisation of a Women's Reserve Army, arguing that 'if there are any functions that can usefully be performed by women, they have a right to claim those functions . . . if once the idea could be got rid of that they must not be exposed to danger.'[85] Combining discourses of patriotism and femininity to argue for an expanded role for women, feminists such as Rathbone argued that military attacks on civilians had demonstrated the futility of attempting to maintain a divide between home front and war front, masculine and feminine, opening up a space in which female non-combatants could usefully undertake an active defence of the nation. It was in this space that quasi-military organisations such as the WVR grew up.

Organised under the aegis of the WEC, with Lady Londonderry as Colonel in Chief, and Eveline Haverfield and Mrs Charlesworth as honorary Colonels, the WVR was a uniformed corps, dedicated to organising women to protect the nation in case of invasion and to serve in any other way possible. The declared aims of the WVR were two-fold: to 'free more men for the firing line' and to 'organise more succour for the helpless ones in the community'.[86] However, although these declared aims sat comfortably within existing concepts of socially acceptable roles for women in wartime, the WVR was, almost from its inception, a controversial organisation. Work and training undertaken by the WVR included running canteens for soldiers, transporting the wounded, camp cooking, first aid and motoring.[87] Although it was founded and led by women of the upper and middle classes, the WVR claimed for itself a classlessness, announcing that all potential members would join as privates, regardless of their social class and standing outside of the organisation. Whilst this claim accorded well with more widespread demands for an equality of sacrifice across class divides, the extent to which it worked in practice however, was questionable. *The London Opinion* reported occasions where 'mistresses have had to transfer to another company because they found themselves forming fours with their own servants, which did not seem quite the thing.'[88] Despite the claim of the London branch of the WVR that the 'rank and file consists of chiefly business girls, typists, shop girls and servants' the perception of the WVR as 'upper-class amazons' was widespread, particularly as employment opportunities for women expanded during 1915.[89] Women working full-time had less time, energy and enthusiasm available for the activities of the WVR, which included regular route marches and attendance at drill at least two evenings per week. Nonetheless, the WVR rapidly expanded, claiming 6,000 members and 40 branches in the United Kingdom by January 1916.[90] The continuing popularity of the WVR illustrates the desire of many women to feel that they were taking an active part in the war, a desire seen in the language of a WVR recruiting pamphlet which claimed that 'the Reserve crystallises into outward form the ardent patriotism of women, and gives them a distinct place in the service of the State, apart from all philanthropy.'[91] The military appearance and quasi-military activities of the WVR allowed women to visibly identify themselves with the 'sacrifice' and service of the male soldiers.[92] However, the adoption of the khaki uniform, so central to the iconography of the male combatant, proved to be one of the most contentious aspects of the non-combatant, female WVR.

Newspaper reports of the founding of the WVR emphasised the organisation's patriotism and devotion to duty, but also drew attention to the military appearance of the women, who wore khaki uniforms, practised drill, named their local groups battalions and their member privates and officers, and some local groups were offered the opportunity of training to bear arms. Although the greater part of the WVR's time was spent in first aid, nursing, cookery and motoring, the highly visible aspects of the Reserve's work, in particular the uniformed route marches and drill which the women undertook, meant that the Reserve was widely seen as trespassing into the military domain of men. Criticism of the organisation began almost as soon as it was formed. Perceived as a female encroachment upon a masculine, military sphere of activity, the WVR embodied for some the worst aspects of the suffrage movement's espousal of the war effort, providing a space for women to dress as men, act as men and generally 'assume mannish attitudes'.[93] Parallels between the peacetime demonstrations of the suffragettes and the wartime drills and route marches of the WVR were made in the press, and the leaders of the Reserve were quick to distance themselves from the political ambitions of the movement. E. D. Smethitt, writing to the *Bournemouth Echo* in

April 1915 refuted 'the idea that the WVR is a suffrage organisation', arguing that like the soldiers in the trenches, 'we have no politics whatsoever'.[94] Nonetheless, the appearance of large numbers of women, learning to drill, sometimes with weapons, and undertaking route marches along city streets was a sometimes disturbing threat to the status quo, in which men were frequently told that they were going to war to protect women and children in the home.[95]

The M. P. Henry Chaplin, speaking at the first meeting of the WVR, attempted to pre-empt some of the criticism of the organisation's military appearance, arguing that

> The use of the force was contemplated only in the case of invasion and even then for purposes only suitable to women ... There was a strong and natural prejudice against the bearing of arms by women, and if the arms were to be borne for the purpose of aggression, he would entirely agree. To arm a woman for aggression was one thing, to arm them for their own defence in the last extremity was a different thing all together.[96]

In Chaplin's representation of the WVR they remain within the female sphere, an extension of the Victorian 'angel in the home', defending themselves and their home against aggression with arms 'only in the last extremity'. Similarly, an article in the *Ladies Pictorial* argued that 'nothing is unwomanly which a woman does to help herself or others.'[97] However, as the organisation expanded, criticism of their militaristic activities and appearance became more widespread. Women in the WVR were accused of 'masquerading in khaki uniforms and aping the bearing of soldiers' and of 'playing at being soldiers'.[98] Soldiering, it was asserted, was firmly and unequivocally a male activity, one letter to *The Morning Post* in 1915 arguing that 'they never can be soldiers and all the drill and marching in the world will never make soldiers of them.'[99] In a similar vein, a letter to the *Newcastle Chronicle* asked 'what useful purpose do women serve by dressing themselves up in khaki, learning to use the rifle, route marching and even forming themselves into regiments?'[100] As the perceived danger of invasion, and subsequent threat to British homes and families, faded, antagonism towards the WVR grew. The appearance of women in the khaki uniform of the Reserve was widely criticised in the press, where women were warned that 'khaki-itis isn't becoming' and reminded that 'khaki ... should be reserved for the soldier, since it symbolises his blood and heroism'.[101] Khaki was strongly associated with the male soldier, the embodiment of masculinity, and was both degraded by its adoption by women and in turn threatened the femininity of the women who wore it.

The response of the WVR and their supporters was three-fold. First, the practical necessity of both a uniform and of drill and route marches were emphasised. E. D. Smethitt, the Organising Secretary of the Reserve, writing in *The Evening Standard*, argued that uniform was adopted because 'a serviceable dress of some kind which shall be the same for all is absolutely necessary in a large body of people', adding somewhat disingenuously that khaki had merely been chosen 'as the least likely to show dirt'.[102] Similarly, an article in the *Midland County Express* asserted that the decision to adopt a khaki uniform was a practical, rather than a symbolic decision as 'you could not have women and girls going about in all their modern costumes...it is rather important to wear a kit in which it is easy to move about.'[103] Drill and route marches were 'intended to keep the girls physically fit and teach them discipline and co-operation', activities which, it was implied, were beneficial not only to the health of the individual women, but to the future health of the nation.[104] Recruitment literature for the WVR asserted that 'Physical fitness becomes a patriotic duty...made possible by the provision of drills in military uniform.'[105] The WVR represented itself as not only training women to release men for the front and to defend their homes and community in times of crisis such as invasion and bombing raids but also as part of the ongoing eugenicist campaign to strengthen the British 'race' by improving the health of its mothers and children.[106]

The sense of duty displayed by the women of the WVR was also emphasised. A poem in the *Women's Volunteer Reserve Magazine*, claimed less prosaic reasons for the Reserve's use of khaki in their uniform, using explicitly religious imagery which evoked the 'sacrifice' of dead soldiers to link the women's voluntary work with the volunteer and, since March 1916, conscripted combatant men:

> When we are gone
> You will remember then
> We wore the sacred khaki soberly
> As did the men...
> For outward sign
> The colour shall suffice
> The inward spirit of the sacrament
> A sacrifice.[107]

A further article in the same journal described a tea party for wounded soldiers and WVR members. When wounded, soldiers wore blue and red hospital uniforms which signified their status as wounded combatants, whilst 'their hostesses' wore 'the khaki they had so lately doffed'. This role reversal, with the enforced passivity of the wounded men and the active women in khaki is not problematised but celebrated, the author claiming that the khaki uniform formed a 'bond existing between them'.[108] This connection between the women of the Reserve and the combatant men was stressed again and again by members of the WVR. The *Women's Volunteer Reserve Magazine* published a poem in its first edition, allegedly by 'a converted admirer' in the army, which stressed the tie between women and men in khaki. Written in an imagined vernacular the poem began by stating that:

> We didn't think much of you
> W'en first you got begun

The poem then goes on to argue that the women had proved that their work was of value to the fighting men, concluding that

> They calls 'em Kitchener's Lizzies
> And I reckon it's all right
> To give 'em the use of 'is name
> 'Oos the best of Britain's might.[109]

The poem thus ends with a grateful recognition of the WVR's help and support for the army, and an assertion that the women, working alongside men, had earned the right to not only wear khaki but to claim a symbolic membership of Kitchener's armies. Although the WVR was not officially recognised by the War Office until 1917, the Reserve repeatedly attempted to distance itself from other voluntary, uniformed organisations and align itself with the male services. An illustration of a woman in Reserve uniform in the *Birmingham Daily Mail*, an area where the WVR was especially active, was entitled 'How to recognise our devoted women' and went on to describe in detail the appearance of WVR members so that they could be identified separately from other organisations and individuals in khaki, whilst Smethitt, writing in the *Daily Mail* in 1915 argued that 'khaki should only be put on as a badge of service', deriding the female 'slackers' who 'put it on just to look smart and military and mannish when they are doing no military service at all'.[110] One letter published in the *Morning Post* from a WVR private emphasised that the khaki uniform was not perceived by the women as an imitation of the soldier's uniform, but instead as an outward symbol of their shared capacity for 'self-denial, discipline and courage'.[111] Established areas of female service, most notably nursing, were also drawn upon to validate the work of the WVR; one article, recruiting for the WVR, used the example of Edith Cavell, the nursing sister executed by Germany as a spy to ask 'will you help to avenge her death by releasing men to go and fight at the front?', whilst members of the WVR attended Cavell's memorial service at St Paul's cathedral dressed in their khaki uniform.[112] The WVR combated claims that their work was 'worse than useless' by attempting to distance themselves from civilian women and align themselves instead with the spirit of sacrifice popularly associated with the armed forces and, following Cavell's death, the nursing services.[113]

Finally, the feminine nature of the work undertaken by the Reserve was stressed. An article in *The Ladies Pictorial* in February 1915 stated that 'there is nothing unfeminine about the Women's Volunteer Reserve. On the contrary, it is distinctly a womanly movement' as the work of rendering 'aid and guidance to the aged, infirm, panic stricken and helpless who can do nothing for themselves' in case of air raid or invasion was simply a wartime extension of woman's established peacetime role as carer and nurturer.[114] In 1915 the Women's Legion was formed. This organisation, also led by Lady Londonderry, began as an offshoot of the WVR, formed 'to include the many kinds of war work that could not be managed on the quasi-military lines of the Reserve'.[115] It is difficult to avoid the conclusion that the foundation of the Women's Legion was also an implicit criticism of the paramilitary tendencies of the WVR. Londonderry was privately convinced that the WVR *was* too militaristic in its appearance and activities, commenting in her autobiography that 'we had to contend with a section of She-Men who wished to be armed to the teeth.'[116] These were perhaps typified by Mrs Charlesworth, the Acting Colonel of the WVR in 1916, who claimed in the *Daily Graphic* that the WVR could provide women to replace men in the army:

> I have with me 250 hunting women, all hard as nails, and each bought up from girlhood to know and understand horses. Why waste us? The machinery to train and discipline a women's army is ready and waiting.[117]

The Women's Legion avoided such contentious language and instead followed more closely than the WVR along the lines which Lady Londonderry had originally imagined for a women's wartime organisation. It comprised both voluntary and paid workers and was far less overtly militaristic than the WVR; they did not drill and the work undertaken by its members, such as cookery and waitressing in military canteens, remained far more clearly within an established female sphere. Indeed, it began to be argued that women were particularly suited for this type of work, the *Evening Standard* commenting approvingly that 'trained women, working in their own sphere, are infinitely superior in it to untrained men.'[118] Perhaps because of this, the Women's Legion proved to be a more acceptable organisation than the WVR, or indeed the FANY, and by October 1915 the Annual Report of the Women's Emergency Corps, which oversaw both organisations, was claiming that the WVR was simply one aspect of the Women's Legion.[119] The Women's Legion was recognised by the Army Council in February 1916 and the Military Cookery Section and the Motor Transport Section began to work directly with the army within the British Isles. These women worked as substitutes for men, taking into the military sphere the already established idea of dilution, by which women in industry replaced men so that they could move into the front line. The work of these women, although it signified the first official acceptance by the British army of the necessity for female labour in total war, also helped to reinforce established, gendered patterns of work and status, as their prime function was to 'take the place of men needed in the firing line' by performing work better suited to women.[120] This work, and the resulting movement of men previously employed in support services towards the front line, was not always appreciated by the departing soldiers, and on occasions the Women's Legion found that their work had been sabotaged, as the women who entered Sommerdown Convalescent Camp near Eastbourne discovered when they found that the departing cooks had blocked the burners of the gas ovens before leaving.[121] Although the activities of the uniformed, quasi-military WVR, and its sister organisation, the Women's Legion, represented a movement of women towards the male sphere of militarisation, they could also be seen as a product of the continued divergence of the sexes in wartime.

Women's voluntary activity during the First World War was both praised as an indication that 'women are not one whit behind the men in patriotism', and widely seen as demonstrating the wide range of activities of which women were capable.[122] Many observers commented that the activities of the suffrage movement in wartime, their 'work for the national good', had demonstrated that they were 'worthy of citizenship'.[123] *The Observer* commented on 'women's right to share in the future of a nation whose very fate is entwined with their very heart strings' whilst *The Hendon Advertiser* argued that women's war work had 'gained the confidence of the nation and earned women the vote'.[124] The initial enthusiasm of the suffragists and suffragettes for war work helped to move the cause of women's suffrage towards the centre of British politics, and when women's organisations began to re-assert claims for franchise reform, they were received more sympathetically than they had been before the war.[125] In the Parliamentary debates about the Representation of the People Bill towards the end of 1917, Viscount Peel, introducing the Bill in the House of Lords, summarised this view, arguing that 'many have been converted (to female suffrage) by the services rendered by women during the war.'[126] The inclusion of women in the Bill, which was originally introduced to secure full citizenship for all the men who had served as combatants in the war, was opposed by politicians who argued that 'women have done all but fight...it is a tremendous exception...typical of the difference between men and women.'[127] Enfranchising women, this argument continued, would give the female population a 'controlling voice' whilst men, in a minority following the high casualty rates in the trenches, had experienced an 'indescribably greater share of the suffering'.[128] Debates in both the Houses of Parliament and in the press concerning female suffrage often returned to the question of comparability: could women's work in wartime stand comparison with the experience of the male combatant? Although women were invariably praised for their wartime work in these debates, a line was firmly drawn between the male work of soldiering, fighting, dying and killing for one's country and the female work of supporting the work of the combatant by nursing, producing munitions and releasing men for the front in wartime. The limited enfranchisement of women, achieved in early 1918, was seen by many at the time as a reward for these wartime services.[129]

However, when women were seen as encroaching too closely on male territory, as in the WVR and other uniformed voluntary corps such as the Home Service Corps and the Women's Reserve Ambulance Corps, they were criticised as suffering from 'khaki-itis' and of taking advantage of the new opportunities opened up to them by the war to 'have the time of their lives'.[130] The very appearance of these women caused enormous anxiety in some quarters and they were often accused of not only being unpatriotic, with their rush to 'get into uniform even though khaki was scarce' meaning that 'the war was delayed on their account', but their adoption of military appearance and activities was seen as 'unsexing' them, *The Daily Mail* viciously claiming that 'a section of them have earned the title "it"'.[131] Both symbolically and practically, female members of the voluntary paramilitary organisations were in a tenuous position in wartime Britain. Symbolically, uniformed women, especially those in the khaki uniform of the WVR, risked being seen as unfeminine whilst being barred by their gender from earning the same status as that accorded to the male soldiers. More practically, women undertaking war service walked a perilous line between being praised for their patriotic service and the accusation that they were taking advantage of the opportunities offered by the war. It was against this background that the Women's Army Auxiliary Corps was founded in 1917.

4 'Eve in Khaki'

The Women's Army Auxiliary Corps

By late 1916 it was becoming increasingly obvious that there was a severe need for more manpower in the front line. One result of the National Register, implemented in 1915, was to demonstrate that almost 3 million men were apparently available for military service.[1] In October of the same year, Lord Derby, Director of Recruiting, organised a recruitment drive which asked men to 'attest' their willingness to undertake military service, on the understanding that the state would take the youngest single men first. This was known as 'The Group Scheme' or, more popularly, 'The Derby Scheme', as men who signalled their readiness to take up arms, if need be, were placed in 46 separate groups, ranging from group one, single men of 18, to group 46, married men of 40. Images of group identity, and of duty to one's country, were accentuated in propaganda promoting the scheme, as men were encouraged to take part as 'it relieves you of responsibility ... Your duty to the country is to enrol and let the local tribunal decide your case'.[2] By this point in the war the initial eagerness to fight had waned considerably, and despite the scheme being presented as a final opportunity to volunteer, less than half the available, single men attested.[3] The Military Service Act, introducing conscription, was passed by parliament in January 1916 and the enforced conscription of men for the forces came into effect in March 1916.

The conscription of men was accompanied by a reconsideration of the role of women and the organisation of women's labour in wartime. Throughout the war, demands for women to undertake service alongside men had occasionally been made, one early correspondent to the *Evening Standard* arguing that 'as there seem to be no men in England, why not appeal to the women? ... they would, at least, have the pluck and patriotism which seem to be almost extinct in Young England now'.[4] Women's war service had been the object of intense scrutiny in 1915, as the introduction of the National Register led to a consideration of the role of women in wartime and their dual duty to the state as war workers and as wives and mothers. However, 1916–1917 saw a reconfiguring of this debate; as men were conscripted, coerced into military service, women's contribution to the war effort became subject to a renewed examination. In a large part, this debate was concerned with the possibility of conscripting women in order to 'free a man for the front'.

Women's war work, both voluntary and paid, was a well established feature of British society by the middle years of the war, and indeed, the introduction of male conscription in 1916 led to calls for parallel legislation allowing for the coercion of women into war service. Female conscription was demanded both as a means of tackling 'slackers in petticoats' and as a way for women to demonstrate their own willingness to serve if 'short of being compelled to make the great sacrifice, they too are conscripted to win the war'.[5] A meeting calling for National Service for women was held at the Albert Hall in March 1917 and elements within the War Office considered the introduction of female conscription a foregone conclusion.[6] There was a sense that women's labour could be used more efficiently, and women were attacked both for doing too little, and for throwing themselves too enthusiastically into the wrong type of work, such as proto-military organisations like the Women's Volunteer Reserve. An article in *The Times* in June 1916 was archetypal in its criticism of 'women who will not work', calling for 'women recruiting sergeants...with the authority to ask any young woman seen restaurant haunting or shopgazing what she is doing for her country'.[7] Conversely, women were condemned for throwing themselves into the war with too much fervour; it was claimed that 'thousands of women are wearing khaki unnecessarily...it is the garb of the fighting man who goes out to war risking life and limb for England, home and his women-kind, and it should not be lightly donned.'[8] Women in military-style uniform and women not undertaking obvious war work were both accused of attempting to profit from the war, either by encroaching on the masculine world of the military in order to 'play' at being soldiers, or simply because they appeared to be enjoying leisure time whilst others suffered.[9] As British society became increasingly rationalised, subject to registration, conscription, food control and emergency legislation under the Defence of the Realm Act (DORA), women's role in wartime increasingly became the focus of official attention. Official attitudes appeared to have come full circle: from rejecting women's offers of voluntary labour in 1914, the War Office was actively anticipating their conscription by 1916.

However, female war service was rarely considered in the same terms as male military service. Women's role in wartime was predominantly seen as that of helping and supporting the vital male 'work' of combat, whether this help be achieved through working in the munitions industry, nursing, or working directly with the armed forces as the cookery section of the Women's Legion had done since August 1915. Even women's work with the army such as this was criticised in some quarters, where, it was argued, women's work in wartime should remain squarely within the home front. Violet Markham carefully delineated between 'compulsion to serve the State in the Army', which she saw as unnecessary for women, commenting on 'the facetious analogies circulating at the moment of an "army of women" mobilised alongside an army of men', and 'compulsion to work for manufacturers or farmers', which she believed was necessary.[10] Concern about the impact of war work on women's reproductive health was also widespread, and a number of articles were published during 1917 on the problem of 'overworked' women in wartime.[11] Necessary though women's war work was, it should not be 'at the expense of her children'.[12] Debates about female war service were thus rarely framed within the same parameters as those concerning male service. Whilst a man could be asked to fight and die for his country, to 'defend . . . mothers, wives and sisters from the horrors of war', women also had the duty of actual or potential motherhood to consider.[13] Although it was becoming increasingly apparent that a formalised system of female service was going to be necessary, early debates about this service reflected the concurrent concerns that if women were to be mobilised, actual and symbolic gender divisions would need to be defended.

Both the Home Office and the War Office recognised the need to recruit more women in order to release men for combat. By the second half of 1916, women were employed, both voluntarily and as paid labour, in large numbers and in occupations closed to them before the war. Yet there had been no over-arching policy monitoring or organising women's labour. War was men's work, and in 1914 the primary role of women was to send men away to it. The contingencies of total war meant that the need for women's labour became apparent in a somewhat piecemeal fashion, as high casualty rates amongst combatants and the economic necessity of maintaining industry and agriculture combined to produce competing calls for female workers. The Women's Services Committee, headed by the former Chief Medical Officer Sir George Newman, which reported to the Home Office, was formed to examine the supply and organisation of women's labour. The final Report of the Committee argued for the necessity for further organising women's labour in wartime, calling for the formation of a centralised organisation, overseeing and controlling women's war work. Focusing upon the munitions industry, Newman argued that 'many women, for lack of organisation and opportunity are either unoccupied or not occupied to the national advantage.'[14] Going further, he suggested the use of women to replace men in non-combatant positions, and although he did not propose that women should actually undertake military service, he did comment on the 'particular value of corps organisation and the wearing of uniform by women so employed'.[15] The female members of the Committee, who included Katherine Furse, head of the Voluntary Aid Detachment (VAD) and later to become Chief of the Women's Royal Naval Service and the anti-suffragist, Violet Markham, appended their own memorandums to the Report. All agreed that there was a pressing need for some type of formally organised service for women. However, they disagreed on whether or not this service should be subject to conscription and which areas of occupation it should encompass. Whilst Markham believed that women's labour should be covered by compulsion, she also thought that it should be kept entirely separate from the masculine world of the military.[16] Furse, on the other hand, argued that whilst 'women do not need compulsion', their work did need to be organised on military lines, suggesting that a state service for women be formed in which women, 'enlisted as men are enlisted in the Army' would 'have the honour of wearing the King's uniform' and could replace uniformed men in hospitals, canteens, as motor drivers and as army clerks.[17] Furse had her way in the final draft of the Report, which concluded that 'large numbers of men, enlisted and otherwise, might be replaced by women in non-combatant positions.'[18]

Despite the influx of conscripted recruits into the forces in 1916, the need for more manpower remained urgent, and following the catastrophic casualty rates of the Battle of the Somme, Lieutenant-General H. M. Lawson was commissioned to carry out a study assessing which occupations within the armed forces could be effectively carried out by older men or by women, thus relieving men for the front.[19] Lawson made a number of suggestions, including raising the upper age limit of the Military Service Act from 40 to 50, and the 'combing out of men and their replacement by women' in ordnance and the Army Service Corps in England whilst 'the male military motor car driver should be everywhere replaced by a woman.'[20] Women, in the form of the Women's Legion cookery and, motoring divisions, were already working for the army in Britain; Lawson suggested expanding the numbers involved, the work being undertaken, and, crucially, the export of women's work to France. Although the Women's Service Committee and the Manpower Distribution Board, which reported directly to the Cabinet, had both recommended the use of women behind the lines by the army, Lawson's report can be seen as the first *military* recognition of some convergence between the war front and the home front in total war.[21] Although women had a long history of servicing the British army as camp followers in the eighteenth and nineteenth centuries, Lawson's Report marks the first official recognition of the necessity of those services in a designated war zone.

However, the suggestion that women should be utilised on a large scale by the British army was resisted in many quarters. Field-Marshal Douglas Haig, Commander-in-Chief of the British Armies in France, whilst broadly acknowledging that the introduction of female labour would enable more men to be released for combat duties, remained sceptical about the type and amount of work that women would be able to undertake. Replying to Lawson's Report in a series of detailed letters to Lord Derby, then the Secretary of State for War, Haig immediately introduced the notion of dilution, a principle which was already being practised in British wartime industries. Women working in munitions and engineering were often employed as dilutees, rather than as direct substitutes for the men they were replacing. Under dilution, skilled workers were replaced by semi-skilled or unskilled workers, a process 'often, but not always, accompanied by simplification of machinery, or the breaking up of a job into a number of simpler operations'.[22] As well as providing an immediate solution to the problem of a lack of skilled workers, and the amount of production which would be lost whilst workers were trained in new skills, dilution ensured that skilled trades such as engineering remained the occupation of a small group of elite male workers. The introduction of female labour into these trades was mediated by the process of dilution as jobs undertaken by one skilled man were broken down into their constituent parts and carried out by several women doing relatively unskilled repetitive labour. Haig argued that this process would be necessary if women were going to be employed in the support services of the army. Where Lawson had suggested that women should be substituted for men, Haig insisted they should be employed as dilutees, proposing a ratio of 200 women to replace 134 men as clerks and in domestic services.[23] Dilution helped to ensure that the introduction of women into the armed services was regulated in such a way as to maintain the separate and higher status of work undertaken by men.

Despite the need for increased manpower in the front line, Haig insisted that there were many areas of support work which could not be undertaken successfully by women. Haig's dominant concern was that any change to staffing should be gradual and carefully managed 'in order that the existing machinery should not be disturbed'.[24] He feared that the introduction of large numbers of women behind the lines in France threatened a severe disruption of army life, arguing that the employment of women in Base Depots, where 'reinforcements are not under such strict control as they are in their Units' was an area of particular concern as there would be 'more likelihood of sex difficulty occurring in these depots than elsewhere'.[25] As well as fearing the disruptive influence of women upon the male world of the army, Haig felt that the specific conditions of service with the armed forces were often unsuitable for women. Whilst accepting that trained women could 'at once be usefully employed as motor-car drivers, motor ambulance drivers ... cleaners, telegraphists and telephonists' he was adamant that other areas of work should remain the sole preserve of men.[26] Nursing, by this point in the war an established occupation for women, was only grudgingly accepted by Haig, who argued that 'it is quite certain that women could not have stood the enormous and incessant strain, both mental and physical' imposed on army medical personnel during the Battle of the Somme.[27] Regarding the employment of women with the Army Postal Service, one area suggested by Lawson, he commented that 'the work of sorting as carried out in France is totally different to that in England, and it is extremely doubtful if women could undertake it.'[28] Work carried out by non-combatant men behind the lines was thus constructed as essentially masculine work which could only be taken on by women in the direst necessity. One way of ensuring that women's work remained separate from that of men working behind the lines was found in Lawson's suggestion that, if women were to be utilised by the army they should not be integrated but 'must form part of definitive units provided with their own women officers and NCO's'.[29] The introduction of women into the army was to be managed in such a way as to not destabilise the existing 'natural' linkage between masculinity and soldiering.

Haig doubted both women's physical capabilities and their motivation for wishing to undertake service with the army. Underpinning his comments about the need for dilution and the careful management of women's work with the army was a deeply held belief that women's aspirations to undertake this work were motivated more by a wish to use the war as an opportunity to demonstrate their capabilities than by a patriotic desire to serve their country. He warned that

> They must be prepared to experience a certain degree of bodily discomfort both in offices and in their dwellings to which they will be unaccustomed; they must be disciplined; they may be called upon in hours of stress to perform long hours of duty; they must realise that there are few or no distractions, and that no-one in this country has time for anything but work.[30]

In this view Haig was reiterating the widespread distrust of women's motivation for undertaking war work, particularly any work which was seen as mimicking that of the men in the armed forces. This distrust of the women's voluntary organisations led to disagreements within the Army Council and the War Office as to the best way to utilise women's labour. Unlike Lawson and Haig who believed that a separate organisation, managed by women but working for the army, was the best means of employing women, Adjutant-General Neville Macready wrote to Lord Derby to insist that any women so employed should be 'part and parcel of the Army, and entirely distinct from any outside organization'.[31] Macready believed that the direct employment of women by the army would ensure that the types of work undertaken would be tightly controlled and regulated, and he suggested that, although women from voluntary organisations could be consulted, 'the War Office organization should be entirely free of them.'[32] Derby agreed with this, his reply that he was anxious 'not to give outside organizations of women an opportunity for agitation . . . I am entirely with you in resisting any outside interference whatsoever' demonstrating a continuing underlying mistrust of women's organisations and their motivations for aiding the war effort.[33] The discussions in the Army Council and the War Office regarding women's work with the army were shaped by a concern to control and regulate women's involvement with the military, ensuring that the War Office and army remain in control. The pre-war suffrage campaign cast a long shadow: women's work with the armed forces was not to become an opportunity for women to prove they were the equals of men and thus claim equal citizenship.

Women were invited to attend the initial conferences held at the War Office concerning the initial organisation of women's employment with the army, but, as Jenny Gould states, 'it is difficult to conclude that either the Adjutant-General or the Secretary of State for War attached much importance to the ideas and opinions of the women they invited.'[34] At the first such conference Florence Leach, then in charge of the cookery and house-keeping section of the Women's Legion, which was already working for the army, was the only woman in attendance. Leach had travelled to France in December 1916 to investigate whether or not the Women's Legion could work with the army abroad. Both Leach and Adjutant-General Leith-Wood were keen to ensure that women recruited from the Women's Legion should be a part of the army, Leach reiterating several times that 'women were anxious to be under every sort of army discipline, and to take the place of soldiers.'[35] The debates which followed show the gulf between the pragmatic need to utilise women's labour in the armed forces and the importance of maintaining a symbolic division between men and women in wartime.

Discussion of the work of women with the army continued at weekly War Office Conferences throughout January 1917. Concerns focused around the terms of employment which would be used, with the women present insisting that 'women would like to feel they were taken on by the Army, and that they were more or less soldiers.'[36] Although it was initially suggested that the new women's organisation be called the Women's Army Employment Department in order to 'show that they formed a portion of the Army', the men attending the Conferences resisted any suggestion that women be enlisted in the same way as male combatants, arguing that as women had not been employed on active service 'that treatment would not do', suggesting instead that women's service could be ensured by increasing 'the moral obligation . . . making it a disgrace to be discharged, the same as it is for a soldier.'[37] It was eventually decided to enrol women for service with the army rather than to enlist them. The new women's service would be 'based on a military . . . scheme of organisation' but its members would have the legal standing of civilians working with the army and not be treated as soldiers.[38] This decision meant that women's legal position was as camp followers, the label which had long been attached to the civilian women who followed large armies and which Cynthia Enloe describes as being 'parasitic' in its implication.[39] Although this definition of women serving with the army abroad meant that they were subject to the Army Act, and were therefore subject to military law and a range of punishments which included dismissal with ignominy, stoppage of pay and detention in special prisons with female police in charge, they were still civilians, and thus defined, remained separate from the male army yet subject to discipline and punishment if their behaviour or 'character' was found to be wanting.

The desire to maintain a distinction between men and women in military uniform permeated much of the discussion of the minutiae of organising a female corps for service with the army. One area which was the subject of detailed discussion was the level of pay applicable to women undertaking this service. Whilst Adjutant-General Leigh-Wood argued that 'if we are to get a satisfactory type of woman and avoid . . . pitfalls, we must pay a reasonable rate', Paterson, in charge of finance at the War Office, stated that if 'women abroad (are) to be paid the same rates as the men they replace, this means paying them as *soldiers*'. (original emphasis)[40] In this case, women serving with the army would be paid more than civilians performing similar duties at home. The use of dilution, as suggested by Haig, and by Sir Auckland Geddes, Director of Recruiting at the War Office, who had argued that 'in civil life it takes 10 per cent to 20 per cent more women to do the work of male clerks', eventually provided the War Office with a means of paying women less than the male soldiers they served alongside.[41] The question of uniforms for the women was also discussed at length. Although uniforms for women were eventually agreed upon, early discussion questioned their necessity, one War Office memo commenting that

> Three thousand women now at work at home have done without it. Why should we incur the expense of uniforming them now? The supply of khaki for the men of the Army is becoming increasingly difficult and there is no cloth to spare for women who can work just as well in garments of other hue and texture provided, as hitherto, at their own expense.[42]

It was eventually agreed that women enrolled for service would wear uniform, as Lawson's original report had suggested, although the reasoning behind this decision appears to be motivated less by a desire to build an esprit de corps than by the belief that the provision of uniforms or badges would 'prevent unauthorised females entering camp areas'.[43] Women's motivation for joining a female corps working abroad with the army was seen as inherently questionable; the patriotic stimulus was virtually dismissed in these discussions and instead the War Office and the Army Council focused upon controlling women whom they believed to be motivated primarily by a desire for excitement, higher rates of pay and the opportunity to mix with the male soldiers.[44]

The creation of the Women's Army Auxiliary Corps (WAAC) by Army Council Instruction 573 was formally announced in the press in March 1917 and the first draft of women, all previously members of the Women's Legion, left for France on 31 March 1917, to staff clubs for officers in Abbeville and Le Touquet. Initially women were only recruited for service in France, though in July 1917 Army Council Instruction 1069 authorised employment of the WAAC both at home and overseas. The WAAC was organised along army lines, and overseen by the War Office with the women's branch of the Adjutant-General's Department, known as AGXI, formed in Janury 1917.[45] Mona Chalmers-Watson was appointed Chief Controller of the Corps, based in London, and Helen Gwynne-Vaughan appointed as Controller of the WAAC in France. Both Chalmers-Watson and Gwynne-Vaughan were professional women from the upper classes, Chalmers-Watson being a medical doctor and Gwynne-Vaughan a lecturer in botany at Birkbeck College. Chalmers-Watson in particular was well connected within the War Office where her brother, Sir Auckland Geddes, was Director of Recruitment. Grades within the WAAC, as in the army, were closely linked to social class.

Although the majority of members were working class, they were led and supervised by women of the upper classes, following the pattern suggested by Katherine Furse in 1916, who had proposed that, if a women's corps were to be organised 'the urgent and immediate need is to select gentlewomen to act as officers'.[46] Although articles in the press made claims, similar to those made for the Women's Volunteer Reserve (WVR), that the WAAC uniform meant 'there is no sense of class distinction whatsoever', existing structures of social class were embedded within the organisation, and the role of the officers, or administrators as they were known, was largely that of supervising the welfare of Corps members, a role similar to that of the lady welfare officers in the large munitions factories.[47] Despite this creation of an 'officer class', these women were not known as officers but as controllers and administrators, the equivalent grades to NCOs and privates being forewomen and workers. In this way, the existing army structure was utilised as an efficient means of organising women without giving them the symbolic male appellations associated with military service.[48]

The appearance of women in uniform officially sanctioned by the state led to a slight decrease in criticism of women 'playing at soldiers' in the press.[49] Initial newspaper articles on the WAAC were keen to highlight the difference between the organisation, where 'there is no playing at soldiers' and the uniformed voluntary organisations such as the WVR.[50] Early articles such as this emphasised the importance of the work being undertaken by women, stressing the need for all available women to join the WAAC and so 'release a fit man for the trenches'.[51] This role of supporting the work of the men in the trenches, and releasing more men for combat roles, was the key function of the WAAC and numbers within the corps were regulated so that 'no woman... is employed unless a soldier is thereby relieved for other purposes'.[52] Women in these first military uniforms symbolised change but also the resilient nature of the existing gender system. Whilst they moved into the armed forces for the first time, they did so in an auxiliary capacity, marked out by their gender as undertaking these new roles simply in order to release men for the more important and higher status job of combat (Figure 4.1).

Army Council Order 1069, which permitted the WAAC to serve at home in Britain as well as in France, clearly set out the gendered nature of the new service, but also highlighted the difficulties of attempting to manage an influx of women into the world of the military without disturbing gender relations. The principle of dilution was written into the formation of the Corps, the Order stating that 'four women clerks will be considered an equivalent to three soldier clerks... four technical women for the RFC and AFC Motor Transport will be considered an equivalent to three technical soldiers.'[53] The feminine nature of the service was also underlined as the Instruction explained that the 'Regimental employments in which it is intended that women be substituted for soldiers' included 'Officers messes, clerks, sergeants messes, tailors, cooks, librarians, company storemen, shoemakers, quartermaster's storemen, regimental institutes, orderlies'.[54] There were five broad categories of employment for the WAAC: domestic, cookery, mechanical, clerical and tending war graves.

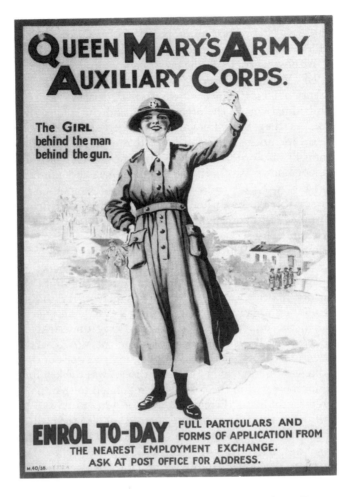

Figure 4.1 Recruitment poster for Queen Mary's Army Auxiliary Corps.

The novelist F. Tennyson Jesse commented in her book about women serving in France, *Sword of Deborah*, that the WAAC 'send a fighting man to his job by taking on the jobs that are really a woman's after all. For is it not a woman's earliest job to look after man?'[55] The work of tending war graves in particular was seen as a proper and correct wartime extension of this nurturing role, and the women who undertook this work were described as undertaking an 'act of reverence towards the heroic dead'.[56] Women were to be employed primarily as carers and providers for the male combatants; although the nature of their employment was in some ways revolutionary, as they wore official uniforms and worked alongside the army; in other ways it reinforced the gendered division of work which existed in civil society.

Their employment in these posts nonetheless had the potential to weaken army morale, as men who remained in the support services saw their occupations as being feminised, and their status, conferred upon them by their uniform, simultaneously diminishing. Men attempted to defend their roles and vigorously argued for their masculine nature. One member of the Royal Army Medical Corps, the 'stretcher bearers' of the war, contended that although he had to suffer the 'jibe' of doing 'women's work', only a very few women who were 'powerful physically and restrained emotionally' would be capable of undertaking work of the 'C3 crocks' such as himself.[57] In this argument, the women who are supposedly the most like men in their physical abilities and their emotional control can only be equated with 'C3 crocks', the class of men barred from active combat because of physical disability. The work of caring for and supporting men, carried out by women in peacetime and in civil society, was defended as male by men in uniform whose responsibility this was in wartime. By emphasising the physical and emotional demands of service work in the army they attempted to maintain their standing as uniformed defenders of the nation and to delineate between the nature of the work they undertook and its lesser nature when diluted and carried out by women.

Although the regulation of women's labour in the support services and the introduction of dilution into this work meant that gender relations were not broken down by the movement of women into the military, they were threatened, particularly when women in uniform appeared to be acting in ways that could be defined as masculine. An early recruitment article for the WAAC in the *Daily Express* was entitled 'Amazonian Auxiliaries' and the *Evening Standard* reported that 'the rules, written and unwritten, include injunctions to abjure powder for the face, to put hats on straight and not at a coquettish angle, and not to smoke in the passages of the barracks.'[58]

Articles such as these emphasised the military nature of the service, an aspect of life in the WAAC played down in interviews by Chalmers-Watson, who chose to emphasise the 'home-like conditions' in the women's barracks and stressed that 'these are no Amazons but the girls we have known, the wives and mothers and sisters who were the light of our homes in the old times and who will return to lighten them again.'[59] Likewise, F. Tennyson Jesse described the homelike appearance of the women's quarters in France:

> In all the camps in France the girls have managed to get not only as individual but as feminine touches as possible. I never saw a woman's office anywhere in France that was not a mass of flowers...Every office too, though strictly business-like, has chintz curtains of lovely colours. You can always tell a woman's office from a man's.[60]

In statements such as these continuity was accentuated over and above change in an attempt to represent the WAAC as an organisation which was female rather than military.

However, the appearance of large numbers of women in military uniform did provide a visual reminder of the shifts in gender roles which had come about since the beginning of the war. The uniform of the WAAC in itself was widely seen as symbolic of women's changing role, and as such, was carefully managed by the War Office and the Army Council in an attempt to ensure that their appearance emphasised their feminine, over and above their military, identity. Early discussions about WAAC uniform attempted to ensure that it was constructed in such a way as to avoid any reference to the uniforms worn by male soldiers. Lawson's 1916 Report had reflected the contemporary discourse which criticised women in khaki, commenting that 'there would be an advantage in having the uniform in some colour other than khaki, possibly blue.'[61] Khaki was, however, eventually agreed upon as the colour of the uniform to be worn by the WAAC as the symbolic appeal of the colour for potential recruits was recognised. Nonetheless, other signifiers of military service were carefully policed. A 1917 conference at the War Office decided that 'no army badges could be worn. All women of the WAAC would wear WAAC badges and no other badges.'[62] Following this decision, the second draft general rules for the WAAC stated that 'uniform will not be modified or added to. The badges of the Corps (but no other jewellery or other badges) will be invariably worn with the uniform.'[63] Letters between Gwynne-Vaughan and Chalmers-Watson illustrate the importance which both the women of the WAAC and the men in the War Office and the Army Council attached to the minutiae of military symbolism. Gwynne-Vaughan had pushed for the fledgling organisation to wear badges of rank, to drill and to take and receive the salute from one another and, more controversially, from men: in short, to appear as militaristic as possible. This resulted in the following plea from Chalmers-Watson: 'I feel sure you ought to take off the badges . . . I am awfully sorry but it will have to be done . . . Also, all saluting will have to stop, and the military salute amongst the women.'[64] Although it was recognised within the War Office that the WAAC did need some means of enforcing corps discipline by visual signifiers of rank and status, established military badges were problematic as they had to be saluted, meaning that conscripted male privates would be saluting uniformed female WAAC controllers who were legally civilians.[65] This threatened the distinction between military and civilian, male and female, which the War Office and Army Council were so keen to maintain. An eventual compromise was reached whereby women did wear distinguishing badges of rank, but the crowns, crosses and bars of the army were replaced by a set of flower insignia, predominantly the rose and the fleur-de-lys which were felt to be more feminine. Military insignia were adopted by the women's organisation but feminised in the process.

The control which the War Office and the Army Council exerted over the appearance of women in uniform meant that women in the WAAC were criticised for their appearance far less than female-led voluntary corps such as the WVR. Every element of their appearance was subject to close attention. The length of skirts was stipulated at 8 inches above the ankle for service at home in Britain and $9\frac{1}{2}$ inches above the ankle in France, where the War Office assumed more physically demanding work would be undertaken.[66] The fine line which the WAAC walked, between appearing too feminine for their state sanctioned work and encroaching too far on the masculine world of the military is apparent in the draft routine orders for the Corps. Civilian signifiers of femininity were constrained by an order prohibiting the use of jewellery whilst in uniform, ordering specifically that 'the practice of wearing badges to fasten frock coats will now cease.' Symbols of overt militarism were also proscribed in the instruction that 'the buttons on great coats have in some cases been exchanged for regimental buttons – this practice will cease.'[67] The woman in uniform had to appear feminine but not too feminine as overt femininity was seen as inimical to military life and discipline. At the same time she could not take on too many of the trappings of militarism as this was seen as devaluing the work and 'sacrifice' of the combatant soldier.

Both overt displays of femininity and female appropriation of symbols of masculinity were criticised in the press. As Susan Grayzel has argued, the appearance of the WAAC in 1917 dissipated some of the criticism of women in uniform which had been made in previous years.[68] However, it never completely vanished, and the presence of women in uniform in British society continued to be an object of some concern throughout the war. A largely unspoken but widely shared view existed which drew links between masculinity in women and lesbianism; the woman in military uniform was taking on one of the key symbols of masculinity and risked being seen as 'abnormal' and 'unnatural'.[69] Although it became widely accepted that a society in total war needed the labour of uniformed, regulated women, some commentators expressed concerns about the impact of war service on women *after* the war. An article in the *Globe* purported to reproduce extracts of a letter from a young administrator with the WAAC who wrote,

> Have just received my commission and I now wear a British 'warm', the dinkiest of riding breeches, a Sam Browne belt and top boots. In fact, I am dressed exactly like a man except I do not sport spurs.

'What effect' the article asked, 'is this passing phase going to have on the womanhood of the nation later on?'[70] Writing a month later in the *National News* M. O. Kennedy argued that 'the danger is that at the end of the war the masterful woman will be in control of the feminine one to the detriment of the race.'[71] The implication of articles such as these was that a female appropriation of military attire and attitudes, whilst tolerable in wartime, had to be just for the duration, acceptable only due to the rigours and demands of a society experiencing total war for the first time.

Women in the WAAC defended their work and their appearance. A letter entitled 'To Our Fellow Countrywomen' and published in the *Spectator* argued that

> Everyone works better for being smart. It is not for mere parade purposes that our soldiers at the front are made to shave and keep their uniforms clean. Women at this moment have a double call to be well-turned out... To be well turned out in wartime is a duty. To be luxurious is a crime.[72]

By implication, this letter linked the work of women in the WAAC with the work of soldiers at the front, also expected to maintain a smart appearance in often arduous circumstances. The WAAC uniform is distanced from that of voluntary organisations, playing on their official status as military auxiliaries. However, in addition it feeds into a parallel discourse which also censured women in wartime: the criticism of female luxury. Since the beginning of the war, when wealthy women cut back on their consumption of luxury goods in a surge of patriotism, the fashion industry was attacked as frivolous and unpatriotic. Money and time spent on fashionable clothing was seen as a waste of labour which 'during the war... should be employed in producing what is really necessary or useful'.[73] Of all the unnecessary extravagances of wartime, there was 'no obstruction so gratuitous, so senseless, and so useless as that of the changing fashions in women's dress'.[74] The Edwardian fashion for extravagant clothing was contrasted unfavourably with the realities of wartime and fashionable women were derided as 'butterfly ladies'.[75] A poem published in the satirical magazine *Punch* in 1916 entitled 'Dress as Usual' informed its readers that

> You who when the world is mourning
> Only think of self-adorning
> Sadden Punch, your friend.[76]

Mrs Alec Tweedie argued that the upper classes had been more patriotic than other groups in society, comparing their 'thriftiness in dress' with the 'thirty shilling a week girls' whom, she claimed, 'were responsible for frequent changes in fashion so as to inveigle new hats and blouses out of the soldiers.'[77]

The increasing rationalisation and militarisation of society had a direct impact on fashions of the period as the fashion industry adapted to wartime conditions, and the need of women in voluntary organisations for practical, serviceable clothing, by producing clothing lines influenced by military uniform. Newspaper advertisements for department stores in 1917 promote 'Zambrene weatherproof raincoats' for women, available in a range of styles including 'The Landsuit', 'The Major' and 'The Flanders'.[78] The 'Beaucourt

Weathercoat', available from Dickens and Jones, was advertised as 'an ideal service coat... Built on military lines, in several fawn shades of drench proof silk.'[79] A 1915 cartoon in *Punch* showed two women fashionably dressed in Cossack style hats and coats, passing shop windows full of military inspired women's fashions with the caption 'signs are not wanting that women are being pressed into the service. Many indeed, are already in uniform'.[80] The appearance of clothing lines such as these, together with calls for 'every woman under fifty (to wear) uniform' as a means of diverting all available resources to essential industry may have helped encourage social acceptance of women in military uniform.[81]

However, despite the early enthusiasm for the WAAC in the press, their behaviour and motivations for joining the service were soon called into question, and by late 1917 it was widely believed that recruitment to the Corps was being harmed by widespread rumours of sexual immorality amongst its members.[82] A letter from Mona Chalmers-Watson to Helen Gwynne-Vaughan set out some of the statements which had been made about the WAAC in France to her:

> Ninety women from Rouen sent back for misconduct (assertor – a woman government official). A maternity home around which the assertor said he himself had done sentry duty. A maternity home, eight hundred beds, every encouragement to procreate, £50.00 bonus to each woman, state adoption... assertor a VAD Commander who is quite prepared to have her name published. Lady Betty Balfour has asked whether it is the case that the recruiting centres are promising a £5.00 bonus to the first case of mother and child. From Scotland a very nice lady writes that her girls (servants) and their friends won't join because they hear that a WAAC who has been to France will have no character left and no-one will care to employ her... Another old and aristocratic bird asserts that the War Office is sending out professional prostitutes dressed in our uniforms.[83]

These rumours reflected concurrent concerns regarding female behaviour in wartime. The widespread absence of men combined with higher wages for women combined to produce a picture of female independence which threatened the established mores and values of pre-war society. Whilst married women were encouraged to have babies and unmarried women encouraged to see themselves as potential, future mothers, sexually active single women were widely seen as internal enemies, threats to the health of the nation and more specifically, to the health and vigour of the fighting man. O. M. Taylor, who had enlisted as a cook with the WAAC and served at a large camp in Woolwich, London, described being 'broken hearted' when, on a trip into Woolwich, the behaviour of the local people demonstrated their belief that 'we had been enlisted for the sexual satisfaction of soldiers'.[84] It wasn't only the WAAC who were vulnerable to such accusations however. Women living near army bases and naval ports were accused of suffering from 'khaki fever' and regulated by the use of the Defence of the Realm Act and the use of female police controls. Female munitions workers, mostly from the working class, were accused of extravagance, drunkenness and subsequent sexual promiscuity.[85] Susan Kingsley Kent has shown how female nurses and VADs could acquire sexual knowledge through nursing duties with the wounded male soldiers.[86] Although the social class of many of the VADs protected them from the worst of the accusations hurled at the predominantly working class munitions workers and WAACs it is not difficult to perceive a resentment of their work as the young women took on the 'motherly' role of caring for the broken and injured bodies of the male combatants, as in the case of the hospitalised 'Sergeant Jones' who 'awoke, a soldier literally in the hands of women. He couldn't so much as bathe his own face. A woman in a white head dress with a red cross in the centre of her forehead was doing it for him.'[87] Whilst all women working in the war were praised for their patriotic devotion to duty, they were also vulnerable to the charge that they were taking advantage of war conditions, benefiting from the new roles which the war opened up to them.

These women were at times resented by the soldiers they were helping or replacing. In part, this resentment reflected a wider feeling amongst the troops that most civilians had little or no idea of the suffering of the combatants in the trenches. Paul Fussell has argued that 'the visiting of violent and if possible painful death upon the complacent, uncomprehending, fatuous civilians at home was a favourite fantasy indulged in by the troops.'[88] Women were closely associated with the home front and the gulf between home and battle could easily be seen by troops abroad as a gender divide. When women replaced men in the support services, their actions were sometimes perceived as motivated by a misplaced enthusiasm for war and an eagerness to send every available man to the front, of which they knew nothing, rather than by a patriotic wish to serve. Volunteers from the Women's Legion, sent to camps to release men for active service, sometimes found that beds had been dismantled and slates removed from the roofs of building where they would live and work.[89] Women serving in France were also subject to this type of resentment and mistrust of their grounds for undertaking work with the army. One private, resting behind the lines in France, confided in his diary his hostility towards the WAACs he met working in Dieppe and his belief that they had come to France in order to sexually entrap soldiers, claiming that 'to my mind they are a disgrace to the country they belong to.' Whilst he acknowledged that 'there are good among them' he believed that 'the good are overshadowed by the bad', implying prostitution in the service by commenting 'girls − I prefer to give them another name altogether.'[90] In this representation, the WAACs are parasitic, preying on vulnerable men who needed to conserve their energies for the male sphere of battle. Even more positive comments about the conduct of the WAAC in France from men serving there acknowledged the widespread rumours about their behaviour. An actor entertaining the troops behind the lines in France, and who generally commented favourably on the WAACs, focused on their appearance and their relationships with soldiers, calling them a 'comely lot' whose uniforms 'are mostly becoming and . . . very pretty', describing how 'Tommy has paired off very quickly with the WAACs.' Unsurprisingly, given his pre-occupation with the WAACs as potential partners for the soldiers, this observer also worried about their supervision and balanced his positive comments with the coda 'if it all works out alright'.[91] Captain Paul Sulman, an Officer with, the 11th Hampshire Regiment who was killed in 1918, defended the WAACs behaviour in his letters home, replying to a letter in October 1917 that accused them of misbehaviour, 'are you sure it's the WAAC? The girls I've seen all seem jolly good class and well educated.' He went on the following month however to enclose a weekly report in one of his letters home, noting that 'it's all rather a libel against the WAAC, but amusing nevertheless.'[92] Women working with the troops were women out of place, acting in the masculine sphere of war and combat, and therefore vulnerable to charges of impropriety and misconduct. Anxieties about the social disruptions of wartime were acted out in concerns about the sexual behaviour of young women.

Women in France, serving with the WAAC, were particularly exposed to these types of rumours and concerns as France was already perceived in the public imagination as a hotbed of vice and prostitution. It was claimed that at least one hospital there for British troops was provided solely for the treatment of venereal disease, and that 380 officers and 100,000 men had been infected.[93] The French system of regulated brothels, *Maisons Toleree*, was a cause for concern amongst hygiene campaigners in Britain, and the Association for Moral and Social Hygiene led campaigns to prohibit their use by British troops.[94] Women working in France may have suffered by association as their lives were hidden from the public eye, only becoming visible through press reports, letters and rumours.[95] However, the social class of the WAAC also contributed to the widespread rumours about their conduct. The VAD, also vulnerable to the same accusations were, to an extent, protected by their social status as many of the volunteer nurses came from the upper and middle classes, and their work could be seen as an extension of the voluntary social work undertaken by such women in the late Victorian and Edwardian periods, and represented by them as an extension of the female domestic sphere, rather than an encroachment on the masculine, public sphere. The ordinary members of the WAAC, by contrast, were predominantly from the working class and lower middle class, employed prior to service primarily in domestic, industrial and clerical work. These women were criticised as lacking in a sense of duty, Mrs Alec Tweedie claiming that 'in lower middle and lower-class education the word "Duty" seems to be unknown.'[96] Their alleged tendency to place individual needs above those of the collective nation was blamed for military setbacks as 'the apathy of cooks, housemaids and scrubbers who have not responded to the National

Service appeal to join the WAAC' meant that potential male combatants were not being 'released for the serving line'.[97] It was widely agreed that, although the work of these women was necessary to the success of the war effort, they would have to be closely monitored by upper-class women administrators, who understood the public school notions of duty, honour, sacrifice and moral rectitude which those serving the nation were expected to embody.

The Hon. Dorothy Pickford, who worked as a WAAC administrator in France in 1918 and 1919, wrote regularly to her sister about the difficulties of enforcing regulations designed to regulate and curtail the social lives of women in the WAAC. She recounted making 'an enemy for life' by 'refusing a pass to a woman to go out with her "friend"', describing a system whereby women were expected to regulate one another as 'they may go for walks with their best boys but they must be two together.' However, as Pickford went on to explain, 'of course they separate at the gate only to meet up again when the pass has to be given up.' Nonetheless, regulations were, on the whole, strictly enforced by the female administrators, and Pickford explains that 'no one is allowed out after seven without a pass' except when 'they go to the YWCA Hut for then they are all marched back together by the forewomen at closing time.'[98] Regulations such as these were designed to guard the women from both actual and suspected impropriety with the male soldiers but were often resented by the women they were meant to protect. Maud Emsley, a worker with the WAAC, told her father that 'after 9.15, one scarcely dare breathe, certainly not loudly. If one dares to whisper, depend on it a forewoman will pounce on you ... I should think some of our keepers will go in for hunting "apres le guerre" '[99] O. M. Taylor wrote after the war that after a few weeks in training camp 'we already hated the officers and anyone in authority ... each time a new rule went up on the board the more daring of us held a competition to see who could be the first to break it.'[100] Women who had experienced some of the freedoms of wartime, perhaps earning a reasonable wage for the first time in munitions work and living independently, away from the strictures of domestic service, resented the imposition of rules and regulations upon them by women of the upper classes. Although women in the WAAC were united by their uniform and their gender, they were divided by the application of the existing rules of social class to the organisation.

The War Office was concerned by the rumours circulating in late 1917 and early 1918 about behaviour in the WAAC, and minutes of the weekly conferences held at the Ministry of Labour, which was in charge of recruitment for the service, record Chalmers-Watson agreeing that 'steps should be taken to further emphasise in the press the provision of welfare measures' in order to counteract rumours, believed to be especially prevalent in Wales and the South West that, in the absence of recreational facilities, the WAAC were spending their leisure time in unsupervised fraternisation with soldiers.[101] Chalmers-Watson resigned as Chief Controller of the Corps in February 1918 owing to family demands and was replaced in London by Florence Leach, previously of the Women's Legion. One of Leach's first tasks on taking over control of the corps illustrates the level of concern in the War Office about the rumours: she was to swear an affidavit declaring that no member of the WAAC had ever been 'requisitioned or sent to France for any immoral purposes whatsoever'.[102] These rumours were normally only referred to tangentially in the press in reports of 'unfounded allegations as to the character of the brave girls who are doing war work in camps' and countered by claims that these rumours were 'so absurd and yet so mischievous that they are surely of pro-German or pacifist origin'.[103] The *Daily Sketch* appears to have been the only national newspaper to print any explicit allegations, and these are a far cry from those reported to Chalmers-Watson, claiming merely 'that they walk about with soldiers, their arms entwined or round waists . . . in light-hearted comradeship', and explaining that 'etiquette in these matters between Tommies and WAAC rank and file is not ours.'[104] The separation of the behaviour of working-class WAACs and private soldiers from the readers of the newspaper is both a recognition that different moral codes existed close to the front and an underscoring of the difference between working-class mores and values and those of the middle and upper classes. In a similar vein Dorothy Pickford defended the actions of the WAACs she supervised, arguing that 'they have their standard of behaviour and very few transgress it, but it isn't always our standard.' Although she went on to comment that, in her opinion, their behaviour was extremely good, the rumours of misconduct continued.[105]

Various attempts were made by government ministries and the army to redeem the WAAC's reputation and so encourage more women to join the service. The number of women enrolling for service with the WAAC had certainly slowed down since its inception. Although over 11,000 women had joined in October–November 1917, this number dropped to just under 4,000 for November–December 1917 and a little over 2,000 for December 1917–January 1918.[106] Conscription for women was again discussed and recruitment parades were planned, where women were told that

> Not only must they maintain the highest standards of honour, conduct and purity, but . . . they must also let others see that they do, and must take an intense pride in the Corps to which they belong . . . you must give yourselves airs and hold your heads very high, and make other women feel that it is a great privilege to belong to the WAAC.[107]

G. H. Roberts, the Minister for Labour, made a series of speeches supporting and defending the WAAC in February 1918, views echoed in the same month by the Archbishop of Canterbury, who had travelled to France to view the troops and the women serving there the previous year.[108] Recruitment rallies focused on dispelling the rumours, a WAAC Recruiting Controller in Brighton reassuring her audience that 'if people heard anything of the stories going round they could rest assured they were a splendid set of girls . . . and that there was nothing to be said against them.'[109] It was announced in the press that 'action will be taken against anybody who is found to be disseminating slanderous statements about the WAACs', and in April 1918 a Primitive Methodist Minister in Congleton was prosecuted under the DORA and fined £40.00 for 'spreading false reports about the WAAC' in a letter to the Secretary of the Purity League.[110] The women of the WAAC defended themselves in the press, one member describing how 'it has surprised and disgusted me to see passers-by in the streets turn up their noses and stand aside when they have seen me approach in a uniform that I am proud to wear.'[111] However, the rumours proved to be persistent, and in early 1918 a Commission of Inquiry was appointed by the Ministry of Labour to investigate.

The Commission, which was made up of six women, published their Report on 20 March 1918. The Commissioners visited 29 camps in France and interviewed over 80 people, including WAAC workers, administrators, medical men and women and officials of the YMCA and YWCA. They found that 'not only are the rumours untrue, but...the number of undesirable women who have found their way into the Corps has been very small'.[112] The Report suggested that the majority of rumours had their basis in letters sent home by troops who, they felt, may have been motivated by 'jealousy and hostility towards the WAAC' if they had been 'dislodged from non-combatant tasks in the bases' by the women's arrival.[113] From 21 pregnancies, the Commissioners found that 2 were to married women and, of the rest, the majority were pregnant before joining the Corps. Indeed, the rate for unmarried pregnancies amongst the WAAC, at approximately 3:1,000, was lower than that for civilian society, a fact acknowledged in the Report's comment that 'the present position of the Corps in France compares very favourably with obvious perils run by girls in ordinary employment at the present time...where neither health nor morality is so safe-guarded.'[114] Nevertheless, the Report recommended that female police patrols should be introduced at WAAC centres in France, that powers of dismissal should be exercised more freely and that women serving close to the front line, an area where they believed 'greater danger exists' and 'special vigilance...is necessary' should be closely monitored.[115] The Commissioners praised the work of the Administrators in 'building up morale and discipline' and 'the maintenance of decorum and good manners among the girls'.[116] However, despite these tributes to WAAC 'morale and discipline' the Commissioners chose to play down the military aspects of Corps life, emphasising instead the healthy 'open air life' of the women, which they believed led to low sickness figures, and arguing that drill and route marches, so criticised when undertaken by the civilian WVR, were 'in the nature of physical exercise, and have a hygienic rather than a military value'.[117] Similarly, the Commissioners, who included the anti-suffragist, Violet Markham, were careful to distinguish between the 'uniformed young women' and the soldiers that they served.[118] This suggests that, despite the generally positive reports of the WAAC in the British press, some antipathy towards women in uniform remained, and it was this antipathy which provided such a fertile breeding ground for the proliferation of rumours regarding women in the Corps.

The publication of the Commission's Report, although acknowledged in the press, is generally seen to have been overshadowed by the sudden and successful German offensive which began the following day.[119] In this offensive, nine members of the WAAC were killed in bombing raids at Abbeville, and their funeral, with full military honours, seemed to show that women, like men, had 'confirmed their right to khaki', making them 'one in sympathy and sacrifice with the fighting services'.[120] The WAAC were renamed the Queen Mary's Army Auxiliary Corps (QMAAC) in April 1918, with Queen Mary assuming the honorary title of Commandant in Chief, 'as a mark of her Majesty's appreciation of the good services rendered by the Women's Army Auxiliary Corps'.[121] Numerous articles appeared in the press emphasising both the femininity and the good behaviour of women in the Corps, and women out of uniform became the focus of criticism and concern, as a renewed campaign for female conscription emerged.[122] The *Daily Express* argued that special uniforms should be introduced to mark out the 'strumpets' who were 'picketing army huts' and the *Evening News* criticised the 'apparently uncontrolled soliciting of our boys by women on the London streets'.[123] Thus as women in uniform became more widely accepted, the woman not wearing uniform was increasingly criticised for her lack of morality and patriotism.

By the war's end in November 1918, between 80,000 and 90,000 women had served in the auxiliary services, the majority in the WAAC and the remainder in the Women's Royal Naval Service, formed in November 1917 and the Women's Auxiliary Air Force, formed in April 1918. They had worked as clerks, store keepers, cleaners, cooks, waitresses, mechanics, telephonists and drivers. Although British women did not take part in combat, they worked close to the front lines in France and Belgium and repeatedly came under fire in the German offensive of 1918.[124] At least nine women died as a result of enemy actions with more injured, and yet more died or had their health affected through illness contracted whilst serving. Their work was widely recognised as an essential contribution to the war effort. However, women's war service was never seen in the same way as men's. Women remained auxiliary, their organisation allied to but separate from that of the military. They worked to serve and support the fighting men, and although they may at times have been physically working alongside men, symbolically, they remained beneath them. Women in uniform were of lower status than the male combatants, able to be injured and killed in warfare but not able to fight for their country. This separate status was reinforced in the Representation of the People Act of January 1918 which extended the male franchise on the basis that no man who had served in the military should be denied the vote; women were awarded voting rights based on their age and marital status, not on their war service. Although the very presence of women in uniform and near to the combat zones threatened to undermine the division between home front and war front, male and female war experience, the regulation and control of every aspect of their service meant that these boundaries were largely maintained. With the war's end they could be rebuilt.

5 Between the wars

Women's military organisations 1919–1938

The First World War ended on 11 November 1918, at 11 a.m. precisely. Individual's experiences of the end of war varied widely. Whilst most combatants who recorded the armistice noted that there was little or no military activity in the hours preceding it, for some, the war continued right until its dying seconds. Private Robert Cude, fighting on the front line in Northern France, recorded in his diary that 'shells, mortars and bullets were fired until 11 a.m. in the spirit of disposing of ammunition and as many of the enemy as possible before the cease fire'.[1] Others described a sense of joy and relief that the years of war were over: Dorothy Pickford, serving with Queen Mary's Army Auxiliary Corps (QMAAC) in France, wrote to friends that the women in her camp were very much in demand as guests at the many dances and entertainments organised by locally stationed troops in the weeks following the Armistice.[2] The lasting impression of the declaration of peace today is probably of crowds in central London, as described by the diarist Frederick Arthur Robinson, who claimed that 'perhaps such crowds have never been known in London... in front of Buckingham Palace was one vast crowd of people'.[3] However, despite the elation felt by many, there were large numbers of people who did not feel able to celebrate, who were perhaps in mourning for loved ones who had died during the war. Vera Brittain is probably the best known representative of this perspective, writing in *Testament of Youth* in 1933 that

> When the sound of victorious guns burst over London at 11a.m. on November 11th 1918, the men and women who looked incredulously into each other's faces did not cry jubilantly 'We've won the war!'. They only said 'The war is over'... I thought 'It's come too late for me'... The War was over; a new age was beginning; but the dead were dead and would never return.[4]

In a similar vein, Robert Saunders, the headmaster of a school in East Sussex wrote to his son in Canada that 'I think that most people feel that some time must elapse before we can properly celebrate peace'.[5] There was clearly no one response to, or experience of, the Armistice. People's experiences of the declaration of peace were shaped by their experiences of war. It is trite, given the range of responses outlined above, to claim one over-riding feeling amongst the men and women who wore uniform. Nonetheless, if there *was* one widely shared feeling, it was the belief that the majority of them would soon be wearing civilian clothes again, discharged from service with the military. However, both the discharge process itself and the experience of civilian life between the wars were strongly shaped by gender.

At the end of the war, there were approximately 3.75 million men and 38,901 women in service with the army.[6] Compulsory military service was suspended one hour after the armistice was declared and demobilisation, overseen by Sir Eric Geddes, began shortly thereafter. Planning for demobilisation had been undertaken well before the end of the war, with military personnel being divided into five separate groups according to the importance of their skills and occupation in the process of reconstruction. Within each group, further priority would be calculated according to length of service, marital status and amount of time spent in the front line. 'Slip men', those with guaranteed jobs awaiting them, were demobilised according to the importance accorded to his occupation in the process of reconstruction. Discontent with this system soon became apparent, as men who had joined the military later in the war were more likely to have retained links with employers, and thus the promise of employment, than men who had joined up in 1914. In December 1918 the Labour newspaper the *Daily Herald* demanded that the government 'Send the boys home'[7] whilst the *Daily Express* commented on 'the depth of hostile feeling that has been raised among all classes and particularly among the fighting men' by the perceived slowness of demobilisation.[8] Demonstrations by men waiting to be discharged took place in camps and cities across Southern England early in 1919: some 20,000 demonstrating in Southampton in January and 10,000 refusing to return to France from Folkestone in February.[9] In response, the government abandoned its planned schedule of demobilisation, replacing it with what was effectively a 'first in, first out' scheme. By the end of 1919, over 3 million men had returned to civilian life.[10]

No such detailed scheme was in place to regulate the demobilisation of women in uniform. As women had enrolled, not enlisted, for military service, they had officially retained the status of civilians serving with the army, subject to military law only as camp followers, not as members of the army. As such, there was no existing model of demobilisation to follow and the pattern which was adopted illuminates the expectations accorded to gender roles in the immediate postwar years. Unlike their male colleagues, released from service according to the need for their skills in the workplace, women's role in the home was the key factor determining their demobilisation. The *Daily Chronicle* claimed that 'homes, not industry or business, are given the place of first importance in the scheme prepared for the demobilisation of the QMAAC'.[11] The War Office *Report of the Women War Workers Resettlement Committee*, published on 18 November, one week after the Armistice, proposed that 'married women and widows with children undoubtedly have a claim for early release with a view to their resuming at the earliest possible moment their domestic obligations'.[12] Married women and women with children were thus released before women with a promise of immediate employment, although single women who 'have either a definite offer of re-employment from their previous employers or who are qualified to under-take work in occupations in which... there is likely to be, during demobi-lization, a strong demand for women's labour' were released before single women without such connections.[13] Some women were retained in service in order to release male soldiers into employment, and Women's Legion Motor Drivers who had spent the war years working in Britain were sent abroad to enable Army Service Corps men to be demobilised. Women were also recruited to serve with the Army of Occupation in the Occupied Zone of Germany, working with the Military Police and searching women suspected of smuggling contraband goods into unoccupied Germany.[14] The QMAAC ceased to exist on active service on 27 September 1921, when the last mem-bers of the Corps were sent home from France. These thirty-one women had been serving at St Pol in France, working at the headquarters of the Director of Graves Registration and Enquiries, the camp from which the Unknown Warrior, buried in Westminster Abbey, had been chosen. The last act of this group of women was to lay flowers at the Cenotaph and to visit the Tomb of the Unknown Soldier in Westminster Abbey.

Attitudes towards women in uniform had shifted during the war, moving from the widespread disapproval of the more militaristic volunteer bodies to a recognition of the essential work being carried out by women in the Women's Army Auxiliary Corps (WAAC, later the QMAAC) and other officially recog-nised and organised bodies such as the Women's Royal Naval Service (WRNS) and the Women's Auxiliary Air Force (WAAF). However, approval of these bodies was always qualified by a suspicion that they were acting outside of the bounds of acceptable femininity, and by demands that, when the war ended, women would return to the home. Numerous articles about the WAAC towards the end of the war stressed the femininity of the women members, a descriptive article in *Everyweek* depicting the WAACs' quarters as resembling 'a school dormitory' where 'posters and pennants adorn the walls; also, pictures of their favourite movie actors and matinee heroes'.[15] Similarly, an edition of *The Mentor*, a magazine published in the United States, described the 'pretty girls in attractive uniforms who have been doing most useful work'.[16] However, in peacetime, opinion shifted away from a qualified approval of female military service towards a concern that it was essentially unfeminine, a threat to the gendered status quo. In June 1919 the *Sheffield Daily Telegraph* ran a story which viciously criticised the impact of army life on femininity:

> in some cases Army life (we omit the nursing and hospital department) in the cases of girls naturally refined or delicately nurtured, has not been an unmixed blessing... they show a tendency to avoid the home and sever

their home ties; the efforts they make to appear 'bold' and masculine, whether it be – to mention one example – in excessive cigarette smoking or the thrusting of their hands deep into their side pockets, all go to indicate the loss of grace and charm which in the old days caused their fathers to espouse their mothers ... we hope that it will represent but a passing phase and that (they) will venture to shed their army manners with their military uniforms.[17]

Reports that the Army Council were considering the establishment of the QMAAC on a permanent basis were greeted with horror in the British press, *The Times* commenting that 'to be frank, the public has grown tired of uniformed women ... The Army in peace has no place for women'.[18] A country recovering from over four years of total war wanted to be rid of the signs and symbols of warfare: women in uniform were one of the most potent of these signs.

Indeed, it seemed that there was little or no place for employed women in postwar Britain. Women's work during the war had often been seen as a temporary feature of a society turned upside down by the demands of total war; when peace came, there was a strong and widely felt desire to return to 'normal' and to return to the pre-war status quo. The slump, which began in late 1920, helped to strengthen an environment in which women working in industry or commerce were increasingly represented as taking work from unemployed ex-servicemen. Women working in industry and commerce had already lost their jobs in large numbers: munitions workers were amongst the first to be laid off, and by the end of 1918, approximately 750,000 women had been made redundant.[19] Women who had been encouraged to join the wartime workforce as a patriotic act were now told that it was their patriotic duty to leave these jobs in order to make way for returning men, a position supported by the National Federation of Women Workers, the largest union representing women. The feminist commentator Irene Clapham, writing in 1935, described a society in which women in employment moved from being seen as 'saviours of the nation' to 'ruthless self-seekers, depriving men and their dependants of a livelihood'.[20] Women workers found that they were no longer the 'brave and busy' heroines of wartime and were instead 'social scroungers', depriving returning male soldiers and their families of an income.[21] Whilst women in the auxiliary services were not under the same pressure as industrial and clerical workers to give up their wartime occupations to the returning men, they were expected to leave their 'masculine' wartime occupations for more feminine roles.

Women returning from service in the QMAAC, expecting to use their skills and training in civilian employment, often found that they were expected to return to the home, if not as wives and mothers, then as domestic servants. Domestic service was an increasingly unpopular area of employment for women: former domestic workers who had found better paid employment in the factories or the auxiliary services during the war were often unwilling to return to the low pay and lack of personal freedom associated with domestic work. In a survey of women outside a Labour Exchange by the Journal *Woman Worker* in 1919, 65 per cent of women questioned replied that they would not take work in domestic service on any terms.[22] By the beginning of 1919, most newspapers were becoming predictably vocal in their disapproval of women refusing to take jobs in domestic service, describing them as 'women slackers' and 'slackers with state pay', the magazine *The Truth* claiming that the availability of an out of work donation for 26 weeks meant that:

> There are any number of vacant situations, but former domestic servants, even if they intend to return to their old occupation eventually, will naturally not elect to do so while they can claim state unemployment benefit...One girl is getting 25 shillings a week unemployment benefit, and she will remain idle for the 13 weeks during which it is payable.[23]

In order to counteract a perceived reluctance amongst women to take the often low paid and low status jobs which were designated 'women's work', the government first cut benefit rates and then withdrew benefit altogether from women who refused *any* offer of paid work. Thus, by early 1919 women were refused benefit if they turned down jobs in the traditional female trades of laundry and domestic service, even if they had never been employed in these areas. Despite the changes of the war: the social and cultural extension of women's role, the expanded range of occupations which opened to women and the limited enfranchisement of women in 1918, postwar government policy and public opinion appeared united in a determination to push women back into pre-war patterns of employment and behaviour.

The Women's Legion, headed by Lady Londonderry, had been the first organisation recognised by the Army Council and had worked with the army since February 1916, its members providing cooks and drivers for the army within Britain and later working with the WAAC in France. Shortly after the end of the war, in January 1919, Lady Londonderry announced a scheme 'to secure that the Legionnaires released from their duties at the front might enter domestic service...under the most promising conditions'.[24] Londonderry planned to create a Women's Legion Household Service Section, which would provide its members with three months training, a guaranteed minimum wage and the right to wear the Women's Legion badge. This proposal was part of a wider movement to make domestic service more attractive to women by rationalisation and professionalisation, as also suggested in the *Report of the Women's Advisory Committee*, published in 1919. A similar plan had been announced in the *Daily Express* earlier in the month under the auspices of the newly launched British Home Help Association. This sought to tackle the 'problem' of munition workers who were unwilling to take up posts in domestic service by adapting the emergent rationalised, Taylorist patterns of working, proposing that domestic service be re-organised along the shift patterns 'to which women war workers had become accustomed'.[25] Early plans for the demobilisation of the QMAAC included proposals for a large programme of lectures in camps supported by training hostels in towns, staffed by ex-QMAAC officials, in order 'to solve the problem of the long-felt want of household workers'.[26] A further plan to meet the shortage of domestic workers was published in *The Times* towards the end of the month, consisting of 'an association or guild established with a uniform, a badge of the order, and distinguishing marks for efficiency'.[27] Thus, the signs and symbols associated with women's auxiliary military service, uniforms, badges and grades, were to be adapted in an attempt to encourage women to (re)enter domestic service.

However, these schemes, which could be seen as the 'carrot' to the government's 'stick' of withdrawing benefit, were not successful and were gradually dropped, in part because of resistance on the part of employers to wage rises and increased autonomy for domestic staff. Despite attempts such as these to raise the status of the domestic servant, domestic service remained an unpopular destination amongst women leaving the auxiliary services.[28] Florence Leach, the Director of the QMAAC, commented that 'the fact that they will be called servants seems to deter so many'.[29] However, ex-auxiliaries were very much in demand as domestic staff, adverts in the QMAAC *Old Comrades Association Gazette* asking for a 'cook-general (QMAAC preferred)', 'QMAAC housemaid' and 'Two ex-members QMAAC wanted as cook and housemaid'.[30] The discipline and training received by women in the auxiliary services, together with the class deference which was built into the organizations' structure, appears to have made former members of the QMAAC attractive to would-be domestic employers, even if domestic service held little attraction for the ex-auxiliaries. The *Daily Telegraph*, discussing the shortage of domestic workers, perceptively commented that although 'there never was any difficulty in recruiting for the domestic branches' of the women's wartime services, the introduction of militaristic uniforms, badges and grades for domestic servants would not attract these workers into private service as the knowledge that they were wearing 'the King's uniform ... performing duties for the state' was the primary motivation for their wartime service.[31] Once this factor was removed, domestic service reverted to an unpopular, low status, occupation.

Women returning from service with the military in the years immediately following the war found that they were returning to a society in which the massive expansion of opportunities for women seen during the war in many areas were rapidly contracting. The postwar backlash against women's new roles extended far beyond the question of women's paid work. In addition to the drive to move women back into the home and traditional areas of labour, the immediate postwar years saw an attack on the social and cultural shifts in gender roles which had occurred during the war. Throughout the war years, and underlying the congratulatory rhetoric which was often used to describe women's war work, a more antagonistic tone could be perceived, which accused women of profiting from the devastation and disruption of war. Early on in the war young middle-class women were attacked for enjoying themselves whilst men fought and died and working-class women accused of profiting financially by soliciting outside army camps.[32] In 1916 the *Pall Mall Gazette* sternly reminded its female readers that 'true sacrifice for country lies rather in doing what we don't like than what we like, and moreover, doing it with a smile'.[33] By the end of the war the *Saturday Review* felt able to publish a savage attack on women whom it felt had profited from the war:

> Let there be no doubt about it; a large part of the female population of the country have had the time of their lives. That time has, we fear, not altogether tended to improve them. They have learnt the joys of freedom, of considerable wages, of swaggering about in every kind of uniform and, above all, of the advantages of the factory over the home life.[34]

A letter to the same magazine two months earlier, just before the armistice, had similarly charged women with benefiting from the war. This time however, women were attacked for remaining within the home, the letter arguing that women had 'married soldiers in the belief that they would never see them again' in order to receive dependent's allowances and widow's pensions. The letter went on to reverse the traditional gendered alignment of men with war and women with peace by arguing that the availability of these allowances would cause 'women, who are half the electorate, to love, instead of loathing, war. The Jingo of the twentieth century will be in petticoats'.[35] Women were thus accused of profiting from the war whether they had undertaken paid work or had married and worked within the home. Catherine Gasquoine Hartley's 1919 essay *Women's Wild Oats* claimed that the disruptions of the war years had led to 'a confusion of values' which 'has led women astray'.[36] The experience of war led Gasquoine Hartley to move from a prewar position of attacking separate sphere ideology to a postwar defence of separate spheres, in which she argued that

> The only rights I desire to claim for my sex are those necessary to the discharge of its own duties; the fulfilment of the instinctive moral craving; the realisation of the deepest impulses of a woman's nature.[37]

Despite, and perhaps in part in reaction to, the partial enfranchisement of women and the general extension of women's roles in wartime, the postwar years were shaped by a vigorous reassertion of traditional gender roles.

Given the conservative thinking which surrounded concepts of gender and helped to limit the opportunities available to women immediately after the war, it is perhaps not surprising that numbers of women who had served with the auxiliary services attempted to pursue a new life in the colonies. Prior to the end of the war the War Office began to look into the possibilities for overseas settlement for QMAAC members, and short lectures were delivered to women in military camps, outlining the possibilities for emigration.[38] Indeed, it was recommended that women who had served in the QMAAC 'would make excellent colonists' due to their wartime training in 'hygiene, discipline, self-control and self-reliance'. In addition to this it was suggested that their experience of 'close contact with large numbers of men' would mean they were unlikely to 'contract undesirable friendships' in the colonies.[39] Emigration had slowed during the war years, and was cancelled out by expatriates returning to Britain to help with the war effort. Almost 1,300,000 British people had left for the Colonies and the United States in 1911 and 1912; in 1918, the figure stood at 23,000. With government assistance, this number had risen to 438,000 in 1920, the peak year for emigration in the immediate postwar years.[40] The Overseas Settlement Office ran a scheme offering free passage to the colonies for ex-servicewomen who had completed a minimum of six months service, complementing the Free Passage Scheme which operated after the war for ex-servicemen. In January 1919 the *Daily Chronicle* commented that 'the girls who are passing out of the women's services manifest much interest in the subject' of emigration, and during the same year representatives from the women's services joined the Society for the Overseas Settlement of British Women.[41] The government agreed to pay third-class passage for women and men wishing to emigrate, and the Overseas Settlement Committee made £250,000 available to the QMAAC for 'the assistance of persons who have suffered as a result of the war and intend to settle overseas'.[42] In 1919 alone, over 10,000 applications for free passage were made, and 1,140 vouchers for travel were issued, enabling 2,000 people (applicants and dependents) to emigrate.[43] By the beginning of 1920, over 200 members of the QMAAC had successfully applied for free passage to the colonies, the majority requesting transport to Canada, Australia and New Zealand.[44] These high figures, accounting for over 20 per cent of all successful applicants, suggest that the lure of a new life in the colonies had a strong appeal for ex-servicewomen, eager to experience new opportunities abroad.

However, women who expressed an interest in emigration were required to complete forms designed to show whether they would prove to be suitable candidates for life in the colonies. Applicants were quizzed on their employment during the war and whether or not they intended to work on the land 'or, in the case of women, to undertake domestic service', and a memorandum from the Women's Legion to the QMAAC noted that applicants for free passage were more likely to be successful if they indicated they were 'willing to undertake domestic service'.[45] Advertisements for female employment in the colonies forwarded to the QMAAC were predominantly for domestic staff and women willing to undertake childcare for salaries of between £80 and £50 per year, considerably more than could be expected from similar posts in Britain.[46] Some positions for female land workers and farmers were advertised, such as the vacancy for 'a land worker on a farm in the hills, eighteen miles from Adelaide, fifteen shillings per week plus board and lodging in cottage with two other women' sent to the QMAAC in January 1920, but these were vastly outnumbered by advertisements for domestic positions.[47] As in Britain, women from the auxiliary services were perceived as being especially suitable for domestic service in the colonies, a Parliamentary Commissioner charged with examining opportunities for British women in Canada commenting that

> The residents of more than one district stated their wish to give preference to women of the war services desiring to settle in Canada as domestic helps ... such women skilled in domestic work should receive a badge of efficiency upon demobilisation in Britain.[48]

Ex-administrators with the QMAAC sometimes obtained posts as supervisors for groups of women travelling abroad, one writing to the *Old Comrades Association Gazette* in 1920 of arriving in Australia with 'my family of sixty domestics' and describing domestic work in glowing terms as 'by far the best work for women in this country'.[49] Women who were still determined to live independently, earning their living by farming or land work, were often at a disadvantage as land settlement facilities organised by colonial governments for demobilised British soldiers were not available to ex-servicewomen.[50] Women looking for adventure abroad were likely to find the same gendered constraints, propelling them into domestic service and other traditional areas of female labour, as they found at home.

Many of the women involved in organising the women's auxiliary services during the war were determined to maintain the organisations as far as possible in peacetime. Following the war, the armed services, and British military policy in general, underwent a period of reappraisal and change. In 1919 the Ministry of Reconstruction published a pamphlet entitled *The Mission of the British Army* which argued that only a large-scale, well funded national army would be able to guarantee the future peace.[51]

This early policy of 'security through strength' was seized upon by women such as Helen Gwynne Vaughan, Florence Leach and Katherine Furse, who argued that the maintenance of the women's auxiliary services was vital to British defence policy. In 1920 a Women's Reserve Sub-Committee met at the War Office to consider plans for a peacetime women's reserve. This was to be the first of several attempts during the inter-war years to establish female auxiliary military service on a permanent footing. Women sitting on the Committee took the opportunity to push for identical terms of enlistment for men and women, arguing that women should be enlisted, not enrolled as in the First World War, and subject to the same codes of punishment as regular, male, soldiers.[52] Other questions regarding women's military service, which had arisen in wartime, were also discussed. The committee was divided over the question of dilution; the ratio by which women would be needed to replace men. Whilst the representative of the WRNS commented that 'on average four women were required to replace three men'

Helen Gwynne-Vaughan, representing the Women's Royal Air Force (WRAF) on the committee, was quick to reply that 'in many cases a woman was quite equal to a man.' This was supported by Florence Leach, representing the QMAAC, who argued that in fact women made more productive workers than men as soldiers were 'notoriously idle' whilst 'a woman is more conscientious and keener,' perhaps because she had to prove her worth.[53] Despite these arguments, the committee agreed that women in a reserve force should receive no pay in peacetime and wages approximating two-thirds of their equivalent ranks in the regular army if mobilised. Men on the committee in particular were concerned about the impact that the organisation of a permanent female reserve would have on home and family life, the Chairman, General Burnett-Hitchcock, asking Gwynne-Vaughan how she felt 'women's feelings would be reflected in the case of the other sex with whom they are connected in home life?' Gwynne-Vaughan replied by emphasising the pride felt by families with women in the wartime auxiliary services, describing 'brothers who were proud of the sisters and even husbands proud of their wives'.[54] Despite these concerns and objections from the representative of the War Office Finance Department, who questioned the need for any such organisation, the committee published its Report in 1920 supporting the organisation of a Women's Reserve.

The Report recommended that a Women's Reserve be established on a permanent basis through the aegis of the Territorial Army. Women were to be recruited through existing organisations, such as the Girl Guides and boarding schools, but also through 'County Ladies', sitting on committees with representatives of their local branch of the Territorial Army. Thus the Reserve would consist of a number of small, County based branches which, in total, would number 100,000 women.[55] Women in the Reserve would attend occasional training camps to ensure that they were ready to work with the army immediately should the need arise. The work that they were envisaged doing was much the same as during the First World War: largely support work such as cooking, cleaning, driving, store keeping and secretarial duties. The proposed system of organisation, under the Territorial Army, which was largely staffed by amateur, part-time soldiers and with society women at the head of the Reserve, represented a move away from a professional status for female auxiliaries. Although women in the planned organisation would be paid on mobilisation, its role as a subsidiary of the Territorial Army, together with the somewhat piecemeal plans for recruitment, which largely depended on the knowledge and connections of local upper-class women, ensured that it would remain on the fringes of British military policy.

However, the planned Women's Reserve was not to be. By the time that the Report was published, opinion was already swinging quickly away from planning for future wars towards planning for peace. Late in 1921 the economist J. M. Keynes described the 'immense change in public sentiment' which had come about since the end of the war, arguing that 'the desire for a quiet life, for reduced commitments, for comfortable terms with our neighbours, is paramount'.[56] These desires became apparent through support for the newly established League of Nations, designed to promote international co-operation and collective security through the peaceful settlement of disputes by arbitration and the imposition of economic sanctions on aggressive nations. The optimistic and widespread belief in the power of the League of Nations to keep the peace impacted on British military policy throughout the 1920s and into the early 1930s. In 1919 the first Ten Year Rule was introduced, a Cabinet policy, re-affirmed in 1928 and only rescinded in 1932, which assumed that no 'great war' was to be planned for or expected for at least ten years. A variety of schemes, such as the Esher proposal of 1922, which attempted to restrict European land and air forces, and the Washington Conference of 1921–1922, which limited the forces of the great naval powers, were planned throughout the 1920s to facilitate disarmament.[57] The Kellogg Pact of 1927 renounced war as an instrument of national policy, and British expenditure on defence fell from £766 million in 1919–1920 to £102 million in 1932.[58] Militaristic women such as Helen Gwynne-Vaughan found themselves increasingly out of step with public opinion and government policy; a nation committed to collective security and to cutting its defence budget was unlikely to look kindly on the creation of a female military organisation, and the planned Women's Reserve was quietly dropped.

Helen Gwynne-Vaughan returned to her post of lecturer in botany at Birkbeck College, University of London, and the majority of the women's auxiliary services of the First World War continued to exist only as Old Comrades organizations. The well-connected women of the First Aid Nursing Yeomanry (FANY) and the Women's Legion Motor Transport Drivers remained as active voluntary organisations and both worked during the General Strike of 1926, driving and running messages between government ministries. Partly as a reward for this work, and also because of their lobbying of male acquaintances within the War Office, both organisations were formally recognised by the Army Council in 1927. Interest in the women's wartime auxiliary organisations declined throughout the early and mid 1920s, in part because of a general desire to move away from the traumas of the war years and in part because of the backlash seen in those years against women's paid work. The QMAAC Old Comrades Association, set up in 1919, reported falling membership figures and a declining circulation for its magazine, the *Old Comrades Gazette*, in 1926.[59] The activities of the organisation, together with minutes of Council meetings and Annual General Meetings throughout the 1920s and the early 1930s articulate the changing attitude towards, and activities of, the women's auxiliary organisations.

A key indicator of attitudes towards women who had served in the war can be seen in the role allocated to women in the official ceremonies of remembrance. Although the last act of the final women to be demobilised from the QMAAC in 1921 had been to lay a wreath on the Cenotaph in memory of 'the boys who, unlike ourselves, would not come back' this tribute was independently organised and not overseen by the War Office.[60] Both ceremonies of remembrance and many monuments to the war dead were shaped by ideals of gender in which men represented warriors and women grieving mothers; there was little space for servicewomen in either the monuments or the parades which followed the war.[61] The QMAAC was only invited to take part in the official Armistice Day parade for the first time in 1926, when approximately 60 women paraded through Whitehall to the Cenotaph with the male military organisations, and in 1929 eight members of the Old Comrades Organization participated for the first time in the annual commemoration of the armistice held at the Albert Hall in London. For the most part the Old Comrades Association focused its attention on benevolent work, providing grants for ex-members requesting financial help with 'training, emigration, sickness and convalescence'.[62] The Association also organised battlefield tours and its members turned their energies to traditionally female areas of philanthropic work, the London branch organising an outing for thirty-six children from poor areas in 1929.[63] Similarly, the news sheets of the FANY for the same period show a move away from the militaristic activities of the pre-war and wartime years towards a concern with benevolent and philanthropic activities. The news sheet for 1932 complained that 'there is so little news to report' and detailed the activities of the Glasgow Branch, which included 'taking children for short runs from the East Park Home for Cripple Children, and also arranging to take patients to their homes from the Glasgow Western Infirmary'.[64] In 1934, during the Great Depression, the news sheet reported that the Ilkley sub-section had 'offered its services as a club for the unemployed in Ilkley'.[65] In this they were part of an essentially conservative wider inter-war movement which was re-asserting the importance of traditional gender roles, and in which spaces for female participation in public life had were shaped by a domestic, nurturing ideology of femininity. Although new opportunities for female employment did begin to open up for women between the wars, most notably in the new light engineering industries, shop work and office work, inter-war Britain remained a society in which a woman's ideal role was as a wife and mother. This ideology of female domesticity was widespread, reflected and promoted in women's magazines of the period, working patterns which showed that in 1931, 90 per cent of married women were not in full time employment and, arguably, in a shift in feminist campaigning towards a focus on the rights of wives and mothers and away from the battle for equal rights.[66] The women's auxiliary organisations, which had been so active in the First World War, and which continued to exist during this period, did so by refocusing their energies and activities back towards the traditionally female sphere.

However, by the early 1930s, war in Europe again began to appear a possibility and international tensions were matched by conflict at home between a government, anxious to provide funding for the social security system during the depression, and the military and the War Office, who were becoming more and more vocal in their demands for increased defence spending. The 'British way in warfare', defined by the military correspondent Liddell-Hart as a reliance on the British Navy to defend the nation and the colonies, appeared increasingly unfeasible in the face of growing air power, Liddell-Hart himself proclaiming in 1937 that 'the air has bridged the sea'.[67]

This growing belief in the importance of air warfare in future conflicts, and in particular the widespread belief that poison gas, used in the trenches during the First World War, would be used against civilian populations, can be seen in military doctrine, government policy and works of popular fiction throughout the 1930s.[68] Concerns about the future role of air power as a weapon to be used against civilian populations had the dual effect of strengthening the Royal Air Force (RAF), the newest member of the military services, and expanding the support base for the pacifist organisations active in the country between the wars. In 1934 the cabinet shifted its funding priorities for the military away from the Navy and towards an expansion of the RAF, focusing in particular on the development of its strategic bombing capabilities. However, although it has been argued that the British public supported this policy as the cheapest form of defence available, this concentration on the importance of air power also helped to strengthen existing support for pacifism.[69] In 1933, the Oxford Union famously resolved that under no circumstances would it 'fight for its King and Country'.[70] The Peace Pledge Union, led by Canon Dick Sheppard, had 100,000 members and collected 120,000 pledges to renounce war in 1937, 2 years after 11.5 million Britons had voted in favour of disarmament and collective security on a ballot organised by the League of Nations.[71] Women also had their own, independent, pacifist organisations, the most prominent between the wars being the Women's Co-operative Guild, which emphasised the maternal response to war, placing the act of nurturing children in direct opposition to the destruction of warfare. This position was also taken by Virginia Woolf in *Three Guineas* (1938), which examined the linkage between militarism and patriarchy, arguing that women, oppressed by both structures, should resist them.[72] However, in direct contrast to these female pacifists, many of the women who had remained involved in women's quasi-military organisations saw the move to re-arm, and in particular the emphasis on the role of civilians in warfare, as an opportunity. If a future war was to target civilians, as many strategists believed, there would once again be a role for women's auxiliary services, who could work on the home front without markedly challenging the re-established gender roles.

The first signs of re-emergent female militaristic organisations came in 1933, when Mary Allen, who had been an active organiser of the early women's police service, wrote to *The Times*, signing herself 'Commandant, Women's Auxiliary Service' and announcing the formation of a 'Women's Reserve, to train and organise women of all ages, with or without previous experience, to be of use to the country in any event'.[73] This new announcement was swiftly censured by the representatives of the existing female organisations.

Lady Londonderry of the Women's Legion couched her condemnation of Allen's organisation in language which served to support both the gendered status quo and widespread pacifist beliefs by arguing that 'any fresh organization of women tending towards militarism is to be deplored,' before going on to point out that the Army Council already recognised both her own Women's Legion Motor Drivers and the FANY, hence there was no need for any new female reserve.[74] Londonderry contacted Gwynne-Vaughan and together they attempted to establish a Council of Women for War Service, which would incorporate the existing Women's Legion, the QMAAC Old Comrades Association, the FANYs and the Voluntary Aid Detachments under the title of the Women's Legion. Attempts to represent the organisation as only undertaking feminine activities, and not threatening the gendered status quo continued, and in a letter to *The Times* in 1935 Londonderry described the organisation in terms which placed its activities clearly within the existing female sphere, explaining that one of its key roles would be to help the St John Ambulance in the event of gas attacks on major cities such as London.[75] In a significant move away from the demands for women to take an equivalent role to that of men seen during the First World War, the re-emergent auxiliary organisation attempted to represent itself as unequivocally feminine and focused on civilian, not military concerns; existing primarily in order to help and protect the home front in a coming conflict.

Londonderry wrote to the War Office offering the Women's Legion services 'if it is thought necessary and desirable by those in authority' to form 'a national reserve of women for emergency services' and reminding them that 'the recognised representatives of the women's organisations which are still in existence' were the most suitable women to approach if such a reserve was to be formed.[76] Londonderry and Gwynne-Vaughan continued to lobby the War Office whilst organising their new corps into two main sections: an ancillary section, which would work with the civilian Red Cross and St John Ambulance on anti-gas work, and an auxiliary section, which would work with the armed forces on the same lines as they had done during the First World War. Within this auxiliary section, Gwynne-Vaughan was given the task of overseeing the training of potential female officers. The newly organised Women's Legion set up in offices in Shell House in London and began to recruit women, offering training in areas such as first aid, anti-gas work, cookery and officer training in locally organised training centres and at its own camp at Abbots Hill in Hertfordshire.

The War Office's reaction was mixed. On the one hand, given the general public's lack of support for any signs of rearmament, they were loath 'to appear to be giving official approval to any organization which might seem to be involved in any preparation for war'.[77] On the other, memories of the piecemeal organisation of women's labour in the First World War were still strong, and the War Office recognised that an existing and efficient women's auxiliary corps would be 'useful in the event of a general mobilization'.[78] However, the War Office remained sceptical at best in its attitude towards the Women's Legion, unable to square its aversion to offering payment to its members with its desire to ensure that any auxiliary military body be organised by the War Office. The War Office were concerned that the Women's Legion was too independent of the military hierarchy and argued that 'a semi-officially recognised body which is not efficient or not what we quite want is a burden rather than a help'.[79] However, official recognition of the new women's corps by the War Office would imply that they were willing to pay members' expenses, and given the relatively low level of defence spending in the early and mid 1930s, they were implacably opposed to offering payment to an auxiliary female organisation for which there was no immediate and obvious necessity. This lukewarm approach to the Women's Legion was perhaps strengthened by memories of many women's determination to appear as militaristic as possible during the First World War, one internal 1935 memo pointedly noting that 'most of these women's organizations have rather a fancy for uniforms'.[80] By 1935 the War Office were moving away from giving practical or financial support to the Women's Legion, arguing instead that women's function in wartime would simply be an extension of their peacetime roles, with women being used to replace soldiers as 'ambulance drivers, waitresses, cooks, domestic workers...telegraphists, wireless operators, telephone operators, clerks and anti-gas personnel'. Given that women were already employed in the majority of these occupations in civilian life, Sir Harry Knox, the Adjutant-General, argued that the female organisation did not need to provide specific training for women but instead could act as a sort of clearing house for the War Office, 'testing, registering and enrolling suitable candidates' for a reserve of trained women on which the military could draw in an emergency.[81] By the mid 1930s the women's auxiliary organisations were no closer to being fully incorporated into the official military structure than they had been in 1917.

In 1936 plans for a renewed women's corps suffered a further setback, when the Women's Reserve Sub-Committee of the Man-power Reserve Committee formed by the Committee of Imperial Defence refused to recommend the setting up of a reserve of women, arguing that the Ministry of Labour could organise and provide all the women's labour needed in wartime. The minutes of this Sub-Committee illustrate the extent to which the essentially amateur approach of the Women's Legion was becoming increasingly out of step with the slowly modernising British military. The Minister of Labour, invited to provide the Sub-Committee with his views on the necessity for women's labour in wartime, argued that organising female labour through a voluntary organisation such as the Women's Legion would result in a purely middle-class organisation, filled with women who did not need to undertake paid work and who thus had the time and energy to expend on unpaid quasi-military training.[82] In part, this was a result of the determination of Londonderry and Gwynne-Vaughan to keep the organisation's expenses at a minimum in order to obtain the support of the War Office, but it was also an acknowledgement of the class-based structure of the women's voluntary organisations during the First World War, in which middle-class women in khaki had predominated, practising drill, cookery and first aid in organisations like the Women's Volunteer Reserve, whilst working-class women flocked to the well paid and essential work of the munitions industry. The government, War Office, Admiralty and Air Ministry, planning for a war which would necessitate massive mobilisation and which, it was widely expected, would entail horrendous civilian casualties in its first days, were anxious to avoid the involvement of amateur, independent organisations as far as possible, preferring to centralise planning within existing government departments.[83]

Perhaps surprisingly, the most vocal supporters of the Women's Legion on the Sub-Committee were the representatives of the most modern branch of the military, the Air Force. The Air Force was the most technically advanced of the three services and also the least bound by tradition and class prejudice. Whilst the army of the mid 1930s was still dominated by the concept of the 'officer gentleman', leading his troops through a natural authority and shared recognition of class hierarchy, the air force 'encouraged individuality, freedom of thought, and a close working relationship between the officers and the rank and file'.[84] Status was achieved in the RAF through technical competency rather than social background. The Air Ministry were keen that they should be able to train auxiliary workers well in advance of a conflict, as they needed 'specialists, drivers and other specially qualified women' with skills that large numbers of women were unlikely to possess in civilian life.[85] The RAF argued that, in the chaos which was assumed to accompany the aerial bombardment expected at the beginning of any coming war, the existence of the Women's Legion to train and organise female labour would ensure that 'we could get the personnel required at two or three hours notice'.[86] In figures collected for the Sub-Committee, the Admiralty estimated that it would need the labour of approximately 5,332 women in the first three months of a national emergency, the War Office approximately 15,000 and the Air Ministry, which needed fewer but more highly trained women, 3,240. In addition to these numbers, the Home Office estimated that 230,000 women would be required to work as nurses and auxiliary first aid workers in the same period.[87] Despite some misgivings from the Air Ministry the Ministry of Labour was confident that these women could be organised and supplied via their Labour Exchanges, arguing that 'more women than in 1914 would be ready trained for industrial and clerical employment in the event of war' and that 'the emergency would call forth the number of volunteers required'.[88] The representatives of the armed forces concurred, though the Air Ministry did so with reservations, and agreed that there was therefore no need to recognise and fund a women's reserve. Indeed, the Sub-Committee concluded, the existence of such an organisation 'might very well prove to be an embarrassment rather than a help to the government's machinery'.[89] Given this lack of support, the Women's Legion closed down its operations in 1936, the victim of interwoven factors, including a public hostile to apparent mobilisation for war, the existence of significant numbers of young, unmarried women working in light industry and the clerical trades, the antagonism of the Ministry of Labour towards an organisation it perceived as threatening its sphere of authority and its own amateur structure.

Helen Gwynne-Vaughan, however, was not to be daunted in her determination to be involved in the organisation of a women's corps which would be prepared for any coming conflict. Her biographer, Molly Izzard, paints a picture of an autocratic, formidable woman with essentially conservative and reactionary social views, who had stood three times as the Conservative Parliamentary candidate for North Camberwell in the 1920s, a eugenicist who criticised the 'deficient and low grade individuals who are artificially enabled to survive' in a Cabinet Memorandum on eugenics.[90] As such she instinctively understood the class-bound organisational structure of the British army, a conservative organisation which was modernising far more slowly than its newer counterpart, the RAF. Coming from an upper-class Scottish family, with generations of service with the army, Gwynne-Vaughan was, in many ways a product of this culture. However, she was also a professionally trained woman, a widow who had to earn her own living and who had taken part in suffragist demonstrations in the early days of the First World War. She had also earned the mistrust of some individuals within the War Office by her insistence in 1917 on wearing military insignia and saluting superior male officers. Although her class position, her politics and her inherent support for conservative army values may have helped her in her campaign for an officially recognised women's corps, her gender and her perceived radicalism during the First World War may have acted against her.

When the Women's Legion scheme collapsed in 1936, Gwynne-Vaughan's section, essentially a female voluntary officers' training corps, continued. The success of this section of the women's organisation reflects the realisation by the War Office that 'many of the women most suitable' for officer training 'would not dream of going to the Employment Exchanges to register their names', a view which illustrates the class-bound nature of the army establishment at this time.[91] Although Gwynne Vaughan's plans were radical in their attempt to create a military auxiliary of women in peacetime, the fact that they only focused on upper-class and professional women helped to make them acceptable to the War Office. Early in 1936 Gwynne-Vaughan wrote to Sir Herbert Creedy, the Permanent Under-Secretary of State for War claiming that 'we really are... getting the right women to train – daughters of senior officers and so forth, who may have inherited some of their father's qualities'.[92] A female officer training corps may have been a challenge to the gendered ideology of the time, in which a woman's ideal place was in the home, but the class-based nature of the organisation sat comfortably with the conservative ideology which still predominated in the War Office. Renamed the Emergency Service, the organisation began to recruit members late in the same year with a recruiting leaflet which both stressed a traditionally feminine, nurturing role and suggested that not all women felt that their strengths lay in that area:

> In a time of national emergency, nursing is usually the best form of usefulness for women who can become good nurses, but there are many with no special turn for care of the sick, yet who want to help and who would make capable officers. It is these whom we ask especially to consider the duty of preparedness.[93]

The Emergency Service thus articulated a national need for female officers whilst reinforcing the idea that a woman's 'natural' role in wartime was as a nurse and carer.

By the end of 1937, 400 potential officers had trained with the Emergency Service, clues to their class position found in Gwynne-Vaughan's memoirs, where she claims that they began by 'enrolling our friends and the friends of our friends, both working and leisured'.[94] Members paid a subscription of 10 shillings per year which entitled them to attend a series of lectures, to drill and to attend an annual summer camp which cost 3 shillings, 6d per day for two weeks, and to which they were expected to bring 'country clothes, low heeled shoes . . . a short skirt or shorts, an overall (and) an afternoon dress for dinner in the evening'.[95] The requirement that all potential members sign a form stating 'whether they are of pure European descent and of British nationality' perhaps reflecting Gwynne-Vaughan's enduring belief in eugenics as much as any desire to monitor the membership of the service.[96] Some upper-class British women were more welcome than others however, with the pro-Nazi Unity Mitford's application for membership prompting a blizzard of letters between Gwynne-Vaughan and her friend and co-organiser Kitty Trenchard as they debated the best means of demanding her resignation.[97] The Emergency Service was recognised by the Army Council and placed on the Army List in December 1937. Thus the plans were laid for a women's wartime auxiliary service which would be run by upper-class women along much the same lines as during the First World War.

Europe in 1938 was moving rapidly towards full scale mobilisation for war. The civilian Air Raid Warden's Service, formed in April 1937, had recruited some 200,000 members by the middle of 1938, and British aircraft production figures began to creep past those of Germany in the same year following the introduction of the Air Minstry's 'Scheme L', which planned for the production of 12,000 new aircraft.[98] In February 1938 Hore Belisha, Minister for War told the Commons that 'the government regards the maintenance of the Forces as the first condition of national security'.[99] Despite the Munich Agreement of 1938, and Chamberlain's famous proclamation of 'peace in our time', the Munich crisis was followed by rapidly escalating rearmament, funds being provided to expand the army from 5 to 32 divisions, and expenditure on Air Raid Precautions tripled.[100] In this atmosphere the War Office was beginning to reconsider its earlier lack of enthusiasm for the creation of a larger women's auxiliary organisation in peacetime. In January 1938 an internal memo acknowledged that 'obviously we are going to employ women in some numbers in the next war', suggesting that the War Office act independently in forming a women's reserve as 'we recruit our own men – why not our own women?'[101] In the same month Sir Harry Knox was replaced as Adjutant-General by General Liddell, who suggested that it was now time for the decision of the Committee of Imperial Defence in 1936 to be rescinded. By February 1938 the War Office had agreed in principle that a Women's Reserve should be organised, and work began on organising a new, large-scale female military auxiliary.

Women of the existing organisations threw themselves into organising women and lobbying the War Office with equal vigour. The FANY news sheets, which had recorded a lack of enthusiasm and a shift of activity to philanthropic pursuits in the mid 1930s reported a renewed interest in the Corps in 1938, London Company No. 1 describing the 'hundreds of recruits who poured in' during the Munich crisis, 'woken at last to the fact that they wanted to DO SOMETHING' (original emphasis).[102] The QMAAC Old Comrades Association offered its services to the War Office, informing them of the 'numerous enquiries they had received from members wishing to offer their services should the need arise' and advising their members to take courses in anti-gas precautions and first aid, so that they would be ready to 'serve wherever needed'.[103] Helen Gwynne-Vaughan, in her position as Head of the Emergency Service, by this point had offices in the War Office and so was able to meet regularly with the men of the Army Council who were addressing the question of women's service. Together with Lady Londonderry she argued strongly that women should be enlisted on identical terms to men and that they should be paid for their time if working women were to be recruited, a necessity as 'the supply of leisured girls is smaller than it used to be'.[104] The Army Council initially suggested that the new organisation would be uniformed but unpaid, following the lines of the Women's Legion during the First World War and thus keeping the women's service on an amateur basis. Londonderry and Gwynne-Vaughan both objected to this, Londonderry arguing that

> It would be impossible to create an organisation on recognised lines of official procedure on a large scale entirely by voluntary part-time effort . . . . The organising nucleus should consist to some extent of whole-time paid personnel. On mobilisation it is assumed that salaries would automatically be received.[105]

The movement of large numbers of young, middle-class women into paid work, together with a shift in feminist consciousness and campaigning away from 'equal rights feminism' and towards a focus on what Susan Kingsley Kent has termed 'an ideology which emphasized women's special sphere' meant that far fewer women could be called upon to undertake voluntary national service for a combination of patriotic and feminist impulses than during the First World War.[106] Recognising this the War Office agreed to pay women in auxiliary services for their time. On other issues however, they remained obdurate.

The main issue of disagreement between the War Office and the female organisers was the subject of the status of female auxiliaries. The women were keen that any female recruits to an auxiliary service be enlisted as soldiers, not enrolled as civilians as had been the case in the First World War. Since 1937 Gwynne-Vaughan had been petitioning the War Office to request that the Emergency Service be enlisted and thus 'subject to the Army Act and not treated as camp followers'.[107] Gwynne-Vaughan's class position shaped her views on this, believing as she did that 'patriotism is more foreseeing among educated people . . . and they will be more willing than other ranks to prepare for a possible need'. However, she continued, the 'officer class' would necessarily 'realise more clearly their status as camp followers, and they will be aware on how thin a thread their discipline must hang'.[108] At a meeting called to discuss the new organisation Katherine Furse, representing the VADs, which were, alongside the FANYs, the Emergency Service and the Women's Legion, to be incorporated into a new auxiliary corps, pointed out that 'members of women's organisations did not favour being regarded as camp followers'.[109] The War Office remained unconvinced, arguing that 'the ladies' desire 'not to be treated as camp followers' and to 'be subject to military law as officers and soldiers . . . was undesirable and in fact unnecessary'.[110] In the approach to the Second World War the War Office was planning to employ women as far as possible along the same lines as they had employed an earlier generation in the First World War.

The Auxiliary Territorial Service (ATS) was formed by Royal Warrant on 9 September 1938. Originally named the Women's Auxiliary Defence Service (WADS), until women unsurprisingly complained about the acronym, the organisation incorporated the existing female auxiliary corps with the FANY and the Women's Legion Motor Driver Corps wearing their own insignia and operating as semi-independent corps within the ATS. Gwynne-Vaughan was appointed Director of the Corps which was affiliated to the Territorial Army. The new corps was shaped by the ideologies of gender and class which had underscored the inter-war years and which were highly visible in the policies of the War Office and the structure of the army. Although the army had begun to modernise during the 1930s, moving away from a structure dominated by the playing field ethos of the public school towards a developing willingness to address tactical issues and mechanisation, this was a slow process, and conservative modes of thought still dominated in the War Office. With regard to women's war service, this led to a conceptualisation of a woman's auxiliary service being run, so far as possible, along the same lines as in the First World War, even being structured with some of the same women at its head. Women were expected to do the same kinds of highly gender determined work, to serve under the same terms, legally defined as that of camp followers and to display the same deference to their social 'betters' as they had in the earlier conflict. Unsurprisingly, this almost obsolete model of women's service sat uneasily with the widely held ideal of a citizen army, fighting in the 'people's war' of 1939–1945. The ATS, despite offering women an immediate and officially recognised route to serve with the armed forces in wartime, thus began on a shaky footing, hidebound by attitudes to class and gender which had more in common with the society of the First World War than the Second.

6 'The Gentle Sex'

The ATS in the Second World War

The 1930s saw a gradual move away from policies of disarmament as Britain began to prepare for the possibility of war with an increasingly expansionist Germany. Despite the initial euphoria of 'peace in our time' following the resolution of the Munich crisis in 1938, war began to seem more and more of an inevitability. Although British war preparations remained inadequate at this point, the crisis produced a new sense of urgency. German rearmament was a very tangible threat to British sovereignty and territory, and, in response, British arms production and preparation for war on the home front both increased. British aircraft production began to outstrip that of Germany, funding to the army was increased, a schedule of Reserved Occupations was published, 38 million gas masks were issued and the new Air Raid Warden's Service was inundated with volunteers. Legislation for national service was put in place and in May 1939 the Military Training Act introduced a compulsory six months military training for young men aged 20 and 21. This was superseded by the National Service (Armed Forces) Act on the first day of the war which made all men aged between 18 and 41 potentially eligible for military conscription. The relative zeal which had marked the first days of the First World War was largely replaced by a resigned determination; an acknowledgement that the steady drift towards war of the late 1930s had finally reached its apparently inescapable conclusion.

The Second World War is often referred to in Britain as 'the people's war'; a recognition of the wartime shift to the left in popular politics and wartime policy, and of the need for the nation to create an inclusive sense of national identity, national aims and beliefs if the demands of a total war were to be met.[1] Nevertheless, it was also a war which, from its very beginning, was deeply divided along gender lines. Planning for war in the 1930s had assumed that civilians would be in the front line, as the aerial bombardment of Spain and Abyssinia had demonstrated the destructive physical and psychological power of the high level bombing of centres of population. With the mobilisation of men, women became ever more closely linked with the home, and, together with children and older people, the likely victims of aerial attack. J. S. Haldane's 1938 polemic on the forthcoming dangers of aerial bombing, Air Raid Precautions (ARP), saw women not only as potential victims of aerial attack, but also partly responsible for it, arguing that female voters 'have not done their duty in this matter'. Women, he argued,

> have allowed themselves to be interested in the latest shows, from the Coronation to the latest murder or fashionable wedding, which serve to divert their minds from things that matter. I only hope their children will not suffer for it.[2]

Haldane saw a natural link between women and pacifism, emphasising women's role as mothers and homemakers. In this conviction, he was part of a widespread set of beliefs regarding gender and war. As in the First World War, men were reminded that one of the things they were fighting to defend was the home, and the woman and children inside it. This gendered division was reflected in many different sites: in state policy which resisted mobilising married women, in advertisements and articles in women's magazines which re-emphasised the importance of the home and the family in wartime, in films in which, as Gledhill and Swanson have argued, the housewife and mother appeared as a cornerstone of the nation and in recruitment literature, which often stressed the gendered nature of modern warfare.[3] Beauty adverts in magazines repeatedly reminded women that the maintenance of 'beauty' was as much a part of their war duty as any officially recognised war service, an advert for 'Tokalon skin cream' from 1940 urging women in the ATS to remember 'your duty to yourself, to your sweetheart, to your husband' by using the skin cream to 'take care of your skin – look young'.[4] Similarly, an editorial comment in *Woman's Own*, one of the biggest selling women's magazines of the period, praised a group of Auxiliary Territorial Service (ATS) recruits for learning to 'keep smart in hair, nails, complexion etc., in about a quarter of the time she spent before', thus combining efficiency, femininity and war service.[5] An article the following week represented these women as an exception to the rule, emphasising that uniform had the potential to undermine the femininity of the woman wearing it in its observation that 'occasionally, one sees an attractive ATS or WREN . . . and one feels compelled to stop and stare unbelievingly'.[6] Potential male recruits for the ARP were encouraged to 'Serve to Save' by a poster image depicting a civilian man with a large shield defending a cowering woman with a baby, whilst women were addressed via a poster asking them to take in evacuated children as 'all women love children and like to help them'.[7] Thus, whilst the threat of aerial bombardment blurred the division between masculine combatants and feminine non- combatants, the war saw the reinforcement of traditional gender roles as dominant representations of masculinity become closely entwined with images of combat, and femininity with the home.

However, the mobilisation of the nation which was a necessary response to the demands of total war was also a mobilisation of women's labour. In addition to managing the home in wartime, women were also needed to replace men in a range of paid positions. Although the existence of the Reserved

Occupations register at the outbreak of war meant that there was not the same immediate need to replace essential industrial workers as there had been in 1915, when there existed, early on in the war, a widespread recognition of the necessity of utilising female labour. Women's magazines however were largely occupied in reminding women that their most important role was to maintain a semblance of normality in the early days of war. *Woman's Own* followed the outbreak of war by inscribing the work of maintaining the home with a sense of national duty similar to the male role of combat: 'we are standing at our posts as the men are standing at theirs'.[8] Similarly, the novelist Storm Jameson, writing in *Woman's Journal* shortly after the outbreak of war, argued that her readers needed to guard against 'that peculiar excitement to which some women succumb in wartime', rejecting the appeal of war work for the less glamorous but equally important work of maintaining the family home. Jameson looked back to the gender disruption of the First World War as a warning to her readers:

> In the last war many soldiers were bitterly disappointed when they came home. They went out believing in certain things, carrying with them precise images of what it was they wanted to defend... They came back to find that we had changed. Our feelings, our ideas had altered... It will be a disgrace if this happens again. Even in small things we must try to keep their 'home' intact.[9]

Unsurprisingly, given this dual address to women, an early reliance on the voluntary principle of labour: the belief that women would be motivated to join the war effort by patriotism alone, soon proved inadequate, and in March 1941 all women aged between 18 and 45 were ordered to register at their local employment exchange so that they could be 'directed' into essential industries. This growing acknowledgement of the need for women's labour however sat uneasily with a sense of nationhood which placed women squarely within the home and men as their defenders; the tension between the demands of production and the demands of patriarchy identified by Penny Summerfield.[10]

This tension was seen most clearly in the debates which surrounded female military service. The War Office in particular reflected the wider ambivalence about women's role in wartime. When war was declared in 1939 three auxiliary services existed for women: the ATS, formed in September 1938 and attached to the Army, the Women's Royal Naval Service (WRNS), formed in May 1939 and attached to the Navy and the Women's Auxiliary Air Force (WAAF), formed from the Royal Air Force companies of the ATS in July 1939. The forces' initial attitude to these services is probably best indicated by the statement of an Air Ministry official in September 1939 that 'there is no need for any recruiting drive in the case of the WAAF', reflecting the belief that women's auxiliary services would not play an important part in the war effort, and indeed few recruiting adverts appeared before 1941.[11]

Despite warnings from women that 'it would be impossible to create an organisation on recognised lines of official procedure on a large scale entirely by voluntary peacetime effort' as in the First World War, women were enlisted rather than enrolled as soldiers and were thus free to leave the services if they so desired.[12] Under this system, the ATS intake of 31,960 between September 1939 and December 1940 was balanced by an outflow of 13,212 women leaving the service during the same period, approximately 40 per cent of the overall corps' membership.[13] At the beginning of the war, the ATS was handicapped by fluctuating membership, an outdated structure and contradictory, and often negative public opinion.

Eileen Bigland, in her official history of the ATS, demonstrated the complexity of public opinion regarding female military service in her description of a conversation overheard on a train in 1938 following the announcement that a woman's daughter had joined the service:

> Someone said the girl guides were carrying a joke a bit too far; another suggested the whole trouble had started when women were given the vote; a third remarked that anyone might think we were living in Russia and a fourth that camp life would be a blessing if it removed some of the paint and lipstick with which young women smeared their faces.[14]

Once again, women's motives for joining the auxiliary services were questioned and compared unfavourably to the male patriotic impulse to fight for one's country. The conversation recorded a disapproval of the militarisation of women alongside a distrust of 'frivolous' femininity. The ATS were perceived as being too 'masculine', allowing women to operate in the male sphere of warfare and as a means of obtaining older feminist demands for an expanded role for women. In the reference to Russia they were also seen as a symbol of an encroaching uniformity, the imposition of public demands on the private world of gender relations. Finally the service was claimed as a boon if it was able to create useful citizens out of allegedly frivolous young women. It appeared that many of the debates of the First World War regarding female auxiliary military service were destined to be replayed.

Early recruits to the ATS could be forgiven for feeling that little had changed since the First World War. The organisation continued to be structured along class lines, with Ellen Wilkinson, the Labour MP for Jarrow, commenting in the House of Commons on the preponderance of titled women amongst the senior commanders of the service. Divisions such as this seemed more and more out of place in a society which was increasingly moving towards a wartime rejection of the class-based ideology of the inter-war years and can be traced back to Helen Gwynne-Vaughan's policy of recruiting 'county ladies' as local officers before the war and her belief that 'patriotism is more foreseeing among educated people.'[15] Occupations on offer to the members of the ATS also appeared to be shaped by the attitudes of the last war, one Territorial Army commander commenting that 'he would welcome women being attached to his Unit, as the average man wanted to deal with searchlights and other military appliances and not to spend his time in camp on cooking etc.'[16] Until 1941 women were only employed on 'non-operational' support duties, the five trades available being clerks, cooks, storewomen, drivers and orderlies, all of which, except perhaps drivers, fitting easily within the accepted definition of a female sphere of activity. Gwynne-Vaughan herself argued that women were particularly suited to these duties, commenting that 'a man required persuasion to enter a cook-house, it was a woman's natural home.'[17] These beliefs were echoed in an early history of the war, in which potential recruits were informed that 'the ATS take over the cleaning, under the proud name of orderlies; they act the part of kitchen maids and housemaids. Those who have been parlour maids are detailed to wait on officers.'[18] Unsurprisingly perhaps, the combination of class and gender attitudes within the ATS acted to hamper recruitment to the service, as many women believed that the ATS 'were little more than general handmaids to officers and even to their wives'.[19] The sense that the ATS was a socially limited anachronism in part grew out of the army's slowness to modernise and professionalise, its attachment to the tradition of amateur 'gentlemen-officers' persisting into the war years. This contrasted with the belief that the RAF, and after July 1939, the WAAF, benefited from a more democratic and technocratic structure and leadership, prizing technical expertise above class background, and thus offering a greater opportunity for progression to the majority of its members.[20]

Women who did join the ATS during the first months of the war often found that the organisation simply wasn't ready for them. By December 1939 approximately 43,000 women had volunteered for the three women's auxiliary services, far in excess of the government's conservative target of 25,000 female volunteers announced in 1938.[21] Potential volunteers were sometimes asked to return home and wait to be called up, as the ATS and the other services attempted to acquire sufficient uniforms and accommodation for their members. Indeed, Helen Gwynne-Vaughan acknowledged in her autobiography that 'the ATS had a bad start' as potential recruits outstripped resources, officers were 'undertrained' and the voluntary principle meant that many suitable women did not come forward to join as they were already occupied running homes or in paid work.[22] The women who did come forward often found that the accommodation provided at training camps and barracks was unsuitable; lack of forward planning for the women's services, combined with their rapid expansion, meant that 'drafts were sent to half constructed camps with huts still waiting completion and imperfectly supplied with lighting and heat.'[23] Early goodwill towards the service rapidly withered, as an outdated structure combined with a lack of facilities to produce a service which had little to offer the majority of its potential recruits.

One of the most unpopular aspects of the ATS was its khaki uniform. Designed by Gwynne-Vaughan, it consisted of a serge, khaki tunic, buttoning to the right in the male fashion, and mid-calf skirt, worn with thick, khaki stockings and low-heeled brown shoes. Only officers initially received greatcoats and a removable fleece for raincoats.[24] Underwear was issued to recruits though it was never made compulsory, Gwynne-Vaughan noting that 'a proportion of the other ranks will not want to wear issue under garments.'[25] The uniforms of the WRNS and the WAAF were widely seen as more flattering, a belief reflected in the spoof poem 'Come Into the Army Maud' published in *The New Statesman and Nation* which described the ATS recruit as 'Queen weed in the garden of service girls' and advised her to 'de-rouge the nails and prune the curls'.[26] One voluntary recruit to the ATS wrote describing the induction process to her mother, commenting that 'we were entirely fitted out and I look AWFUL!'[27] Another recruit described her uniform as 'stupid and inelegant', going on to explain that it consisted of

> Thick lisle stockings, which went a sickly yellow colour after repeated washings, balloon shaped khaki knickers and the sort of vests which our Grannies wore, the sturdy Oxford brogues and that miserable creation, the groundsheet, which doubled as a rain cape. Being square, one corner hung down the back and dripped into one's shoes.[28]

A recruitment pamphlet of 1941 recognised the mixed feelings which women may have had about the militarisation of the previously personal area of appearance, reassuring potential recruits that 'you are not obliged to wear army issues of underwear unless you want to do so, but since it is really attractive, most members do wear it.'[29] This contrasts with the complaints about ATS clothing documented in an unsigned letter to Sir John Wardlaw Milne MP. The author described the experiences of his daughter, commenting that

> Theoretically, each girl is supplied with two uniforms. In practice, many of them, after six months service, have only received one and (in their own words), they stink. The majority of girls in my daughter's bunch have taken their greatcoats to Harrods to be reshaped at the waist at their own expense . . . Most of the girls are wearing, and wearing out, their own civilian underwear.[30]

Whilst the social class of the recruits discussed here, able to afford the sartorial services of Harrods, was not typical of the service, their endeavours to personalise their clothing do highlight the problems of attempting to impose a uniformity of appearance onto individual women of differing backgrounds and tastes, who were at the same time trying to maintain elements of the private, the individual, which were so closely associated with femininity.

These attempts to combine a military consistency with elements of civilian femininity resulted in numerous attempts to discover the views of women both within and outside the auxiliary services regarding female uniforms. A Mass-Observation visit to an ATS Camp, undertaken for the Ministry of

Information, found a widespread dislike of the khaki uniform amongst ATS recruits. Women complained in particular about the standard issue khaki stockings, suggesting they be replaced with silk stockings, a potent symbol of sexuality and femininity during the war, despite the impracticality of the material. An interview with the camp commandant revealed a distinct ambivalence amongst the women regarding uniforms; an instinctive dislike of uniform was partly countered by a sense of pride in the recognition of work of national importance it bestowed upon the wearer:

> The commandant said 'I don't think any woman really likes uniform, but when I went into the ATS I found most of us disliked it, but we soon grew used to it and feel now that the wearing of a war uniform is grand...we regard it as part of our war work.'[31]

In contrast with the First World War, when many women were keen to wear uniforms as an outward symbol of their patriotism, female uniforms were widely regarded by those who wore them as a necessity, a necessity which often threatened to undermine their sense of a desirable femininity.

The ambiguity with which women in uniform were often regarded is evident in J. B. Priestley's campaigning book of 1943 *British Women Go To War*. Whilst Priestley wrote the book for propaganda purposes, as an attempt to ensure more women came forward voluntarily for service, especially in the relatively unpopular ATS and in industrial work, Priestley displays an ambivalence about the desirability of militarising femininity. In a discussion of the women's services as a whole, he concluded that a 'feminine Combined Operations Force' would have been preferable to the three separate women's services which existed as not only 'would there have been no suggestion of their being female imitations of soldiers, sailors and airmen' but 'experts could have decided what colour and cut of uniform flattered the largest number of girls and...our eyes might have feasted on some new and delectable combination of shades, with all manner of strange and romantic badges and insignia.'[32] Despite Priestley's avowed aim of improving voluntary recruitment for the war effort amongst women, the book emphasises again and again the fundamental incompatibility of war service with femininity, commenting that in the early days of the war 'the girl in khaki' had 'an awkward look about her as if both her tunic and her skirt were not meant for her' whilst describing ATS drill as 'the right compromise between feminine anarchy and a burlesque of the Prussian Guard'.[33] The ambivalence towards women in uniform which permeates Priestley's book was a reflection of a wider sense that femininity and war service were essentially opposed to one another and that not only was femininity threatened by women's inclusion into the military, the military was threatened by the feminising effect of so many women.

In July 1941 Helen Gwynne-Vaughan retired as Commander-in-Chief of the ATS, and was replaced by Jean Knox. Although Gwynne-Vaughan had been largely responsible for the formation of the Corps, and had brought her knowledge of military matters drawn from her time with the Women's Auxiliary Army Corps (WAAC) to bear on the ATS, she was becoming increasingly anachronistic. Under her leadership, ATS officers were largely drawn from the aristocracy and the upper classes, an organisational structure which was out of step with the dominant rhetoric of the levelling 'people's war', helping to contribute to the unpopularity of the Corps and publicly criticised as inefficient by the Parliamentary Select Committee's critical Report on the ATS in August 1940. In addition, Gwynne-Vaughan had maintained the militaristic bearing and attitudes which had so irritated many in the War Office during the First World War, and which appeared to be no less irksome in the Second. Certainly Lesley Whateley, Director of the ATS from October 1943, believed this was the main factor behind her early retirement, commenting in her memoirs that

> our Director was so imbued with military spirit that she was quite unable to see that women could not be treated like men, and I am quite certain it was this factor which was responsible for her not remaining longer in office.[34]

Knox, younger and more archetypally feminine than the militaristic Gwynne-Vaughan, oversaw a redesign of the ATS uniform along more feminine lines. The jacket was restyled to button to the right, and to flatter a conventionally feminine shape, with tighter waists and padded shoulders. Potential recruits to the service were assured that the uniform was both feminine and practical; an article written for *Women's Employment* in 1941 purported to represent the experiences of a newly appointed ATS officer:

> the recruit on joining is provided with three pairs of stockings, three shirts, panties, Milanese khaki knickers, ties, gloves, jacket, skirt, great-coat, shoes, a comb, a toothbrush, a complete outfit of every necessity in fact ... After six months service a second uniform is issued and as each article wears out it is reissued free of charge. The ATS member who loses all her clothes in an air raid never finds herself faced with the appalling prospect of buying a completely new wardrobe, (Quartermaster's Stores) sees to all that.[35]

Women considering joining the ATS were thus reassured that, by joining the Corps, they would be able to maintain their wardrobe, and therefore their femininity, to a degree unavailable to the civilian woman increasingly constrained by rationing.

Despite these moves however, the ATS remained an unpopular choice of war service for British women. The growing need for female labour in all areas was identified by the Department of Labour's Manpower Survey of 1940, and the question of recruitment to the women's auxiliary services began to be seriously considered by the War Cabinet. Of all the women's services the ATS appeared to be the least popular, having, as a percentage of members, the highest wastage rate and one of the lowest rates of recruitment, between June and August 1941 only recruiting 6,647 new members, whilst 15,827 women applied to join the far smaller WAAF.[36] An inter-departmental committee, bringing together the armed services, the Ministry of Information and the Ministry of Labour launched a recruiting drive in 1941, aimed primarily at obtaining more women for the ATS. Advertise-ments, posters, radio broadcasts and newspaper articles attempted to improve the appeal of the Service by emphasising both the femininity of ATS members and the wide range of occupations available to them. The campaign specifically addressed the widespread belief that for most of its members, the ATS offered little more than a militarised form of housework, one advert stating that 'the idea that the ATS girl is a sort of domestic servant to the army is now obsolete. Duties of the humdrum type do not occupy 10% of the ATS programme.'[37] Whilst some adverts drew on an imagery and language more suited to the First World War than the Second, telling women that 'Your help is needed today' and asking whether soldiers should 'be kept on work a woman could do, while you stand back', most recruitment literature for the ATS attempted to combine an appeal to female patriotism, addressing women as equal members in the 'people's war' with a more feminist inflected discourse which emphasised the opportunities available to individual women in the service.[38] Some of the propaganda attempted to subjugate individual desires to group identities, with women reminded that

> Whoever you are, rich or poor, young or middle aged, wife, mother or daughter-at-home, highly qualified or willing to learn, the ATS need 100,000 recruits. They are crying out for women like you.

The same article uneasily combined a language of equality and egalitarianism, arguing that the ATS offered 'a life of equal chances where influence cannot help', with an emphasis on the continuity of civilian gender roles in the ser-vice, concluding that 'women are different from men and the army respects your feminine needs. It feels chivalrous towards you.'[39] Recruitment propa-ganda for the ATS endeavoured to appeal as widely as possible, combining a call for women to act patriotically by subsuming their individuality to a group cause, whilst still emphasising both the femininity of women in uniform and the wide range of opportunities available to them.

The fine line which had to be walked between a desirable, individualistic femininity and the demands of an increasingly collective wartime society is well illustrated by the fate of one recruitment poster. The image of an ATS recruit designed by Abram Games, the Official War Office Poster Designer, showing the profile of a beautiful, blonde, carefully made-up young woman in ATS uniform was withdrawn from circulation as it was believed to be too glamorous and sexual, 'too daring for public consumption'.[40] Games' poster was replaced instead by an image of a well scrubbed, vigorous, marching brunette, based on a photograph and described by his contemporary Eric Newton as 'slightly Russianised' and consequently more suitable to a nation being asked to 'pull together' in a total war.[41] Glamour had come to symbolise a pre-war ideal of beauty, signifying a focus on the self which was out of place in a wartime nation where collective needs were replacing individual wants. Although the importance of maintaining beauty regimes was stressed within the pages of women's magazines, their foremost value was as a morale boosting exercise in which the management of the material self signified national determination. By 1941 acceptable tropes of femininity had moved away from the glamorous, leisured woman of the early and pre-war years and towards an embrace of a less spectacular, less sexualised, concept of beauty.[42] Other advertisements were more successful in drawing together femininity and military service; one advert which began 'Time I got a new hat', went on to point out that job opportunities within the ATS included radiolocation, described as 'a man-sized job, with all a man's opportunities' alongside cookery courses, and concluded by assuring readers that by joining the ATS they would 'be part of the Army and help the men'.[43] Thus in one paragraph it attempted to draw together a traditional image of femininity, an emphasis on the new opportunities war work was offering to women and a reassertion of established gender relations in its conclusion. The promise of female fulfilment through war service had to be contained within a discourse which emphasised both the national need for this work and the ongoing maintenance of traditional gender relations.

The recruitment campaign alone, however, did not produce the necessary number of volunteers for the ATS. The direction of female labour was increasingly seen as a necessity as the country entered its third year of 'total war' and the introduction of the Registration for Employment Order (REO) in April 1941, a piece of legislation similar in intent and organisation to the National Register of 1915, gave the government the power to direct women into industry. The Year 1941 saw an ongoing debate about women's role in wartime. Under the auspices of the REO, the Ministry of Labour could direct women aged between 18 and 24 who were unemployed or working in non-essential occupations into industry but not into the Forces. However, women interviewed by Ministry of Labour officials could be pressured to join the services in order to enable the movement of men to front-line duties. The government's new powers over women were seen by some as an attack upon fundamental social values; the overwhelming of the private life of the family and home by an autocratic, authoritarian state. Agnes Hardie, the Labour MP for Glasgow, Springburn, was one of the few members of Parliament to speak against the REO, basing her objections in part on the movement of women away from the private world of the family home and into lodgings and hostels in unfamiliar areas. Although Hardie did not deny the need for women's labour, she argued that it could be met through voluntary means, and that work should be organised locally, so that 'young people, instead of being dragged away from their own homes and districts, could have been provided with work in their own areas'.[44] Whilst women with responsibility for children were not subject to the directives of the REO, the Secretary to the Ministry of Labour arguing in the House of Commons that 'there is no higher form of national service for any woman than the guidance of a home and the upbringing of young children' single women, designated as mobile, were.[45] The Woman-Power Debate of March 1941 in the House of Commons contrasted a heroic, liberating discourse of female war service with concerns that state control over women threatened both essentialist constructions of femininity and the maintenance of family life. Whilst two Conservative MPs Thelma Cazalet and Irene Ward argued that 'women will not be found wanting', and 'this debate creates another milestone in British parliamentary history', Agnes Hardie stressed the importance of women's maternal role over and above their economic role in the wartime economy, commenting that women bringing up children were 'doing a far more important job for the future generations, for which we are meant to be fighting, than filling shells with which to kill some other mother's son'.[46] Debates about women's war service thus echoed those of the First World War as the representations of female labour as a modernising, liberating force were answered with a reassertion of the overarching importance of motherhood and the home during wartime.

Although mothers with children at home were never going to be subject to direction or conscription, young women in the parental home were. The division between the symbolic need for women to remain within the private, domestic sphere and the wartime necessity of mobilising these women for war work shaped public debate about the role of young, unmarried women. These young women were positioned differently within the family from young men, who had been subject to conscription since 1939 with little public outcry. Whilst the absence of men was largely accepted as a necessary feature of war, and the state recognised the position of mothers as the 'immobile' cornerstone of family life, government policy was out of step with public opinion in its view of young women as independent, as 'independence and adventure were unlikely to be consistent with parental expectations of daughters'.[47] Whilst state intervention in family life in the form of male conscription, rationing and evacuation was generally accepted as necessary, attempts to extend mobilisation to the nation's daughters were widely resented. As Penny Summerfield has demonstrated, although young women had previously worked outside the home, the government's introduction of powers of control over the labour of young women was widely seen as an unwanted 'intervention into the realm of private life'.[48] The ATS appeared to be particularly unpopular with many parents and Leslie Whateley's memoirs often make reference to the problem of overcoming parental resistance to daughters joining the service, exacerbated in part by the 'whispering campaign against the ATS' and in part by widely publicised examples of the Corps' inefficiency, such as the newspaper reports of January 1940 which described the la[?] of warm coats for ATS members.[49] Whateley claimed that in her role

ATS Director she 'had to ask myself always whether the decision I was about to take was one I could justify in the eyes of a parent' whilst balancing this concern with the private domestic family with a recognition of the needs of a nation in wartime as 'at the same time, I had always to remember that this was war'.[50] Ministry of Information propaganda was produced which attempted to address these parental concerns, particularly those regarding the welfare of young 'mobile' women, living away from the parental home for the first time. One advertisement in *The Evening Standard* attempted to reassure parents:

> You, her mother and father, need have no fear for her whilst she is away from you. Careful measures have been taken to ensure her health, happiness and well-being. She will be well looked after. Friends and sisters are encouraged to join together. And as a high standard of conduct is required by the ATS, your daughter will be in good company and will make good friends.[51]

In this address to parents the state was positioned in a parental role, taking responsibility for the moral and social welfare of the young women in its care. Parental concern about the welfare of their daughters was seen especially clearly in the public response to the recruitment drive for the ATS.

The ATS, together with the other women's services, was incorporated into the Army Act in April 1941, giving its members military status commensurate with men and, for the first time, leaving behind the demeaning term 'camp followers'. As well as giving the ATS full military status, the Act ensured that discipline was tightened in the ATS and that women could no longer leave the service at will. Importantly, given the general move to the left amongst the British public during the war, the appointment of Officers by virtue of birth and background, rather than by merit, ceased, as Officers were drawn from the ranks of the Corps and had to go through a lengthy selection process which included examinations, public speaking, practical tests and a psychological assessment.[52] It also provided the framework for women's occupations within the service to expand into 'operational areas' such as anti-aircraft and radio location. Women could now be superior in rank to men, an aspect of gender confusion summed up in *Punch* magazines' contemporary cartoon of a soldier on the London Underground standing up to give his seat to a uniformed women with the words 'Take my seat, Miss – MADAM – SERGEANT.'[53] Combined with the powers of persuasion the REO bestowed on Ministry of Labour interviewers the award of full military status to the ATS led to increased levels of membership, with 16,408 women enrolling in the three months following the introduction of the order.[54] However, the ATS overall remained an unpopular service in comparison to the other female services, its average enrolment of 1,600 women per week falling well below the War Office's target of 5,000 per week.[55] Mass-Observation were employed by the Ministry of Information to collect views on the Service from civilian women, service women and serving men. In their surveys they found a deeply held antipathy to the service, with objections ranging from the belief that 'it's all peeling potatoes' and 'they just do all the dirty work for everybody' from women to a widely felt objection to female military service from men in the army.[56] Male objections were focused on a belief that the ATS was a repository for women of a low social class and con-currently low standards of moral behaviour. Displaying a hatred and even fear of female sexuality, men described the women as 'nothing but a league of amateur prostitutes' and 'bloody whores the lot of them', belonging to an organisation in which 'the rougher type seems to predominate... ready for a good time, drunk without much provocation, sexually promiscuous and in language as blue as the men'.[57] These views resonated with wider views of the organisation, in which the Ministry of Information's attempt to 'rebrand' the ATS as 'Adventure Through Service' was replaced in popular discourse by 'Auxiliary Tarts Service'.[58] As in the First World War, the dislocated nature of wartime life, with its transient relationships and the constant proximity of death and injury, was widely believed to have led to an increase in sexual activity outside marriage. Double standards applied here as young women were overwhelmingly the focus of concerns about such behaviour, their new-found 'mobility' and independence believed to combine with the absence of the 'head' of the family and the presence of uniformed young men to create the 'problem of girls running wild' and 'out for a good time'.[59] Women in the ATS were seen as transgressing the acceptable bounds of femininity; by moving into the male sphere of the military they were believed to take on male standards of behaviour, behaviour which, whilst suitable for combatant men, was widely seen as incompatible with even a militarised femininity.

Unsurprisingly, given such views about the Service, ATS recruitment continued to fall short of its target. Reluctantly, the government began to consider introducing compulsion to female military service. As part of a wider debate about the extension of national service to the general popula-tion, the Cabinet met to discuss the possibility of extending conscription to women. Churchill initially opposed the introduction of conscription for women on the grounds that the 'vociferous opposition' of men in the Forces would cause unrest, an argument he was supported in by the representatives of the Forces on the Defence Committee, who believed that male concerns would 'cause unrest and opposition'.[60] Nevertheless, female conscription was agreed in principle, on the conditions that there would be no compulsion for married women, only volunteers would be asked to go into operative roles, and that women could register as conscientious objectors.[61] Although the government was anxious to avoid using the term 'conscription' the National Service (No. 2) Act was passed in December 1941, enabling all young unmarried women, aged between 20 and 30, to be called up.

The National Service (No. 2) Act was the first attempt by the British government to apply compulsion to women's service with the armed forces and, as such, was accompanied by a public debate about gender roles and responsibilities in wartime. All the main aspects of this argument were voiced during the debate on 'Maximum National Effort' which occupied the House of Commons for much of December 1941. The debate was opened by Winston Churchill, arguing that 'a very large proportion of the population, principally women, is occupied in ministering to the needs of the more actively engaged'.[62] Churchill went on to state that married women would not be directed into the auxiliary services, but that any woman who did join the ATS 'not only renders a high service herself, but releases a man – actually 4/5 of a man – for the active troops'.[63] The work that women who had been conscripted into the ATS could be asked to do had been the subject of lengthy debate in the War Office before the Bill was introduced, particularly the question of whether or not women could be directed into work on anti-aircraft sites, the closest that women in the service came to active combat. It was eventually decided that women would only work on anti-aircraft batteries if they volunteered for such work.[64] This was reiterated by Churchill, who argued that individual women would decide whether or not they wanted to undertake this type of work and that such decisions would not be directed by national need, but rather by 'quality of temperament... which every woman must judge for herself'.[65] Churchill's daughter Mary, a member of the ATS, volunteered to work on an anti-aircraft battery. The final barrier between male combatants and female non-combatants was thus maintained: although women could volunteer to work on anti-aircraft sites they could not be directed to do so, and once there, they would not be able to fire lethal weapons.

Ernest Bevin, the Minister for Industry, restated many of the ideas expressed by Churchill. Discussing the necessity for the increased involvement of the state in women's lives, he emphasised the symbolic importance of women's work of maintaining home and family during wartime, claiming that married women played 'just as great a part as a citizen as if she were in any other vocation.' The weight that the state placed on women's role in the home was implicit in his statement that women called up to the auxiliary services would be posted 'as near to their homes as practicable'.[66] Bevin recognised that disquiet about female conscription was centred on women being directed into the services rather than industry, and, like Churchill, attempted to answer this unease by emphasising that no woman would be forced to work with lethal weapons, suggesting that women's natural patriotism would ensure that sufficient numbers volunteered for work on anti-aircraft batteries.[67] Thus female patriotism was stressed within a proposed framework for conscription which ensured continuity, so far as possible, for the linkage of femininity with home and hearth.

Nevertheless, many MPs continued to voice concerns about, and objections to, the effective extension of conscription to women. These concerns were focused on the extent to which the state was seen to be interfering with the private life of home and family, a sphere still very much associated with women. Echoing debates of the First World War, the public world of the services was represented as morally hazardous, unsuitable for young women used to the protection of the private, familial, home. Agnes Hardie again invoked the maternalist position long held within a section of the Labour Party, arguing that 'war is not a woman's job... women share the bearing and rearing of children and should be exempt from war', going on to claim that 'barrack life and camp life is not suited for women'.[68] The movement of young women from the parental home to more public accommodation was also a source of unease for Gordon McDonald, MP for Ince, who stressed the dangers inherent in removing women from the moral guidance of the home, 'which has helped her to withstand all the temptations to which a girl of that age is subjected' to a new environment 'in which their characters will be undermined'.[69] Although women's ongoing contribution to the war effort was stressed within the debate, again often through a language which looked back to the First World War by stressing women's 'self-sacrifice', many MPs argued that traditional gender divides needed to be reinforced, and that young women in particular, belonged within the morally secure world of the family home.[70] The state's proposal to coerce these young women into more public forms of service was seen as a threat not only to the private family but also to public morality.

The opposing argument, that women should be more fully absorbed into national service, drew on a discourse which combined images of female patriotism with a feminist inflected emphasis on women's abilities. In this argument the wartime rhetoric of a unified nation, pulling together in defence of shared national values and beliefs, cancelled out the belief that wartime roles were shaped by gender. Eleanor Rathbone, who had helped to found the Women's Volunteer Reserve during the First World War, maintained that 'women want to serve their country', arguing that lack of recruitment to the ATS could not be attributed to a lack of patriotism amongst women, but rather to 'blunders in... their method of recruitment and in conditions of service'.[71] Rathbone contended that ability was more important than gender when allocating wartime roles, suggesting that instead of limiting the types of service that women could perform, the state should be concentrating on assessing women's abilities, and placing them in the most suitable occupation, whether these were defined as combatant units, as anti-aircraft batteries were, or non-combatant. Rathbone expressed contempt for the recruitment campaign which had attempted to highlight the attractive nature of ATS uniforms, proposing that an emphasis on the femininity of the ATS actually 'repels the best kind of girl', who felt that 'it is as if what the army wants is chorus girls rather than soldiers'.[72] These arguments were echoed by Edith Summerskill, Labour MP for Fulham, and a long-standing advocate of an expanded role for women in the war. Summerskill explicitly addressed the gender divisions of war, arguing that any blame for the lack of voluntary recruits for the ATS was not due to women's lack of patriotism, or unwillingness to join a uniformed service, but rather could be laid at the door of the War Office, whom she described, accurately, as 'traditionally masculine'.[73] Unequivocally discounting the argument that women had been slow to join the ATS because of the khaki uniform, Summerskill dryly remarked that the initial unwillingness of the War Office to organise a women's auxiliary service, leaving the organisation of the Corps, in its early days, in the hands of Gwynne-Vaughan and other veterans of the First World War, had led to the creation of an outdated organisational structure, in which upper-class women dominated. Summerskill argued that it was the class-based structure of the organisation, and the widespread perception that only women of 'wealth or influence' were able to reach 'higher positions' in the Corps, that had led to its relative unpopularity, especially when compared to the WAAF, widely perceived as more meritocratic.[74] In the arguments of Summerskill and Rathbone, the ATS was represented as a modernising force with the potential to provide new roles that women were eager to undertake if only the male-dominated War Office would provide them with the opportunity.

The immediate impact of the extension of compulsion to women was to slightly increase the numbers of women volunteering for the auxiliary services under the National Registration Act in order to have some degree of choice over the occupations they were placed in. In the first week of 1942, 2,446 women enrolled for service with the ATS, an increase of approximately 400 on the numbers of recruits for the last weeks of the previous year, and during the first three months of 1942 volunteers for the ATS came forward at the highest rate since July 1941.[75] The first group of women to be conscripted into the ATS were unmarried women born in 1920–1921, conscripted in March 1942. The War Office initially agreed to accept 3,500 conscripts a week into the ATS, although its desire for more female labour was balanced by a concern that there was not enough accommodation for the larger numbers of women coming into the service. In a very visible illustration of gender relations in wartime, ATS recruitment patterns were set by the concurrent need of the army for more men, and from 1942 until the end of the war, staffing of the women's services was dependent upon the numbers of men needed in the front lines. The extension of the war to the Pacific, together with naval losses in the Mediterranean and the ongoing conflict in North Africa combined to stretch the army over a wider arena of conflict in 1942 than at any point previously during the war. This led the War Office to revise upwards the numbers of women it needed for the ATS in order to release more men for service abroad. In particular, it began to argue that more women were needed to replace men on the anti-aircraft batteries. This work appealed to some of the recruits as it offered the clearest chance to undertake visibly active, patriotic wartime activities, the closest that most women could get to the high status masculine occupation of combat. Employment on anti-aircraft sites seemed to offer opportunities for heroism and excitement unavailable to women working in the more traditionally feminine occupations, predominantly as office and domestic workers, in which the majority of members of the ATS were occupied.[76]

Anti-aircraft batteries had been identified as a potential area of employment for the ATS by the Joubert Committee which reported on anti-aircraft organisation in March 1941. The Committee argued that 140,000 men who could be used in active service were 'immobilised' on anti-aircraft sites, 'causing a serious drain on army personnel' and recommended that the ATS could be brought in to work as 'track reporters, plotters, teleprinter and searchlight operators', suggesting the opportunities for this type of work might also have the added advantage of 'attracting the more intelligent type of recruit to the women's services'.[77] General Sir Frederick Pile, Commander of Air Defence, put the figures even higher, claiming that by late 1940, and the beginning of the Blitz, Britain's air defences were short of 1,114 officers and 17,965 other ranks.[78] Air Defence was particularly vulnerable to being 'combed out' by the operational Army; in the state of trench warfare which seemed to exist between the different sections of the armed forces represented at the War Office, the Field Forces (those serving abroad and in combat) often demanded that fit men working in air defence be moved into the main body of the Army, resulting for example in 30,000 searchlight operators being lost from Air Defence in the middle of 1941.[79] Pile saw the ATS as an efficient means of replacing this shortfall in manpower and perhaps of improving on it, commenting that 'women would actually perform their duties more efficiently than some of the low-category men who were being allotted to us.'[80] The first mixed batteries became operational five months later in Richmond Park London and quickly became something of a public attraction with crowds often gathering to 'stand and gaze in fascination'.[81] The site of women working alongside men on these sites must have soon become commonplace however as by 1942 more women were working on anti-aircraft sites than men, and approximately 50 per cent of new ATS recruits were choosing to work in Air Defence.[82] However, although women working on these batteries assisted in the targeting and shooting down of aircraft, they remained officially 'non-combatants', unlike their male colleagues. Women worked as radar operators, height finders, spotters, predictors and locators on the sites, but men alone fired the guns.

Sir Frederick Pile had successfully persuaded the government of the necessity for women's labour on the gun sites but had been unable to break down the prohibition on women acting as combatants. Writing four years after the war, Pile recalled that although he could 'see no logical reason why they should not fire the guns... I was not going to go so far as to suggest employing them on lethal weapons'.[83] Despite the example of the Soviet Union, where more than 300,000 women were successfully deployed on women-only air defences around large cities, the War Office remained strongly opposed to the use of women in combat positions.[84] The distinction between male combatant and female non-combatant on the batteries extended to a ban on women firing on the pilotless V1 and V2 rocket attacks of 1944 and 1945. Although women did take part in the campaign against these rockets, codenamed Diver, in which many batteries were moved to remote coastal areas in order to target the rockets before they came over land, their participation in this aspect of the war was criticised in Parliament, the MP Tom Driberg condemning the women's living conditions. Pile claimed however that letters from the ATS showed that 'they were proud of the fact that they were at last allowed to rough it with the men'.[85] One experiment, in which women did load and fire the guns on a mixed anti-aircraft site, was short lived owing to widely voiced disapproval in the press, in the War Office and in parliament.[86] Pile himself, who favoured allowing women to play an equal part with men on the anti-aircraft sites complained that 'There was a good deal of muddled thinking which was prepared to allow women to do anything to kill the enemy except actually pull the trigger.'[87] The prohibition on women firing guns did nothing to prevent women on anti-aircraft batteries being injured and killed whilst on duty. Private Nora Caveney, aged 18, was the first woman to be killed in this way, hit by a bomb splinter during a bombing raid.[88] Betty Holbrook, who served on the large anti-aircraft battery in Victoria Park, East London, vividly described the experience of bombardment, recalling that, during the V1 and V2 attacks 'we never went around alone . . . the feeling of not wanting to die alone was very, very strong'.[89] Symbolically excluded from combat, women working on the anti-aircraft batteries were not eligible for the service medals their male colleagues could receive and were paid approximately two-thirds of the equivalent male wages. Women worked with the Royal Artillery, who ran and staffed the sites, but remained members of the ATS, subject to the separate code of ATS discipline and ultimately answerable to the authority of ATS officers. This somewhat confused chain of command sometimes led to problems of identification for the women working on the gun sites, whom Pile claimed 'wanted to feel they were members of the artillery', a part of the higher status male organisation actively defending the British Isles, an identity which was 'actively discouraged' by the upper echelons of the ATS.[90] Thus although women worked with, and sometimes died alongside, men on the anti-aircraft batteries, they remained lower status members of a separate organisation, on lower pay and, defined as non-combatant, unable to be awarded combat medals.

The memoirs of women who served with Anti-Aircraft Command describe the disparity between their sense of themselves as active, patriotic citizens and the oft-expressed wider perception of them as transgressing acceptable boundaries of gender. Marian Mills, who served on anti-aircraft sites between 1942 and 1945 contrasted her feelings about this work with the negative reactions she sometimes received from civilians. Mills drew on a discourse which equated women with the maintenance of national morality in her claim that 'Many women saw the defence of the country and the demon of Nazism as a moral crusade and therefore not incompatible with feminine values and a dislike of violence.'[91] Whilst Mills followed feminist arguments dating from the First World War which claimed the defence of the nation and the home as women's moral duty, others seem to have believed that women in uniform, particularly those living and working in close proximity with men on the anti-aircraft batteries, were acting outside of conventional morality and gender roles. Mills recalled how some civilians, 'seeing girls in battledress, made pointed remarks about women aping men', demonstrating the durability of traditional models of gender relations in wartime.[92] Betty Holbrook's recollection of arriving on a gun site for the first time demonstrates how misplaced the belief that these women were acting outside their prescribed gender roles could be. Holbrook, who was a member of the first group of women to be posted to this particular gun site, described how they were detailed to scrub the Navy Army and Air Force Institutes (NAAFI) floor by the male Officer in command of the camp when they arrived.[93] However, despite an initial reluctance to accept women as members of the battery, Holbrook explained how, as the women proved that they could do the work allocated to them, 'a feeling of friendship' developed between the women and men who worked and lived together, and recalled how, towards the end of the war, the women from the battery were applauded by civilians as they shopped at a local market.[94] The integration of women into the anti-aircraft sites proved to be an operational success; the challenge that they were seen to offer to existing gender roles was perhaps less easy to negotiate.

Women working on anti-aircraft batteries, often in isolated sites, living and working in close proximity with men, were positioned in such a way as to make them more vulnerable than some other groups of women to charges of immorality. Like the women of the WAAC who served in France during the First World War, they were often geographically separate from the mass of the civilian population and thus became the focus of a popular concern with the impact of the war upon women's morality. Although the ban on women loading and firing guns allowed society to believe that gender roles were being maintained when women worked on the gun sites, there was more widespread unease about the potential for sexual relationships. The ATS overall had a reputation for promiscuity; a reputation they shared with the women working in war factories and which was perhaps closely linked to the social class of many of the women working in both services. This reputation was touched upon by MPs during the Maximum National Effort Debate of December 1941, *The Times* reporting one MP's objection to conscription on the grounds that 'the ATS has a thoroughly bad reputation . . . it is not the sort of service a nice girl goes into'.[95] Remarks such as these had their roots in dual concerns about both the social class of recruits to the ATS and their position outside the familial home. In wartime, the traditional female sphere of the domestic home is enlarged to include the nation, reconfigured as the home front. This reformulation of home and nation allows women to undertake more public roles without having to, ideologically, move outside of the home; it helps to provide a discourse of nationalised femininity. Nevertheless, women operating in this new, extended definition of home, however necessary their labour, were unmistakably more independent and less subject to the discipline of parents or husbands, than those who remained within the domestic sphere. Although there was widely voiced unease about the morality and sexual activity of many groups of women in wartime Britain, including those in the domestic sphere who were still believed to be likely to succumb to the temptations of American GI's or other men remaining on the home front, mobile women, particularly those in the low status ATS, were particularly vulnerable to rumours concerning their morality.

It was widely believed that rumours about immoral behaviour in the ATS were contributing to a continuing shortfall in numbers of recruits, Nancy Astor commenting in Parliament that 'there has never been anything more villainous than the campaign against the morals and the state of women in the ATS'.[96] The government's response to these rumours and to complaints about the living conditions for women in all three services was to form an investigative committee.

Violet Markham, who had served on the Ministry of Labour Commission during the First World War, chaired the Committee on Amenities and Welfare Conditions in the Three Women's Services whose Report was published in 1942. The remit of the Commission was wide-ranging: whilst its ostensible purpose was to review amenities and facilities for women in the services, the introduction demonstrates an underlying discourse of concern regarding the impact on recruitment of rumours regarding the services:

> Rumours derogatory to the Services began to circulate. Sometimes they took the form of concrete charges about bad conditions, sometimes of vague accusations about drink and immorality. Growing uneasiness was shown by parents as these stories gathered force and volume.[97]

Thus, as women's military service was necessary for the war effort, the Committee set out to dispel these rumours and improve both recruitment figures and the morale of women in the services.

The Markham Committee obliquely acknowledged that many of the concerns regarding immorality had their basis in public perceptions of the social class of women in the ATS. The service was widely believed to predominantly recruit women from the working class, a belief reflected in responses to the Mass-Observation survey on women's service which described the ATS variously as 'rather rough', as having a 'bad reputation' and, in one extreme example as 'a load of whores'.[98] These concerns were reflected in the Markham Committee's assertion that, upon recruitment it was 'the girl from the sheltered home, who has not known the hardships of daily work ... who may find it difficult to make the necessary arrangements'.[99] Some of the Committee's recommendations, such as the introduction of minimum standards for accommodation, warmth, food, medical attention and hygiene, were designed to ease the passage of middle-class women into the services, but the Report also took care to assert that the war was a levelling experience, bringing the different classes together. Despite the ATS's emulation of the army's class structured division of labour the Report argued for an egalitarian and patriotic aspect to women's service:

> The country is engaged in a struggle for existence and the first business of each one of us is to fit our lives into the war effort...young women, without distinction of class, have been bought together to share a common life, while fulfilling a common duty to their country.[100]

Although the Markham Committee acknowledged the existence of concerns linking the social class and the morality of women in the services, they also maintained that the needs of the nation in wartime overrode individual anxieties. In the people's war, individual concerns were to be subordinate to national needs.

The 1943 film *The Gentle Sex* represented the film industry's contribution to these attempts to overcome the negative image of the ATS. Although the ATS had formed the backdrop to earlier films, ranging from broad comedies such as *Old Mother Riley Joins Up* (1941) to romances like *Somewhere on Leave* (1942), *The Gentle Sex* was the first dramatised narrative to specifically follow the lives of ATS recruits. Directed and narrated by the film star Leslie Howard, himself a powerful symbol of wartime resolution and unity, whose radio broadcasts had replaced Priestley's *Postscripts* series of 1940/1941 as one of the most popular BBC programmes, *The Gentle Sex* used elements of documentary realism in its endeavour to represent the ATS as ordinary women, identifiable counterparts of the women in the cinema audience. The opening scene, an image of the busy concourse at Victoria Station, viewed and described by Howard from a balcony, both represented the ATS recruits as members of the ordinary people, and situated Howard, and by extension the audience, in a position of power in relation to them. The camera picks out seven women from the crowd and follows them as they train and serve with the ATS. Like Launder and Gilliat's film *Millions Like Us*, released later in the same year, which focused on women working in industry, the characters in *The Gentle Sex* are clearly intended to operate as archetypes of women: with women of different classes, regions, educational backgrounds and character types all represented. In *The Gentle Sex* the seven women include middle-class Anne, an officer's daughter, goodtime girl Dot, a beautician, the cockney waitress, Gwen, sheltered Betty and Erna, a Czech refugee. These disparate women learn the importance of collectivity over divisions of class and character in wartime Britain and, after they have undergone the rigours of training and service, experienced bombardment and suffered bereavement, the film ends with a panning shot of all seven queuing together for tea and sandwiches from a mobile Women's Volunteer Service (WVS) canteen. In this final scene the individual backgrounds of the women have been erased by the communal identity of the services.

Howard intended the film to act as a recruitment aid to the ATS, commenting that 'women's wartime role' was 'so far reaching and important that the least a mere maker of films' could do was to 'express on the screen

the significance of their work'.[101] However, *The Gentle Sex* also expresses the
tensions which existed between women's new role as active participants in the
war and more traditional conceptions of femininity. The film's title and its
credit sequence, which uses embroidery to contrast this earlier domestic and
submissive femininity in which 'a spirit of modesty, humility, obedience and
submission will always be required' with the more active lives of modern
women, tells the audience that women in uniform are a recent creation, a
facet of the war's modernising tendencies. Although the film's narrative
reminds the audience that women have in fact served in uniform in wartime
before, one character reminiscing about her days as a WAAC in 1917, this is
undermined by the repeated use of imagery which harks back to the more
clearly defined separate spheres of the Victorian era. Whilst the film's title
and use of this imagery were no doubt meant to be ironic, their function,
especially for the male members of the audience, uneasy about the movement
of women into uniform, would have been to reassure them that these women
were a necessary if perhaps unusual and certainly transitory, response to
wartime conditions. The unstable nature of femininity in wartime, when
women were expected to symbolise the continuity of home and domesticity
whilst manpower and economic pressures demanded their presence in the
forces, fields and factories, is central to the representation of women in *The
Gentle Sex*. Although women's labour was required for the war effort, and
although women in the audience are encouraged to consider themselves as
potential recruits for the ATS, the film ends with a reassertion of masculine
superiority in Howard's final speech:

> Well, there they are, the women. Our sweethearts, sisters, mothers,
> daughters. Let's give in at last and admit that we're really proud of you.
> You strange, wonderful, incalculable creatures. The world you're helping
> to shape is going to be a better one because you're helping to shape it.
> Pray silence gentlemen. I give you a toast. The gentle sex!

Whilst the film undoubtedly appealed to women, 19 of the 104 women who
replied to a Mass-Observation Directive naming it as their favourite film of
1943, this closing speech imagines the spectator as male, reasserting masculine superiority and power over the female characters.[102] The threat which the
ATS posed to gender roles can be seen in the attempt of *The Gentle Sex* to combine a narrative appeal to women to come forward as recruits for the corps by
emphasising the opportunities for adventure and romance which service
offered, with a reassurance to men that gender relations, and masculine
power, remained essentially unchallenged.

Despite the ongoing need to recruit women for the ATS, one group of
women, black women from British Caribbean colonies, were initially unwelcome in the Service. The decision to eventually recruit black Caribbean
women for the ATS came out of a battle between the War Office, reflecting
the entrenched conservative values of the Army, and the Colonial Office,

which was concerned that revolutionary ideas would take hold more easily amongst a population which felt itself excluded from the war effort. Despite the recurrent requests of the Colonial Office, which was trying to meet demands in the Caribbean to play a greater role in the war, the War Office repeatedly refused to consider recruiting members of the ATS from amongst the black population of the islands. Although there was never any official colour bar in the ATS, the War Office did all that it could to discourage recruitment from the Caribbean, announcing in 1941 that volunteers would only be accepted if they paid their own passage to Britain and stating in December 1941 that

> The Army Council considers it would be wrong to encourage coloured women to come from the West Indies...as they would be unused to the climatic conditions and modes of life in England...any demand by West Indian women to be enrolled in a uniformed service would be better met by local organisations.[103]

However, the War Office was forced to reconsider its policy of unofficial exclusion in 1942, when Jean Knox, then Chief Controller of the Service, began to consider recruiting ATS members from the Caribbean to work with the British military mission in Washington. A small number of ATS had been working in secretarial positions in Washington since 1941 and the War Office argued successfully that any Caribbean ATS recruits for Washington would have to be white, as the US Army, with whom they would be in close contact, operated a policy of segregation. The Colonial Office replied that if only white women were to be recruited for Washington, black women should be accepted for service in Britain. Although the War Office prevaricated, insisting that whilst they were happy to receive any 'suitable European women from the Colonies' they could not 'agree to accept any coloured women for service in this country', in May 1943 James Grigg reluctantly agreed to recruit thirty black Caribbean women into the ATS as a symbolic act.[104] Thirty women eventually arrived at Guildford for training in December 1943, although the majority of Caribbean women to volunteer for service were employed at home. Altogether 600 women volunteered for the ATS from the region, one hundred came to Britain, two hundred, all white, worked in the United States and 300 remained in the Caribbean.[105]

As the numbers of women in the ATS increased, reaching a peak of 214,420 in June 1943, so did the amount of advice published about maintaining femininity whilst in uniform.[106] Women's magazines, with their ongoing concern with the preservation of traditional tropes of femininity in wartime, were a fertile source of such advice. Indeed, within their pages, the uniformed woman began to replace the civilian as an ideal, *Woman* and *Woman's Own* both running a number of covers adorned with images of glamorous servicewomen.[107] Although the magazines did, as the war went on, sometimes position women's service within a feminist narrative, articles on this service were primarily concerned with the safeguarding of femininity in uniform. These two discourses did not always sit easily together: whilst uniformed women were praised on the one hand for showing 'courage and endurance...under the most trying circumstances', on the other they were criticised for being too masculine, hiding their femininity 'under a patchwork cloak of masculine heartiness'.[108] Uniformed service, a powerful visual symbol of wartime citizenship and sacrifice for men, was more problematic for women. Women's dual wartime role, as homemakers and carers, maintaining the home and the nation despite the disruption of total war, contrasted sharply with their labour as workers and servicewomen. Women in uniform were both expected to subjugate their individual desires and identity to national needs and to maintain their individuality and femininity whilst in uniform.

This division was clearly seen in the final year of the war. Small numbers of ATS servicewomen had served abroad since the early days of the war, predominantly the women of the Motor Transport Corps and the FANY, a socially elite group within the service who, whilst being absorbed into the ATS in 1940, had maintained a separate identity visually represented by the FANY arm badge which most chose to wear on their ATS uniform. These women worked as drivers and mechanics, and all women working with the Special Operations Executive behind enemy lines joined the FANY, most famously perhaps Violette Szabo, subject of the 1958 film *Carve Her Name With Pride*, who was captured and executed at Ravensbruck Concentration Camp in January 1945. Many other members of the ATS who served abroad were recruited locally, and the ATS in the Middle East was described as 'a virtual women's Foreign Legion', as out of its 4,605 members, 3,684 originated in the various countries of the region.[109] Small numbers of ATS also operated in East Africa and in India and Asia: the nearly 500 members of the No. 1 and No. 2 Clerical Companies in East Africa were formed of women from Britain and a local FANY branch of white upper-class settlers whilst small numbers of ATS trained the Women's Auxiliary Corps of India and 250 others supported Mountbatten's troops in Southeast Asia as clerical officers.[110] The small numbers and high social class of the FANY and Motor Transport Corps, and the national identity of most of the members of the ATS in the Middle East, meant that these women were largely exempt from the kind of criticism levelled at women who had served abroad during the First World War.

However, following the D-Day invasion of continental Europe by Allied troops in June 1944, larger numbers of women in the ATS began to serve overseas, supporting the army in its offensive against Axis troops. The opportunity to serve overseas appealed to many women as offering both the prospect of excitement and an escape from the often drab realities of wartime life in Britain. Sybella Stiles, an upper-class driver with the Motor Transport Corps who served both in South Africa and in the Middle East, described the increased sense of comradeship she found with soldiers when they were united

by living and working abroad.[111] Similarly, the letters of the Honourable
Miss L. E. Lawson, who worked with the Allied Expeditionary Force in Paris
following the city's liberation, express both a comradeship with other
members of the forces and an opportunity to socialise with male soldiers and
officers denied to her in Britain.[112] A more sombre note was sounded by Mary
Doherty who was billeted in the old Gestapo Headquarters in Brussels and
recalled Jewish families arriving to search for a trace of relatives who had been
held there.[113] However, the increasing numbers of women working abroad
were a cause of some concern. In part, this concern was a response to the tim-
ing of the decision to send women overseas; the Home Guard had been stood
down and there was a widespread feeling that, if the war hadn't actually
ended, it was beginning to come to an end and any extension of wartime compulsion was something of a blow. Women's roles behind the lines were
believed to place them closer to official combat zones than at any other point
during the war. As Penny Summerfield has argued, close proximity of women
to combat, and the possibility of their participation, undermined the
'wartime gender contract' in which 'men were pledged to fight for women,
who undertook to maintain home and family'.[114] Although approximately
80,000 women had been enlisted as armed fighters in the Soviet military the
prospect of women fighting, or being caught up in combat, with the British
army caused considerable anxiety.[115] This was not just a concern for the safety
of individual women; after all, the numbers of civilian dead had outnumbered
service personnel killed in the war until 1943. Whilst combat was widely
understood as a natural aspect of masculinity, combatant women were
'unnatural' and thus out of control, posing more of a threat than the combatant man to the social order. Women in combat threatened the division
between masculinity and femininity, combatant and non-combatant which
had been so carefully preserved during the war.[116]

Women serving abroad were, like the members of the WAAC who served
in France during the First World War, largely removed from the public gaze,
working far from home with large numbers of men. These women were the
subject of contradictory discourses regarding their behaviour whilst abroad.
Whilst a memo from the Secretary of State early in 1944 argued that 'it is
desirable to have as many British women as possible overseas' as the policy of
non-fraternisation between soldiers and civilians could only be maintained by
the presence of 'British and Allied women in occupied Germany', there was
widespread concern that women overseas would be unsupervised and more
likely to act 'immorally'.[117] The implicit recognition that the presence of
British women abroad could be good for soldier's morale was undermined by
fears about the morals of these same women. Predictably, rumours began to
circulate regarding 'immorality among the ATS serving overseas'.[118] Leslie
Whateley was concerned that as 'the majority' of ATS who had 'never yet set
foot on foreign soil' were especially vulnerable and 'might easily fall – through
ignorance – into pitfalls'. She was determined that rumours about the Corps
behaviour abroad should not affect the flow of women to continental Europe

where they performed important support roles for the occupying Allied armies there. Whateley emphasised that, in addition to performing their work efficiently, women serving overseas had to remember that 'their personal appearance and behaviour was as important as their work'.[119] Whateley saw public relations and the maintenance of morale in the service as important, intertwined aspects of her role as Director, and, as such, made many visits to ATS abroad, visiting Egypt, Palestine, Greece, France, Belgium and Italy in 1944 and 1945. At times she found conditions which, if they had become widely known in Britain, would have amplified the rumours regarding ATS immorality and apprehension about the living conditions of women abroad, such as the group of ATS in Bari, Southern Italy, who, she discovered, had been billeted in a run down hotel next door to a brothel.[120] In many ways the concerns regarding the role of women outside the British Isles echoed earlier anxieties regarding women on anti-aircraft batteries. Both were working in areas which were conventionally associated with men, and although they were still working in support roles and not directly taking part in combat, the women serving in Europe predominantly working as cooks, clerks, drivers, signallers and orderlies, they were still perceived as threatening established gender roles. Concerns which were expressed as anxieties regarding the welfare of women serving abroad can equally be read as a disquiet regarding this latest expansion of women's work.

Nevertheless, many members of the ATS did serve abroad following the invasion of continental Europe. When women left Britain the Army Act ceased to apply to them, and until this was altered in September 1944, they reverted to the official status of camp followers. Until the final months of 1944 only volunteers could serve overseas, and approximately 1 in every 30 women took up the opportunity.[121] In addition to volunteering, these women had to provide a written letter of permission from parents or husbands. Although permission was often refused, reflecting the widespread anxiety about the movement of women overseas, by January 1945, 4,000 members of the ATS were serving in North West Europe, including many working in mixed anti-aircraft batteries defending the cities of Brussels, Antwerp and Rotterdam.[122] When compulsion was introduced in February 1945, women could be directed to serve abroad but only women who were unmarried and aged over nineteen. James Grigg, the Secretary of State for War, announced the government's decision to post members of the ATS overseas just before the House of Commons' Christmas break in December 1944, stating that women would be sent abroad in order that 'the maximum number of men are released for operational duties'.[123] Despite Grigg's emphasis on 'the best possible standard' of accommodation for women serving overseas, and his statement that they would be undertaking work 'similar to that which they have performed with such success at home', objections to the plan were made, and the Commons agreed to debate the measure when it returned after Christmas.[124] The debate demonstrated both the strength and continuity of both women's symbolic relationship with the home and the longevity of concerns about the moral welfare of women in the services. Pethwick-Lawrence, speaking against the Bill, argued that women serving outside Britain were especially vulnerable to 'other dangers besides those arising from enemy action', whilst Colonel Viscount Suirdale described letters he had received from parents concerned that their daughters would be 'exposed' to 'the importunities of licentious soldiers'.[125] Mr Reakes contrasted the 'idling' Home Guard with the 'frail young women who are to be sent overseas' whilst Mr Beaumont stressed women's symbolic linkage with the home in his claim that 'the difference between a man and a woman' was evidenced by 'the home ties of members of the Women's Services'.[126] Although the Bill was passed, the debate demonstrated the extent to which traditional ideas about femininity had been maintained during the war. The decision not to compel married women to serve abroad, demonstrates yet again the symbolic importance of the home in wartime and the linkage of femininity to the maintenance of this symbol. With so many men abroad, the posting of wives overseas would mean that the home was empty, both symbolically and physically. When women stayed within the home front, even when not actually living in or maintaining a marital home, the ideal of home could be preserved. Whilst, as Antonia Lant has argued, the home could be extended in wartime to encompass the home front, the decision to compel members of the ATS to serve abroad challenged this symbolic linkage. Even women who did serve overseas were encouraged to think of themselves as, first and foremost, potential wives and mothers, as Leslie Whateley's letter justifying the decision to introduce compulsion and sent to all members of the Corps explained:

> Many of you will marry and bring children into the world and we are not going to have it laid at our door that for want of a little more unselfishness on our part now our children or our husbands might have to go through the horrors of another war ... Selfishness has bought us into this war and only unselfishness on the part of us all can bring a lasting peace.[127]

Thus, women were asked to conceive of their military service as both an extension of, and a means of protecting, their key role in society: that of wives, mothers and homemakers.

As the war drew to an end, this traditional female role was foregrounded as attention turned to the reconstruction of postwar society. Conscription, rationing, evacuation, the fear of invasion, the disruption and danger bought about by bombardment and the shared anxiety of having loved ones in danger had helped to weaken many of the class and political divisions of the inter-war years. Although the nation had moved to the left in many ways during the war, resulting in the landslide election of the reforming Labour government of 1945, ideas about gender and the rebuilding of the family unit in peacetime remained fairly conservative. Whilst the policies contained in the Beveridge Report of December 1942 had laid the foundations for the postwar welfare state by combining the 'doctrines of Liberal individualism' with the 'revolutionary sentiments of the People's War', women's main role in this brave new world was to return to the home and help to rebuild the domesticity which had been disrupted by the war.[128] Whilst the war was seen to have provided new opportunities for women, opening doors that could not simply be shut by the cessation of hostilities, support for equal rights was often combined with an emphasis on women's domestic role. The woman's magazine *Woman and Beauty*, for example, ran a 'Post-War Career Planning' series alongside articles arguing that 'the rebirth of home life is what 99 out of every 100 of us are living for'.[129] The postwar woman was expected to combine a new interest in politics and citizenship, the result of living through six years of total war with its merging of public and private life, with a renewed focus on the traditionally female areas of the home and domesticity. Women would not only help to reconstruct society, they would also be rebuilding the private world of the home and family.

Women's role in the reconstruction of the postwar nation was addressed in the two programmes of army education which were running: the Army Bureau of Current Affairs (ABCA) and 'British Way and Purpose' (BWP), both of which were designed to educate British soldiers in issues of citizenship. Both aspects of this education programme can be broadly understood as aspects of the 'people's war', left-leaning attempts to develop a sense of citizenship amongst soldiers through a discussion of war aims and potential schemes for postwar reconstruction. However, in their approach to gender roles, the education schemes were distinctly conservative. Although originally intended to be delivered to the male army, both schemes of education were extended to the ATS, ABCA in 1941 and BWP in 1943, although neither was ever compulsory and women attended classes in their leisure time, rather than as part of their service duties, as male soldiers did. Whilst there were some mixed ABCA classes in the anti-aircraft batteries the ATS were usually taught separately, and citizenship classes for women tended to focus on the domestic and the personal. This reflected an apprehension regarding postwar gender roles which ran through much of the programme, seen for example in BWP 13 which addressed 'The Family and Neighbourhood'. This edition focused on the imagined anxieties of its largely male audience, asking them to consider whether they 'approve of married women having careers' and whether 'a woman who is mistress of her own home and lives there with her children is necessarily unemancipated?'[130] Official histories of education in the forces, published in the late1940s, claimed that the women of the ATS had less interest in current affairs than men, preferring instead to study 'embroidery, soft toy making and leather work'.[131] It was argued that, in order to interest women in issues of reconstruction and citizenship 'ABCA would have to start near home, and stress the human problems involved in war, or in reconstruction, rather than in strategy and politics.'[132] Accordingly, W. E. Williams, the liberal, civilian Director of ABCA, advised that when leading sessions on postwar reconstruction, ABCA tutors would find that 'women wanted to argue about the best height for the kitchen sink, or the necessity for running hot water'.[133] Women were thus primarily educated for the domesticity which they were expected to return to at the war's end.

Demobilisation began six weeks after Victory in Europe (VE) Day, with married women the first to be released from service with the ATS. The earlier pre-occupation with feminine individuality and appearance was reflected in the demobilisation process as, unlike their male counterparts, demobilised women did not receive a 'demob suit' on leaving the ATS but instead were provided with 56 clothing coupons and a small amount of cash, in order that they could choose their own clothing. *Current Affairs*, the fortnightly ABCA publication for soldiers, commented that 'no one would venture to prescribe women's taste in civilian clothing'.[134] Wilson's history of army education reflected in 1949 that 'women in the forces were looking forward even more than the men to having homes of their own' resulting in frequent requests for 'lectures, talks and discussions on town planning, housing, interior decoration and colour schemes'.[135] As women moved from the highly organised, public world of the forces to the more private civilian sphere, the concept of an individualistic femininity, always present but so problematic to the collective nature of the armed forces, began to dominate.

During the war, many thousands of women served with the ATS, both at home and abroad, undertaking a wide variety of jobs which ranged from the very controversial, working alongside men in anti-aircraft sites, to the domestic, serving as cleaners and cooks in army camps (Table 6.1). Amongst their many other roles, women worked as secretaries, drivers, mechanics, bakers, telephonists and store keepers, and sixty-seven died whilst serving with the ATS.[136] However, as in the First World War, the female soldier's role remained that of an auxiliary, secondary to and serving the male soldier;

Table 6.1 Number and percentage of women utilised by the armed forces in the Second World War

	No. WRNS	WRNS as % of Navy	No. ATS	ATS as % of Army	No. WAAF	WAAF as % of RAF
1939	3,400	1.56	23,900	2.08	8,800	3.93
1940	10,000	2.92	36,400	1.72	20,500	4.01
1941	21,600	4.59	85,100	3.51	98,400	10.80
1942	39,300	6.49	180,700	6.58	166,000	15.06
1943	60,400	7.84	212,500	7.35	180,300	15.51
March 1944	68,000	8.20	206,200	7.14	175,700	14.94
December 1944	73,400	8.60	196,400	6.64	166.200	14.44
June 1945	72,000	8.42	190,800	6.13	153,000	13.87

Source: Statistical Digest of the War, London: HMSO, 1951.

existing primarily to enable more men to enter into combat, recruitment figures being ordained by the needs of the male army. The conflict between the military need for uniformed, conscripted women in auxiliary roles, supporting the armed men, and the ideological threat, which these women posed to traditional models of both femininity and masculinity, was never resolved, continuing to inspire debate about women's role in the forces until the war's end. Despite the importance of the term 'for the duration' during the war, used especially in relation to the expansion of women's roles in traditionally male, public spheres of activity, the ATS was not entirely demobilised at the end of the war and was maintained in smaller numbers whilst the government and the War Office considered its future. Volunteers were offered the opportunity to continue to serve with the ATS, officers for three years and other ranks for two. Although British society and most of the wider world was returning to a form of peace, albeit a peace shaped by the concerns and paranoia of the Cold War, there did appear to be space for small numbers of women to serve in an official capacity with the military. The ATS, which had grown out of the desire of Helen Gwynne-Vaughan and her associates to create a class-bound organisation which would enable small numbers of upper-class women to express their patriotism within the military sphere, was going to find a place for itself in the very different postwar world.

7 'Gentle in manner, resolute in deed'

Women in the postwar army

The celebrations which marked Victory in Europe (VE) Day in May 1945 and Victory in Japan (VJ) Day in August 1945 were accompanied by a widespread belief, expressed in women's magazines and in newspapers, that the return of peace would be accompanied by the general return of women to the home. *Woman's Magazine* published a lengthy article by Ella Thompson, a member of the Women's Auxiliary Air Force (WAAF) during the war, in which she articulated her desire for 'a return to a sane and sweet normality'. This normality was symbolised by her desire to marry as 'marriage is the aim, confessed or unconfessed, of the healthy, normal girl'. However, this marriage was to be a creation of the war years, which had shown that 'comradeship can exist between men and women'. It was to be a marriage of equals, companionate rather than patriarchal, in which she would combine marriage and motherhood with 'a small niche somewhere in business as a part-time typist, teleprinter or secretary'. The purpose of this paid work though was not self fulfilment, nor the sense of personal achievement expressed by many women working outside the home during the war, but to develop the author's role as a citizen and, centrally, to make her 'a more interesting wife and a mother of broader understanding'.[1] Whilst Thompson's war experiences, as a useful member of a public body, helping to win the 'people's war' alongside combatant men, are described as important, formative events, this public role is to fade into the background in her imagined postwar life, where the role of wife and mother takes uncontested priority.

The small public role which Thompson imagined for herself in the postwar world was very different from the large-scale movement of women into the public sphere seen during the war. Women's withdrawal from the workplace in the immediate postwar period was the result of a combination of factors: personal, political, practical and ideological. Whilst the postwar welfare state was socially progressive in its attempts to redistribute wealth and to provide a 'safety net' of insurance and health care for all of the population, it was also deeply pro-natalist, its policies built around the idea of a nuclear family where the man was the principal breadwinner and the woman had primary care for the house and children. The policies of the Labour government, elected by a landslide majority in 1945, paid little attention to the idea of women workers, implementing as they did the recommendations of the 1943 Beveridge Report. Beveridge's Report laid the foundations for a welfare state in which the married woman was essentially dependent upon her husband, her rights as a citizen based upon her unpaid work as a wife and mother rather than upon paid work outside the home. Under Beveridge's system of social security benefits, the married woman who worked outside the home could choose to pay a lower rate of National Insurance for which she would receive lower benefits, as Beveridge assumed she would be provided for by her husband and that 'during marriage...most women will not be gainfully employed'.[2] Beveridge shared the assumption with many of his contemporaries that after the war women would simply return to the home, his pro-natalist beliefs leading him to assert that women would replace paid work with the 'vital work' of 'ensuring the adequate continuance of the British race'.[3] The postwar welfare state which was built on Beveridge's wartime recommendations thus positioned women inside the home, bringing up children and dependent upon their husbands for financial support, with the safety net of the state providing for those families whose income was too low to provide a reasonable standard of living.

The principal address to women in the policies of the reforming Labour government of 1945, and in the welter of publications which made proposals for the reconstruction of Britain, was as wife and mother. Although the Royal Commission on Equal Pay, set up in 1944 as a response to the wartime working conditions which had challenged gendered ideas about employment and male and female rates of pay, reported in 1946 and made a limited argument for equal pay, it was rejected by the government. Fears about inflation combined with an anxiety that higher wage rates would encourage more women to choose paid work over unpaid domestic labour and childcare, resulting in a continued decline in Britain's birth rate.[4] The ensuing retreat from the wartime workplace into the more private space of the domestic home did not mean, however, that women were no longer the subjects of social policy. Indeed, schemes for the improvement of women's lives seem to have taken up much of the time of policy makers in the mid 1940s. Suggestions of potential ways to improve women's lives in the immediate postwar period included rest homes for tired housewives, the provision of official babysitters, after-school play centres and free holidays for poorer families. Houses on the new council estates and in the new towns being built to replace the slum areas of cities which had often been decimated by bombing were designed with rationalised kitchens and access to utility services such as hot water, gas and electricity in order to make housewives' work easier. Pro-natalist inspired concern about the declining birth rate meant that these houses were designed with enough bedrooms to accommodate the larger families which women were encouraged to have following the war. Women were to be educated not only in citizenship but also in household management and childcare, through an education policy which helped to shape the curriculum for girls in the new Secondary Modern schools. Whilst the provision of communal restaurants and laundries was also considered, these were meant to give relief to the tired housewife, not the hard pressed woman combining paid and domestic labour of the war years.

Although women were expected to take an interest in public and political issues, thus continuing the role of active citizen which they had been encouraged to adopt during the war, the key image of the postwar woman was that of a wartime worker or member of the auxiliary forces returning to a normality symbolised by domesticity. Although there was plenty of work available for women after the war, almost two million women had left paid work by 1947.[5] In part these figures reflected a desire on the part of many women to rebuild pre-war lives. The dual burden of paid work and the management of home and family was one which numerous women were glad to abandon, and the return of men from the forces to civilian employment allowed many women to dedicate more of their time to family life and, in many cases, to start the families which had been deferred by the disruption of war. Most commentators of the period shared a concern that the war had done much to disrupt family life, leading to a plummeting birth rate and a rise in delinquency amongst children brought up in their father's absence. In his *Essays on the Welfare State* Richard Titmuss discussed the falling birth rate which, he argued, characterised working-class life in the twentieth century, commenting that 'family building habits have settled at a little below replacement level'.[6] J. C. Spence argued in *The Purpose of the Family* that 'our economic system' did not 'recognise the right of every mother to possess the means of homemaking if she so desires it' whilst the Women's Group on Public Welfare published a 1948 Report entitled *The Neglected Child* which concluded that one common feature in all problem families was 'the capacity of the mother'.[7] This anxiety about the impact absent fathers and working mothers had upon children was reflected in the work of the influential child psychologist John Bowlby, who argued in 1946 that the wartime disruption of the family led directly to juvenile delinquency and in 1951 that young children who were denied full-time maternal care would suffer psychological damage.[8] The ideological drive to return women to the home and family was accompanied by a withdrawal of much of the practical support women undertaking the dual role of housewife and paid worker had relied upon during the war. British Restaurants, the communal feeding centres which had provided hot meals for workers and their families during the war, disappeared, and, as Denise Riley has shown, the financial strictures of the postwar economy led to the closure of the majority of workplace nurseries.[9] Neither was there any escape for women in fiction; *Brief Encounter*, one of the most popular films of 1945, acted as a metaphor for women's responsibility for rebuilding the home in its story of a married woman giving up her opportunity for romance in order to return to her husband. The wartime tension between the state's need for women's labour and the ideological need for women to remain within the home was to be resolved by the return of women to domesticity.

Amongst women who had worked during the war, servicewomen were a group with a specific, and uncertain, postwar identity. Whilst many assumed that they too were impatient for a return to normality and an opportunity to rebuild the domestic home, others thought that the relative autonomy and sense of citizenship which service life was believed to have bestowed upon them may have created a new sort of modern woman, ready to claim a 'new form of feminine citizenship'.[10] However, the concept of the modern woman emerging from the forces appears to have been marginalised in much of the public discussion of demobilisation, which overwhelmingly imagined servicewomen's postwar role in the domestic home. Mass-Observation's report on demobilisation, *The Journey Home*, found that 'the large number of opinionated women want to return to or start on domestic life when the war is over' whilst magazines such as *Woman and Beauty* reassured their readers that 'the rebirth of home life is what 99 out of every 100 of us are living for'.[11] Whilst observations such as these often appeared alongside discussion of the new opportunities which might open up for women after the war, such as the author Monica Dickens' article of March 1944 for *Woman's Journal* which specifically addressed servicewomen in its suggestion that their wartime experiences would equip them 'for a peace-time job that requires organizing ability' the servicewoman who wanted to take her new-found skills into the workplace was more widely regarded as a problem than an aid to reconstruction.[12] Indeed, the freedoms which the war was widely believed to have awarded British women, were themselves sometimes seen as a problem for both the wider reconstruction of postwar society and for the individual returning soldier. Three anonymous Infantry Platoon Commanders expressed exactly this view in a letter to the *Sunday Graphic* in 1944. Using a language reminiscent of that used by the wartime poets and novelists of the First World War who had expressed a profound bitterness at the continuities of civilian society, they articulated a resentment of the civilian population whom, they believed, had not suffered the horrors of war, specified here as combat, as they had, instead losing themselves in 'a wild fandango of pleasure—mad sensation seeking'. This ungrateful civilian population was represented here as women who had been subject to 'the unsettling action of war' which had 'given a new freedom' to them. 'With this new freedom' the men argued, 'enhanced by a greater feminine income than ever before, women have given themselves over completely to experimenting with these new sensations', in the process forgetting their debt to the returning combatant men. The authors condemned the social changes of wartime, denouncing most of all the changing attitudes of women. Although servicewomen could be exempt from the 'wild fandango' of civilians they described, they were arguably the women who had been changed the most by their wartime experiences, donning uniform, leaving home for communal life, undertaking new work and perhaps travelling abroad.[13] The uniformed, mobilised woman was, as Antonia Lant has argued, 'a highly unstable category', a necessary part of the war effort, but inherently problematic in a nation attempting to rebuild the domestic home and nuclear family.[14]

The Manpower Debate on demobilisation which took place in the House of Commons in November 1944 gave an early warning of dominant discourses of femininity in the postwar years. Whilst the debate overwhelmingly visualised the returning soldier as male, there was some discussion of servicewomen and their return to civilian life. With only two exceptions, the discussion of female demobilisation saw them returning to the home, the centrality of which to the postwar world can be seen in Lieutenant-Captain John Profumo's opening remarks that

> The nucleus around which we shall build all our future hopes and plans for a happy nation must be the home, and the sooner we can unite those whose intentions were thwarted by the outbreak of war, the better.[15]

Women overwhelmingly appear in the debate as waiting at home for men to return, a process which the House agreed it must undertake as quickly as possible as it was 'a duty to the men...and a duty to the womenfolk who have waited for them'.[16] Female service, when it was mentioned in the debate, appeared as a duty, something undertaken by women out of a sense of patriotic obligation and a desire to support the serving men, one MP remarking that 'we owe a great deal to these women who gave up their safety, their comfort and their privileges to stand shoulder to shoulder with the men'.[17] The different futures imagined for servicemen and servicewomen were emphasised in the discussion of demobilisation dress. As discussed in Chapter 6, whilst demobilised men were to receive clothing from civilian clothing depots on leaving the forces, women would be 'given facilities to purchase civilian clothing' as part of their demobilisation process, receiving a grant of £12.10s with which to buy their own clothes.[18] Profumo stressed that the reasoning behind the decision to allow women to choose their own clothing was that demobilisation would allow women to reclaim their femininity, arguing that the House should be generous in 'affording them the means of becoming once again adequately and gracefully dressed'. Elaborating on this he emphasised that men and women had a different relationship to clothes as 'no one would venture to prescribe a woman's taste in clothes' and whilst 'a man can do with a good suit of clothes and a coat and they will last him a long time...women's clothes appear to be somewhat different'.[19] Within Profumo's discourse women in the services had given up one of their essential feminine characteristics, the desire to be 'adequately and gracefully dressed', and by providing women with an opportunity to choose their own clothes once again, the government was both ending wartime uniformity and re-establishing traditional gender differences. The return to civilian life was an opportunity to reconstruct traditional gender roles and, although the House of Commons and the nation as a whole was grateful for the 'sacrifice' of the women in the services they were overwhelmingly expected to return to the home on demobilisation.

The numbers of women continuing to serve in the Auxiliary Territorial Service (ATS) immediately after the war's end reflected these trends.

Numbers of women in the ATS had fallen towards the end of the war, dropping from a peak of 214,420 in June 1943 to 197,230 by August 1944.[20] Although conscription was still in place, priority began to be given to the needs of industry for more labour as factories struggled to meet the demands for armaments following D-Day. Volunteering had re-opened for the women's services with a focus on recruiting young or married women who were designated non-mobile and thus could not be moved around the country into industry, and on ex-servicewomen. War Office records indicate that, more often than not, the ATS had to rely entirely on volunteer recruits after June 1944, recruitment figures showing that for most months, no women were conscripted for the service.[21] The Army had struggled against this fall in recruitment, consistently requesting that more women be drafted into the ATS than agreed by the War Cabinet. In 1944 for instance, the ATS had asked for 26,900 women, but the War Cabinet only approved 12,000, less than 50 per cent of those requested.[22] By this point in the war it was difficult to meet these numbers almost entirely through voluntary recruitment, and the ATS in fact only received 8,500 new recruits in this year.[23] This conflict in demand for labour from the ATS and restriction in recruitment imposed by the government carried over into the demobilisation process. Whilst the armed forces were focusing on the need for personnel in occupied Germany, in the Middle East and in British colonies, the government's priority was the reconstruction of Britain, and the need to increase the numbers of workers available for civilian industry. A meeting of the Manpower Committee in June 1945 recommended that 200,000 women be released from the three auxiliary women's services by December 1945, almost 50 per cent of the total women serving, but the services argued that only 16 per cent could be spared. The Cabinet intervened to propose that 135,000 women should be demobilised by the end of the year, although Churchill had made the case for a higher figure of 250,000, arguing that 'all women should be free to retire as soon as possible from the services' as he believed that 'those who like to stay will be sufficient to do the necessary jobs'.[24] Once again, women were caught between two opposing poles of argument: in this case, the desire of the services to retain women's labour and the desire of the government to release women both as a morale boosting symbol of the return to peacetime normality and as a reserve pool of labour for the reconstruction process.

However, women's role in reconstruction lay more in the home than in the factory. When women were prioritised for release from their wartime service because their work was seen as vital to the rebuilding of postwar Britain, they were released into occupations traditionally associated with femininity, and often a long way away from their wartime work. However, while there was a widely shared expectation that women would either return to the family home or to their pre-war employment, there was no direct pressure on women to undertake employment in domestic service, as had been the case following the First World War. In the very different political and social circumstances of the 1940s, domestic service was not perceived as the essential work it had been just over twenty years earlier. In answer to a query in the House of Commons as to whether a woman from the forces or the Land Army who 'qualifies herself in domestic science, or undertakes to take up domestic work on demobilisation will be given priority of release' Bevin replied that he was 'not prepared to introduce or impose conditions of release which would interfere with the liberty of these women to choose the profession they wish to follow on release'.[25] Nevertheless, women leaving the services for paid work did largely move into areas of employment traditionally associated with women, and in 1951 the census showed that there were still 750,000 women employed in domestic service.[26] Service personnel waiting for release were divided into three groups: Class A, those 'found surplus to military requirements', who would be released according to age and length of service, Class B, who were to be 'released on grounds of national importance' and Class C, to be 'released on compassionate grounds'.[27] Men demobilised under the Class B Release Scheme in 1945 were returning to jobs in construction, industry and coal mining; women released in the same scheme were predominantly going to work in the wool and cotton industries and in laundries, all traditional employers of working-class women. The 17,180 men released for essential services were teachers, university students and lecturers, theologians and potential candidates for the Colonial Service; the 1,500 women released in the same category were hospital cooks and telephone and telegraph operators.[28] The Reconstruction Committee of 1942 had already considered the scheme of demobilisation for conscripted women, and argued that although the plans for discharging women and men should be similar, both based on age and length of service, with those who had served the longest being released first, there should be one essential difference – married women should be released before unmarried, and before those needed for civilian jobs.[29] Although the eventual scheme of release was broadly similar to that used at the end of the First World War, with men and women divided into release groups according to their occupation, and demobilised in turn according to their length of service, the Ministry of Labour booklet published in November 1945 to explain the demobilisation scheme stated that 'married women have the right to claim priority of release over all other women'.[30] Women needed for the reconstruction of British industry were thus to be released after those who were reconstructing the marital home.

The rebuilding of this peacetime home was emphasised in the lectures given to women on demobilisation. Marian Mills, who had served on anti-aircraft sites during the war recalled one of these lectures in some detail:

> The good homemaker will rise as early as possible ... In winter the fireplaces that are used the day before should be cleaned and the fires relaid before breakfast. The room in which this meal is to be served should first be swept and dusted.

The horrified Mills commented that 'what we really needed were pep talks about all the wonderful opportunities that might be open to us in the brief periods when we were not shopping dusting, nursing and mangling', wondering 'what lectures they gave to the men?'[31] As the 'gunsite poet' and regular contributor to *Punch* magazine E. S. Turner wrote,

> Behold how flatteringly glows
> The sun on burnished boss and shaft!
> What happens when the whistle blows?
> The girls fall in for Mothercraft![32]

The shift from a mobilised, wartime society, in which the state had control over many areas of citizen's personal lives and in which many men had learnt to kill was to be managed by the rebuilding of the home and the reassertion of traditional gender relations. Whilst the armed forces trained men to act violently, tutoring them in the aggressive skills of warfare, there was no concurrent programme for the demobilisation of these men; although army education lectures encouraged them to consider their options for peacetime employment, there was little attempt to help them manage the psychological transition to civilian life with its taboos against killing. It was feared that these combatant men would be unwilling to return to the constraints of peacetime society, the military historian John Laffin arguing somewhat floridly that one of the best 'inducements to the end of a war' was 'the intense desire of men to return home to women and bed'.[33] If large numbers of women were to remain in their wartime occupations in industry or the auxiliary forces, this inducement would disappear. Women's magazines tutored their readership on what they could expect when servicemen returned home. 'Back to Real Life', an article about the postwar world in *Woman's Own* in January 1945, warned women it was 'essential' that they 'readjust their outlook' as husbands who 'before they went away, led quiet, regular lives' had 'faced the dangers of the battlefield, and passed through experiences so gigantic that they are bound to have left their mark on them'. As well as helping men adjust to their civilian lives once again, women were counselled that it was their duty to combine the wartime sense of community and comradeship with family life, building family units which were outward, rather than inward, looking. Indeed, the article concluded, this would be 'a woman's main task in the reconstruction of life after the war. She will be the mainspring of a new and better way of living.'[34] Similarly, an article by Louise Morgan in *Good Housekeeping* in 1945, entitled 'When They Come Home', argued that 'the adjustment of the demobbed to civilian life is the most difficult demand that society makes on any human being'. In order to better understand what these men were experiencing, the article advised its readers to read novels of the First World War, such as Robert Graves' *Goodbye To All That* or Remarque's *All Quiet on the Western Front* as 'the mentality of the demobbed soldier in the last war was fundamentally the same as now'.

Women were also told to 'rub up' their general reading, as men would be returning with 'a wider outlook, a keener brain, and a thirst for knowing the world about him'. However, Morgan argued that the most important thing that women could do was to patiently emphasise 'the comfort of your love and understanding' as men would be feeling 'hurt, angry, profoundly home-sick for what he has lost' and would probably be 'very difficult to get along with and very unhappy in himself'. Although Morgan recognised that women too had experienced profound changes in wartime, she emphasised that their wartime experiences were less dramatic than those of 'a mechanised man, trained to do only one thing – kill the enemy'. Working in the Auxiliary Services or the factories, Morgan argued, women had 'been spared the experience of fighting and killing', and would thus have less adjusting to do than the returning ex-serviceman.[35] Women in the home were to be a nor-malising force, mediating between the ex-combatant man and the mores and values of civilian society.

Although the desire to rebuild a peacetime society ensured that the con-flict between 'production and patriarchy' which had dominated wartime debates about women's role was largely resolved in favour of the patriarchal status quo, women were still needed in the armed forces. At first, women departed at such a rate that men from the army had to be drafted in to replace them. The task of reconstruction in mainland Europe was enormous, and the labour of auxiliary women was a necessity if Britain was to maintain any influence in the rebuilding of this postwar world. However, the main reason that the government agreed to the continued employment of women by the army in Occupied Germany appears to be influenced less by the need for manpower than by the desire to prevent soldiers from fraternising with German women. This issue had been raised in the 1945 ATS Overseas Service Debate in the House of Commons, when Colonel Thornton-Kemsley, the MP for Aberdeen, had argued that the presence of 'a large ATS element in the Army' would ensure that there was 'no fraternisation with the Germans'.[36] In this he was echoing a long running debate within the War Office about the relationship between the Allied forces of occupation in Germany and German civilians. As soon as Allied forces crossed the Rhine in 1945 the Supreme Headquarters of the Allied Expeditionary Force (SHAEF) implemented a 'policy of uncompromising non-fraternisation' between Allied troops and German civilians.[37] The aims of this policy were two-fold. First, substantial resistance to the occupation was expected to be organised by Nazi sympa-thisers including both 'civil disorder, including sniping, assaults on individ-uals, sabotage, provoked riots, perhaps even organized raids' and 'attempts to influence sympathy and support' through fraternisation with civilians, 'especially children, women and old men'.[38] Second, non-fraternisation was intended to 'impress upon the Germans the prestige and superiority of the Allied armies and to demonstrate to the Germans their complete defeat'.[39] If Allied troops kept themselves aloof from German civilians, not only would they be immune to attempts to win their hearts and minds but their attitude would also emphasise their role as victors and the Allied disdain for Nazi actions.

However, as the memos and telegrams which shot backwards and forwards between SHAEF, the Cabinet, the Adjutant General's office and the military intelligence unit MI 11 illustrated, there were at least two fatal problems with the policy: the troops' unwillingness to act upon it and the ensuing shortage of civilian personnel available for employment by the forces. The utilisation of significant numbers of ATS personnel was seen as a means of solving both of these difficulties as not only could they replace soldiers in clerical work and other day to day tasks which might otherwise be undertaken by civilians, but their presence would 'provide the essential female element which a self-contained community must have if it is to remain self-contained'.[40] The importance which the government placed upon the need for a female presence in Germany can be seen in Manny Shinwell's statement to the House of Commons that 'the members of the women's services are an excellent influence on the troops', emphasising the social significance of their presence there in his comment that 'the men have already received them with open arms'.[41] Although the employment of ATS personnel in Germany had initially been tightly restricted, with no women allowed to serve East or North of the Rhine before VE Day, this restriction was soon lifted, though women who did serve there were largely confined to their units, only allowed to travel or leave the Allied camps when accompanied by armed soldiers.[42] Discussion in the army and the War Office about the non-fraternisation policy between soldiers and civilians centred largely on the possibility of relationships developing between German women and Allied soldiers. In particular, the War Office was determined to 'prevent German women marrying British subjects solely in order to escape the consequences of their nationality', and it was suggested that as well as outlawing any such marriages, the government should look into the legalities of forcibly dissolving those which had already taken place.[43] The army attempted to warn troops away from German women in the handbook issued to soldiers leaving for a tour of duty in Germany. In this book, they were warned that

> Numbers of German women will be willing, if they can get the chance, to make themselves cheap for what they can get out of you . . . Be on your guard: most of them will be infected . . . Many German girls will be waiting for the chance to marry a Briton, whether they care for him or not.[44]

Despite these dire warnings, and despite it being an offence punishable by court martial, fraternisation was still expected to take place and levels of VD infection amongst troops were expected to be high.[45] The employment of large numbers of ATS and women from other voluntary organisations was intended to make the British troops more self-sufficient and self-contained, able to avoid contact with German civilians both in the workplace and, implicitly, in their romantic and sexual relationships.[46]

The policy of strict non-fraternisation was gradually dropped from July 1945 following the relaxation of the policy for United States' troops and Montgomery's insistence that 'the ban on fraternisation should be lifted at once' in order to begin the process of 're-education' believed to be vital to the integration of Germany into the postwar world.[47] Concern was already being raised about the activities of the Soviet Union in the zones of Germany and Austria which it occupied, and in a precursor to the Cold War, a secret memo circulated within the War Office warning against the popularity of propaganda issuing from the Soviet zone of occupation:

> The programmes from the Russian controlled Berlin radio have given the impression that life in the Russian zone is vastly happier than that in the Allied zone ... (it is) an area which produces a food surplus, railways and cinemas are open and concerts in full swing ... the Red Army has played a football match against a German workers team.

Although the memo noted wryly that in fact

> The Red Army lives largely off the land – paying for the produce not being part of the bargain ... (and) the area between Vienna and the Allied zone is like a dead country in which no man exists and women are afraid ever to work in the fields.[48]

Concern remained strong that for civilians in Allied zones, unable to interact with troops stationed there and suffering from all the hardships of life in immediate postwar Germany, the promise of plenty in a Communist nation was attractive. Postwar hopes that Britain, the United States and the Soviet Union would continue to work together were beginning to fade and the pre-occupation with resisting a perceived Soviet threat to the democracies of the West, both physical and ideological, was beginning to shape British military policy.

The developing Cold War shattered public optimism that the end of the Second World War would herald a new era of peace. The state of mutual mistrust and suspicion which soon came to characterise relations between the Soviet bloc and the Western democracies, led by the United States, came to dominate both international policy and military planning and strategy. By 1947 the Soviet Union was in control of most of Central and Eastern Europe and was increasingly running East Germany as a separate entity from the British, French and American controlled zones in the West. Tensions between East and West were heightened by the appearance of new weapons with the potential to literally bring about Armageddon. The use of atomic weapons against Japan in August 1945 signified the beginning of a new era in warfare; Clement Attlee, the new Labour Prime Minister, noting at the end of that month that 'the modern conception of war to which in my lifetime we have become accustomed is now completely out of date'.[49] Whilst British scientists had worked on the 'Manhattan project' in the United States to develop the bomb, the passing of the McMahon Act by United States Congress in August 1946 effectively ended any collaborative nuclear research between the two nations, leaving the United States as the world's only nuclear power. A secret Cabinet Committee of senior Ministers decided in 1946 that it was imperative that Britain have nuclear weapons, both to maintain its position as a world power and to act as a counterbalance to a perceived threat to Western Europe from the Soviet Union. The financial cost of developing a nuclear bomb was enormous for a country trying to rebuild homes, industries and public services after the war and proved to be an extra strain on the defence budget, already stretched by the need to maintain forces in Europe, the Middle East, North Africa and colonies in Asia and Africa. Continuing economic pressures both abroad and at home led the government to impose an annual limit on defence spending of £600 million in 1947, and pressures on recruitment led to acute manpower shortages within the army as it could not compete with the wages on offer in the rising postwar labour market.[50] In order to ensure that the Army was supplied with the necessary manpower to meet all its obligations, the Government took the decision in late 1945 to re-introduce conscription, a reasonably inexpensive, if unpopular, means of guaranteeing that the armed forces would be able to cope with their various overseas commitments. Although conscription, or national service as it was known, was only to apply to young men, initial discussions show that the re-introduction of conscription for women was also considered.

The debates regarding the possible re-introduction of conscription for women in peacetime are interesting as they shed some light on contemporary thinking about both gender relations in general and the roles of men and women within the armed forces. The National Council of Women of Great Britain, a voluntary organisation which has long campaigned on issues such as equal pay and equal status for men and women, discussed the matter of women's national service at its Executive Committee meeting in February 1946. The Committee argued that 'in the war period...the principal of equality of liability was broadly recognised' and that if conscription was to be re-introduced for men, the same regulations should apply to women, with 18-year old women being directed into a range of services including 'the auxiliary forces, nursing, land army, public institutions and domestic workers, residential and nursery schools, holiday camps (and) national industry'.[51] However, although the Committee based its argument on the principle of equality of service for men and women, it drew the line at conscripting married women, concluding that 'exemption from further national service obligation would be granted on marriage, whether there were children or not'.[52] This recommendation echoed the government's decision during the Second World War not to include married women without children, whose husbands were away in the services or on other war work as mobile: in peacetime or in wartime, the position of the woman within the marital home remained almost inviolable and certainly incompatible with any type of national service. Indeed, the Annual Meeting of the National Council of Women narrowly rejected the call for compulsory national service for women, arguing that it would disrupt married life, despite the argument put forward by one delegate that 'national service training would make for better wives and happier homes'.[53] Concern about women's role as wives, mothers and housewives appears to have been almost universal in the immediate postwar years.

Although the Manpower Committee of the Ministry of Labour discussed extending national service to women, its suggestions for a system of this kind were prefaced with the observation that 'a scheme of this sort would be undesirable'.[54] Whilst the re-introduction of conscription for men was also known to be unpopular, state control over women's labour encroached more deeply upon the idea of the private life of home and family. The overwhelming tone of the debate within the Ministry of Labour was one of reluctance. When national service for women was considered, it was not within the same parameters as national service for men; instead the Manpower Committee's remit was to deliberate upon women 'being made liable to direction to national service of a civilian character' rather than service with the forces.[55] A similar pattern was followed when the matter was debated in Parliament. When the National Service Bill was debated in March 1947 only Barbara Gould, the Labour MP for Hendon North, suggested that National Service should be applied to women in the same way that it was applied to men. Drawing on the memory of women's war work, Gould argued that 'the wonderful things that women did during the war' meant that it would be 'uneconomical, unrealistic and unfair to exempt the women power from national service, if there has to be national service'.[56] Gould combined a belief in the principle of equality of opportunity and service with the conviction that women would be motivated by patriotism to undertake national service, arguing that

> The women were called up in the war. Of course, there was an outcry at first; but it was very soon accepted and everybody was throwing bouquets to the women – and rightly so – for the magnificent job they were doing, and pointing out that the war could not be won without them. Is it – I hate to think it – but is it that our Government are being thoroughly prejudiced and old-fashioned? ... citizens' rights are being increased, and rights involve obligations. Those obligations are just as much on women as on men ... Women want their rights and opportunities ... but they are prepared also to undertake their responsibilities.[57]

Gould however was a lone voice in a parliament reluctantly debating the extension of national service from 12 to 18 months; her appeal for women to be included in the scheme was described as an attempt to 'reproduce all the most dreadful conditions of war' and national service continued to be only applicable to men.[58]

There was however one aspect of Gould's argument, also voiced in the Ministry of Labour debates, which did receive some serious consideration.

This was the idea that, by taking young men out of the labour market for over a year, women were being given an unfair advantage. Gould argued that a male-only conscription policy would give young women an 'unwanted privilege' in the workplace as 'girls are being taken on instead of boys' by employers unwilling to see their workplaces disrupted by the movement of men into the forces.[59] This point was echoed in a Ministry of Labour memo which suggested that 'from the point of view of preserving equity of opportunity' in the workplace 'a similar sacrifice' should be imposed on young women as on young men. However, the terms of national service suggested for men and women were perceived here as being quite different. Whilst national service for men was imposed in order to 'have a reserve of men who can be used to build up highly trained modern mechanical forces' national service for women was imagined as training as 'land workers or members of a domestic corps'. In fact, the memo continued, 'the most obvious form of compulsory training for women is training in domestic employment because this is likely to prove of some value in the women's subsequent life'.[60] The concept of separate spheres for men and women, with men in the army and women in the nursery, appeared to be alive and well in Whitehall in the years following the Second World War.

However, whilst the debate about national service was raging, women were still serving with the armed forces. Although large numbers of women had left the ATS following the end of the war, a small but significant number remained in uniform, seeing work in the military as a future career prospect. In the immediate aftermath of war these prospects must have appeared fairly fragile, as the government was reluctant to commit itself to the definite maintenance of any of the women's auxiliary services. Although there was no rush to disband the units, as there had been following the First World War, the government was hardly enthusiastic in its pronouncements on the future of the women's services. Whilst, as Leslie Whateley commented in her memoirs, the decision to maintain a female presence in the armed forces was 'a foregone conclusion', the task of organising a woman's corps proved difficult and lengthy, as the three services attempted to unify their approach to pay, conditions of service and status.[61] Despite the many ringing endorsements of the work of the auxiliary services during the war the initial announcement of the decision to create permanent female Corps within the Army, Navy and Air Force was distinctly low key. In an echo of the auxiliary forces' role during the war, when they had been formed and utilised in order to release more men from the forces for combat, the decision to make the women's services permanent was dependant upon the forces' ongoing need for men. In a debate about the re-introduction of male conscription in May 1946 the Minister for Labour announced to the House of Commons that

> In order to lessen the needs of the services for men, it has been decided to call for recruits for the women's Auxiliary Services to volunteer for a period of not less than two years. It has also been decided to continue the

WRNS, the ATS and the WAAF on a voluntary basis as permanent features of the Forces of the Crown.[62]

Women's military service was once again contingent upon the military's need for men, in this case as a means of reducing the demands of an unpopular policy of national service.

The official announcement confirming that women's auxiliary corps were to become a permanent feature of the armed forces was made in Parliament on 20 November 1946.[63] Although all three women's services were to be continued, only the ATS and the WAAF were to become members of the armed forces, with the Women's Royal Naval Service (WRNS) remaining as a civilian service. The government and the War Office were keen to both retain women who were already serving in the corps and to encourage women who had left the services following the war to return, a recruitment campaign in 1947 emphasising that 'the army needs the women who made this badge famous . . . to give the lead to new arrivals'.[64] Women already serving with the ATS were encouraged to extend their service, officers for three, four or five years, other ranks for two, three or four years. Married women were accepted back into the ATS provided they could prove that 'they are likely to be fully mobile for the period of their service' whilst women who married whilst in the service could leave, remain in the corps or transfer to a Reserve.[65] The new women's corps, which retained the title of ATS whilst a new name was considered, was expected to consist of approximately 27,000 women, just over 10 per cent of the size of the regular, male army, which was formed of between 220 and 250,000 men.[66] As numbers of women in the ATS had fallen sharply after the end of the war, women who had not served with the forces before also needed to be recruited, although as the recruitment campaigns demonstrate, the early appeals to women emphasised that service with the ATS would be an opportunity to help men, rather than an opportunity for independence, travel or a career. Reiterating the appeal to women during the war, one poster from 1947 stated that 'they can't get on without us', over the large image of a smiling brunette in uniform, placed in front of a smaller black and white drawing of men loading anti-aircraft guns. If this image echoed the wartime discourse of 'serving with the men who fight', which placed women symbolically behind the men, other recruitment literature was resonant of the First World War. One leaflet from 1945 used the language of housewifery and domestic service, with the words 'You are needed now to look after all of this' placed over a picture of an army camp, whilst inside potential recruits were reassured that 'it becomes quite homely once you have put a picture or two on the wall'.[67] This emphasis on domesticity, femininity and serving and supporting men would presumably have had little appeal for women looking for a career in the services as a means of escaping the constraints of postwar Britain, such as Eva Buckingham, who joined the ATS towards the end of the war and later described her service in Sri Lanka during 1945–1946 as 'exciting, adventurous and madly romantic', reflecting instead an ongoing concern that there would be public opposition to the maintenance of military service for women.[68]

Despite the decision to create a permanent role for women within the armed forces, much of the discussion within the War Office about the organisation and administration of the women's corps was resonant of the discussions which accompanied the founding of the Women's Auxiliary Army Corps in 1917. Mary Tyrwhitt, who had replaced Leslie Whateley as Director of the ATS in May 1946, was anxious for the Corps to be properly integrated into the armed forces, with issues such as discipline, conditions of service and titles of rank discussed and decided long before the Corps was established on a permanent footing. Much of the debate which took place in the policy committee she established to consider these questions was focused around the need to differentiate between the as yet un-named women's corps and the male sections of the armed forces. In a discussion at the War Office between male representatives of all three services about how to apply the Army Act to women, debate focused around the questions of discipline, titles of rank, saluting and chains of command. As in the years preceding the Second World War, the representatives of the Air Force appeared to deserve their reputation as members of the more egalitarian of the three services. The establishment of a unified policy amongst the services proved problematic because of the RAF's readiness to allow women a greater measure of authority over and equality with men than the other two services. For example, in the discussion of chains of command, which focused around the issue of women being placed in a position of command over men, representatives of the Army were concerned that the 'divergence between RAF and Army over chains of command' would lead to 'WAAF women having powers of command over junior Army men'.[69] Philip Noel Baker, the Secretary of State for Air wrote to the Secretary of State for War to assert that the Air Force structure of command was one which should be followed by the Army, arguing that 'in these days when we have women Cabinet Ministers and M.P.s, women Mayors, Magistrates and J.P.s, it would in our opinion be indefensible to withhold from women Officers in the services disciplinary power over men'.[70] However, the representatives of the army opposed the idea of a non-gendered chain of command, arguing instead that 'it would not be advisable for general disciplinary powers over men to be granted to women except in specific cases such as when men were "specially placed under their command, e.g. in mixed A.A. batteries." '[71] The same pattern was seen in discussion of the issue of saluting between men and women, with the Air Force arguing that men in the RAF would salute superior women, whilst the army countered that 'men resent saluting women unless they are well known to them'.[72] Underlying the army's antagonism to the extension of women's powers of command over men was a fear that 'the men will resent it'; a belief which suggests that, although women were to be established in permanent positions within the postwar army, opinion concerning the formation of a permanent women's corps within both the armed forces and the wider public was divided.[73] In the years following the war the idea that the 'return to normality' of peacetime would mean the re-establishment of traditional gender roles was difficult to dislodge.

Whilst the army recognised that it needed women's labour in order to support the work of men in the forces, and to avoid the extension of National Service, it was concerned to ensure that these women remained separate from the men, both symbolically and organisationally. Women remained an organisationally discrete unit of the army, separated from men in their own Corps, nominally led by women but organised and controlled by the men of the army and War Office, and the question of integrating the ATS into the regular army simply never arose. The War Office recommended that members of the new women's corps should be subject to the same disciplinary procedures as men, including the death penalty, excepting 'field punishment', which was seen to be 'quite unsuitable for them', but that discipline should be administered by female officers as a male Officer 'might not always appreciate the nuances of a women's mentality and troubles'.[74] As had been the case during both world wars, the female officers of the new women's corps had a role reminiscent of the philanthropic middle-class women of late Victorian and Edwardian Britain who had attempted to oversee the moral and physical welfare of working-class women in homes and factories through their work as health visitors and industrial welfare officers. They were to be responsible for the welfare and discipline of their subordinates but not to have any say in larger questions of military policy and organisation. As a further means of differentiating female soldiers from male, they also recommended that 'normal Army titles for officers were not suitable for women officers, particularly in the higher ranks' and female officers continued to be known as Controllers and Administrators.[75] Although the armed forces' continuing need for labour after the war ensured that there would be a permanent place for women within the services, these women were to continue to be classified as separate and distinct from the higher status combatant men.

Combat remained a key means of differentiating between military men and military women, arguably taking on a new significance in the postwar world where the threat of invasion and the concurrent possibility of women having to defend the home, was less pressing than it had been during the two world wars. Indeed, the growing threat of nuclear weapons meant that the physical defence of the home was becoming an increasingly unlikely possibility, and despite the brief and unpopular revival of the Home Guard in the 1950s, military policy was becoming gradually more concerned with the role of traditional modes of combat in the nuclear world.[76] As the army refocused its attention on field warfare the need to distinguish between the combatant male and the non-combatant female became an issue of intense discussion within the War Office. Major General McCandlish, the postwar Director of Personnel Administration within the War Office, chaired a Committee which examined the relationship of women to combat during 1948–1949 as, 'Now that the WRAC has become a Corps of the Regular Army, it is necessary to clearly define the function of its members in the face of its enemy.'[77] The Committee was divided between those such as Mary Tyrwhitt who argued that members of the Women's Royal Army Corps (WRAC) should be trained in the use of weaponry, a view broadly shared by McCandlish, and those who strongly opposed the arming of women in any circumstances. The language used in the discussions is illuminating: McCandlish was directed by the Adjutant-General's office to undertake an examination of 'the defensive role and status of the WRAC in war', demonstrating a continuity of thought which placed armed women as defenders of the home and the self rather than as aggressive combatants.[78] Within this context debate focused around exactly what role women should take if they should by some chance be confronted with the enemy.

Running throughout the memos and minutes of meetings is an underlying concern with the impact that arming women would have on the morale of the male soldier. Whilst the use of women's labour on anti-aircraft sites during the war, although never as actual combatants, could be condoned as it was understood to be a temporary response to exceptional circumstances; a 'just for the duration' experiment which allowed the release of more men for the higher status combat units, the arming of women in peacetime, even for self defence, threatened the male-only status of combat. McCandlish produced a list of 'pros' and 'cons' regarding the arming of women, including in his list of issues which weighed against the decision the note that 'The arming of women in any circumstances is distasteful to the British people. There are many soldiers who would find it incongruous to say the least that women officers would take part in a battle.'[79] This was echoed in a later discussion paper which recommended that the WRAC's defensive role 'should consist of such duties which do not involve the use of personal arms or the actual firing of guns, projectiles etc.' as 'neither the Army nor the nation are yet sufficiently accustomed to the idea of women in the fighting services.'[80] Combat was still seen as an activity which was crucial to the difference between masculinity and femininity, articulated in the comment from one male member of the Committee that

> The fact that 'little Olga' is trained to kill and prides herself on the number of notches cut on her revolver butt is no reason why we, too, should cry 'Annie get your gun'. It is still the soldier's duty to protect his womanfolk whatever they are wearing. Even in these days when war means total war let us at least retain that degree of chivalry.[81]

Even when women wore an army uniform their gendered identity took precedence; 'the soldier's duty to protect his womanfolk' over-riding any duty that members of the WRAC might feel to defend themselves or their positions.

Arguments put forward in the debate which supported the arming of the WRAC for self-defence also focused around their femininity, with gender being seen as both a reason for arming, and for not arming, women.

McCandlish's first draft of his discussion document noted somewhat controversially that 'I do not think that there is any doubt that most women would much prefer to be shot rather than raped', a comment which was deleted following Tyrwhitt's understated rejoinder that 'it is not sufficiently clear that most women prefer shooting to being raped.'[82] However, the question of arming women remained intimately linked to their femininity, with the suggestion that a woman's gender should be defence enough against an enemy assailant being asserted again and again. The Director General of the Army Medical Service reiterated exactly this point in his argument that 'their non-combatant status and the fact that they are women are sufficient protection' going on to comment that women's possession of arms might in fact endanger them as 'if one member was found in possession of fire-arms the tendency would be to assume that all members of the corps were militant, and to deal with them accordingly'.[83] Despite Tyrwhitt's observation that 'most women would rather put their faith in their own skill with a rifle than in the finer feelings of an invading enemy', McCandlish included the argument that 'if women shoot to kill they might forfeit the measure of protection which, unarmed, their sex would demand and which our opponents might concede' in his list of points weighing against arming the WRAC.[84] A sense of British national identity which rested in part on fixed ideas of gender, and the racist stereotyping of an 'enemy other' as uncivilised and untrustworthy can also be read through these documents in the repeated references made to perceived Asian, and particularly Japanese, attitudes to women and warfare, such as McCandlish's comment that 'the ruthlessness of modern war' could be seen 'particularly in the case of Asiatic opponents', and in Tyrwhitt's description of a 'largely uncivilised enemy'.[85] The underlying belief – that British women should be defended by chivalrous British men, combined a long held ideal of the noble warrior as an essentially British archetype with a prurient fascination with the actions of an imagined enemy who would rape and murder British women.[86] Women in military uniform may have been members of the armed forces, but their gender was interpreted by those who supported arming them as a potential vulnerability, and by those who opposed this course of action as a means of protection in wartime.

McCandlish eventually put forward three different proposed courses of action. The first proposed that the WRAC be regarded as civilian and ordered to take shelter with the civilian population if they were in danger of coming under fire. The second suggested that women be employed in providing first aid, communications support and other non-combatant duties as 'the obvious occupation for women in the case of enemy action is succouring the wounded'.[87] The third course of action proposed that as a last resort, the WRAC be allowed to use small arms in self-defence. Although McCandlish initially recommended the third option weight of opinion both on the Committee and more widely was against women being armed even in self defence and the WRAC remained a strictly non-combatant unit within the army until 1980, when women were allowed to volunteer to train with small arms for self-defence.[88] Far from challenging the combat taboo, the creation of a women's corps as a permanent feature of the British army further reinforced it.

The issue of maintaining the femininity of women in military uniform which had been so important a feature of discussions during both world wars appeared again in the debates which accompanied the foundation of the WRAC. Tyrwhitt chaired the Committee on Post-War Dress for Queen Alexandra's Imperial Nursing Service and the WRAC which sat between 1946 and 1949 to decide upon an appropriate uniform for these two services. Despite the decision of the WAAF to design its own uniform, the Committee decided to use civilian designers as they believed this would have 'recruiting value', hopefully attempting to alleviate the widespread perception of the ATS's wartime uniform as both uncomfortable and unflattering and which Mass-Observation had argued 'is a very appreciable factor in making women feel they don't want to join the ATS'.[89] The Committee approached designers including Norman Hartnell, Charles Creed, Edward Molyneux and Aage Thaarup, and Hartnell's design was eventually chosen as the most suitable as 'it has a feminine line and yet is reminiscent of military uniforms of the early nineteenth century'.[90] Hartnell, who was best known for his glamorous designs for the Royal Family and other aristocratic clients, in producing a uniform which was seen to provide the elusive combination of feminine elegance with military uniformity that had been missing from the ATS uniform had at last achieved his wish that the government 'would invite him to become a camofleur'.[91] Hartnell's design was certainly more stylish than the 'drab looking' and unpopular uniforms worn by the ATS, reflecting the influence of the 'New Look' in fashion in its use of tight, fitted jacket with fuller skirt.[92] The jacket had three diagonal seams running in a 'V' shape across the front towards the centre and the back of the jacket was longer than the front, cut in a way 'similar to those of the Scottish regiments'.[93] The skirt was cut slightly wider than that of the ATS in order 'to allow more freedom' and was seen to be 'suitable for walking out and marching without discomfort to the wearer'.[94] The Committee were concerned that as well as being recognisably feminine, the new WRAC uniform be recognisably distinct from other women's uniformed groups, especially 'the various voluntary women's organisations' whom, it maintained in an echo of the controversy around uniformed women in the First World War, should not be confused with the new, official organisation.[95] In addition to being distinct from any voluntary organisations, the WRAC uniform also had be easily distinguished from male army uniforms, and bottle green was chosen as a colour specifically because it was a recognisably militaristic colour yet differed from the rifle green and light infantry green worn by several male units within the army. By choosing a uniform which combined 'a smart military yet feminine appearance', the Committee demonstrated not only the need to appeal to more recruits for the new corps but also the continuity of the idea that femininity was somehow inimical with militarism, and that it needed to be protected once women were in uniform.[96]

However, despite the popularity of Hartnell's designs, recruiting for the new Corps proved to be a problem, at times even making it difficult for the Committee to find WRAC models for the designs they were considering.[97] Austerity was hitting army budgets as well as producing the civilian short- ages which led to an increase in rationing in the immediate postwar years. Although women in the services and their families had tolerated uncomfort- able living quarters, at times even welcoming them as proof that they were 'doing their bit' alongside the men, this did not prove to be the case in peace- time, and the Army's financial inability to provide little other than 'squalid conditions based on wartime hutted camps' did little to encourage recruit- ment.[98] Patriotism and a desire to be of service meant that recruits may have endured hardships in wartime; they proved less willing to do so in peacetime. A new recruiting campaign was devised which focused less on the sense of duty which the campaigns of wartime and the immediate postwar period had attempted to mobilise, concentrating instead on the desire of potential recruits for independence and adventure. The new campaign, which ran between 1948 and 1950, was entitled 'two sides of an exciting life' and emphasised the new opportunities which were awaiting women who joined the WRAC (Figure 7.1). The adverts consisted of two contrasting pictures of women in the WRAC, one at work and one at play. The images of work showed women busy in a wide variety of occupations: height finding, chang- ing car tyres, sewing, operating a teleprinter and cooking. Contrasted with these were images of women at leisure and these demonstrate an interesting shift in emphasis over the two years that the campaign ran. The two earliest adverts showed women spending their leisure time with army officers, danc- ing and playing tennis, calling potential recruits' attention to the opportuni- ties military service offered to meet and socialise with the opposite sex. However, over the next two years these images vanished to be replaced first by a series of images which emphasised the communality of army life, show- ing women singing, swimming and putting on make up together, and then by images which stressed the independence of WRAC members, showing them in Arab markets and at a desert oasis. The language too underlined the opportunities for independence and adventure that the WRAC offered, ask- ing recruits 'are you keen to travel?' as 'adventure begins when you join the WRAC' and emphasising both independence and collectivity in its declara- tion that service offered 'a chance to strike out on your own, to develop your independence' whilst at the same time being 'a member of a grand team'.[99] The WRAC attempted to present itself as a means of escape from the constraints of traditional femininity which were being re-imposed in the immediate postwar years.[100]

Although the ATS and WRAC struggled to recruit women in the 1940s, the War Office was unwilling to extend its offer of service to black women. In a debate which highlighted issues of national identity, and the importance of armed service to British conceptions of nationhood, the War Office spent many hours deliberating upon the race and nationality of women eligible for

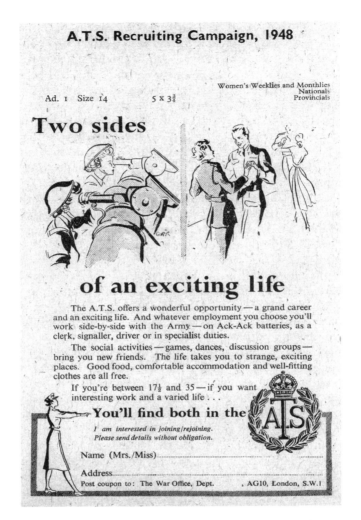

Figure 7.1 'Two sides of an exciting life': Recruitment poster for the Auxiliary
Territorial Service/Women's Royal Army Corps.

service with either the regular women's army corps or with the Reserve,
which served as a part of the Territorial Army. As in the war, there was no
official colour bar which excluded black women from military service, but
enrolment by those of a 'non- European race' was certainly not welcomed.[101]
Britain was experiencing something of a postwar crisis of identity, renegoti-
ating its relationship with a resurgent United States and attempting to come
to terms with the growing desire of many colonies for independence. At the
same time a need for labour to aid in the process of reconstruction meant that
migrants from British colonies were beginning to arrive in Britain to take up

work in important but low paid occupations such as transport and health care. These new arrivals, whilst widely seen as 'our people' when living in far flung parts of the empire, swiftly became 'other' when they took up residence within Britain. The treatment of potential recruits for the WRAC who were not of 'European race' is indicative of a wider set of attitudes towards migrants in postwar British society.

In a confidential memo to HQ Home Command in May 1948 the War Office stated that in order to be eligible for enrolment into the ATS a woman should be either 'a British subject of European race' or 'a British subject or protected person of non-European race'.[102] In the case of this second group of potential recruits however, any applicants were to be referred to the War Office for consideration before enrolment. This was an extension of the wartime policy which had eventually grudgingly allowed non-European women to serve with the ATS in Britain despite the misgivings of James Grigg, then the Secretary of State for War.[103] The War Office set different standards of enrolment for black and white women, arguing that

> A volunteer of non-European race who is of the required standard for enrolment must further... satisfy the selection authorities that she is likely to mix with other auxiliaries and hold her own in the corporate life of the ATS.[104]

ATS recruiting officers were expected to decide 'whether the applicant is considered to possess these qualifications' as 'some volunteers of non-European race may not possess them'.[105] Unlike the US army the British military did not operate an official policy of segregation, but an unofficial policy of resistance to the movement of colonial subjects and immigrants into the regular Units of the British army. Whilst many of these migrants had served with the armed forces during the war, and some were returning to the nation where they had been stationed, they would find that they were not welcome in the postwar British army.[106]

The WRAC was a small part of a much larger, and profoundly conservative organisation decidedly resistant to change of any kind, mirroring in some ways the conservatism of Britain in the late 1940s and 1950s. Although Britain had undergone profound and deep rooted change during the war years and in the reconstruction of the nation as a welfare state, it retained an antipathy towards some underlying shifts in social structure, seen, for instance in the government surveys of 1943 and 1958 which indicated that 58 per cent of women believed that married women, with or without children, should not undertake paid work.[107] As such, it should not be surprising that the employment initially offered to women in the WRAC was less varied than that which had been available in wartime. Despite the statement to the House of Commons by Manny Shinwell, then Secretary of State for War, in March 1948 that in order for recruiting to 'produce better results' the WRAC would have to 'offer varied employment which should suit any women's taste', women who had remained in the Corps or joined since the war generally found themselves employed in positions traditionally associated with femininity.[108] In the new Corps women were overwhelmingly employed as clerks, drivers, switchboard operators, cooks and storewomen, with just a very few occupied in anti-aircraft work. The motto of the new Corps, finally confirmed in its existence by Royal Warrant on 1 February 1949 was '*saviter in modo, fortiter in se*', which translates as 'gentle in manner, resolute in deed', a linguistic attempt to combine the demands of military strength and determination with discourses of femininity which emphasised gentleness and sensitivity which had so concerned policy makers and military leaders since the formation of the WAAC in 1917.[109] Although the work of women in the military had finally been recognised and rewarded by the creation of a permanent space for them within the British armed forces, this space was one which was entirely defined by their gender.

The WRAC, like its counterparts in the Royal Air Force and the Royal Navy, was created, organised and employed along lines which firmly delineated the work and character of the women's Corp from that of their male colleagues in the regular army. Whilst the WRAC was less class-bound than its predecessors, with Officers being predominantly chosen by aptitude and skill, rather than on grounds of birth and social class, its identity was defined by dominant contemporary conceptions of femininity. As such, its members, who wore a uniform which reproduced many aspects of the 'new look' in female fashions, were largely employed in occupations traditionally associated with women, and were designated as a non-combatant corps, unable to defend themselves with arms even in the face of enemy attack. Although dilution was no longer in use the WRAC Charter made it clear that the Corps had been formed in order to 'provide replacements for officers and men', coming into existence as a means of supporting and replacing men, freeing them for the higher status occupation of combat in much the same way as the WAAC and the ATS had been formed.[110] It was assumed that members would leave on marriage and although they had rank parity with men in the army, women in the WRAC were paid at a lower rate than men.[111] In the 1960s, women on officer training courses at Camberley received training in 'beauty culture and flower arranging' as 'it was important for the girls to maintain their femininity' and 'in any officers' mess it will always be the female officers who are asked to do the flower arranging'.[112] Whilst the formation of the WRAC may have offered opportunities for travel and independence to individual women, its overall structure and organisation acted to reinforce traditional gendered identities, placing militarised women squarely behind the military man, both in terms of occupation and in terms of status.

Conclusion

The story of women's work with the military in the first half of the twentieth century is a story of paradoxes, at once a narrative of recognition and progress and at the same time a tale of containment and constraints. Whilst the state and the military recognised the need for women's labour in the armed forces, the appearance of women in military uniform repeatedly challenged existing conceptions of gender. Women in the army threatened both the feminisation of military service and the militarisation of femininity. This dual threat to existing structures meant that the military attempted to constrain female military service, constructing a role for women in the armed forces which was able to draw on their necessary labour whilst at the same time containing them within a space designated as female, preventing them from corrupting the masculinity of the army by controlling their occupations, their appearance and their behaviour. Femininity's links with nurturing and peace, and masculinity's links with combat and warfare, were largely maintained even when large numbers of women served with the army as they did in the First and Second World Wars. As Cynthia Enloe has argued 'militaries need women – but they need women to behave *as the gender "women"*'. (original emphasis)[1] The utilisation of female labour, whilst necessary to the maintenance of large armies such as those which existed in Britain during both of the total wars of the twentieth century, acted as a challenge to underlying structures of gender.

There are striking continuities in the history of women's work with the British army. Most conspicuous perhaps is the ongoing perception of women's military service as a threat to both femininity and masculinity. This was, of course, not just the case in Britain. Time and time again, women who joined armies and undertook military service found that they were treated very differently once they donned an army uniform. Their sexuality was questioned and women were at times subjected to abuse for a perceived lack of femininity, stereotyped as 'unfeminine' 'mannish' lesbians as in the First World War description of 'finely-built girls who called each other old chappie'.[2] More common however was the belief that women in the military had abandoned socially acceptable tropes of moral behaviour when they joined the forces, resulting in the conviction that they were sexually available. This belief had its roots in both the social class of most militarised women and in the history of women's involvement with the army as camp followers, and it was certainly widespread. Maria Botchkareva, the founder of the Women's Battalion of Death in Russia during the First World War recalled how her first night in barracks was spent fighting off the men who took her for 'a woman of loose morals who had made her way into the ranks for the sake of carrying on her illicit trade'.[3] In Britain rumours circulated that the Women's Army Auxiliary Corps (WAAC) of the First World War was merely a front by which the War Office was sending out prostitutes to the troops in France and members of the Auxiliary Territorial Service (ATS) in the Second World War found themselves described by soldiers variously as 'good time girls', 'sexually immoral', 'a league of amateur prostitutes' and 'bloody whores'.[4] Women's military uniform was repeatedly depicted as unfeminine, with an article in *The Globe* in 1917 questioning the impact that women's perceived love affair with uniforms would have 'on the womanhood of the nation later on' and ATS uniforms described as 'taking all the femininity out of a woman'.[5] The separate treatment and status of the women's military units can be understood to a large extent as a means of attempting to maintain the femininity of women in uniform.

Equally present though less often articulated was the belief that the movement of women into the armed forces constituted a concurrent threat to the masculinity of the men who had traditionally formed the entirety of the services. The appropriation of khaki by the Women's Volunteer Reserve (WVR) during the First World War was criticised as undermining the respect due to the 'King's uniform ... rendering it ridiculous by adopting it for themselves as playing at soldiers'.[6] Uniform was a particularly keenly contested area, with the War Office's determination that 'military uniform is not to be adopted' by the WAAC appearing to support Marjorie Garber's contention that 'the sight of women wearing medals or 'orders' attached to their chests' suggests that 'such orders can be unpinned, detached, from men'.[7] The feminisation of military service was felt particularly keenly by men working behind the lines, outside of the uniquely masculine combat zone who may have already felt that their masculinity was somehow lacking when compared to that of the male 'heroes' and 'warriors' in the front line. They attempted to defend their status and their work, arguing that the special conditions of wartime meant that only a small minority of physically powerful yet emotionally contained women would be able to undertake the work of caring for and supporting the combatant men.[8] A similar pattern could be seen in the Second World War, despite earlier moves to ensure that the ATS was established from the beginning of the war as a separate, auxiliary organisation. Two areas in particular, both of which could be seen as marginal to the traditional definition of combat, were the sites of struggles to defend the masculinity of the men occupied there. Women's employment on anti-aircraft sites alongside men was carefully controlled in order to ensure that they did not fire the guns which bought down either planes or pilotless rockets, thus ensuring that they remained non-combatant. Campaigns by women to be accepted into the Home Guard, an organisation which, in its tenuous claim to combat status, could be compared to non-combatant members of the army in the First World War, were also seen to threaten the masculinity of its male members. Whilst for women who wanted to join the Home Guard as full, that is armed, members, 'the unifying force of the rhetoric of national identity' overpowered the concurrent discourses of male and female roles in wartime.[9] The men of the Home Guard for the most part strongly resisted the arming of women members, Lieutenant-General Sir Ralph Eastwood, the Director General of the Home Guard drawing on the 'natural' linkage of men with combat and women with peace in his argument that

> under no circumstances should women be enrolled in the Home Guard...it is undesirable for women to bear arms...and I do not think anyone should be enrolled in the HG who is not under an obligation to bear arms when called upon to do so.[10]

The unstable gender status of men occupied in positions which were peripheral to combat, and which could be theoretically undertaken by women, was defended by the exclusion of women from these roles, even though, as in the case of the anti-aircraft batteries, women worked directly alongside, and were in as much physical danger as, the men. The non-combatant status of women was codified and formalised when women became a permanent feature of the British army. When the Women's Royal Army Corps (WRAC) was founded as a permanent unit of the British army, it was established along lines which stressed both its separate status and the femininity of its female members – as a non-combatant support unit for the male units of the regular army.

However, although the movement of women into the military has been marked by resistance and a determination to ensure the maintenance of existing gendered identities, there has nonetheless *been* a movement of women into the military, and, with a few steps backwards as well as forwards, a gradual process of gender integration. The recognition by the War Office of the usefulness of women's labour which resulted in the formation of the WAAC in 1917 was a result of the much derided work of the various women's voluntary organisations such as the First Aid Nursing Yeomanry (FANY) and the WVR. Without their determination to attest to the possibility of an expanded role for women in wartime, it is unlikely that the army would have established an official women's corps. Although the end of the First World War saw the standing down of the WAAC, alongside a more general postwar backlash against the new roles undertaken by women, the experience of working with the army was remembered by both the women and by the War Office, and when war appeared inevitable in the late 1930s, the ATS was organised relatively quickly and amicably. Women were further integrated into the military during the Second World War, both by the extension of conscription to women and by the incorporation of the ATS into the army in 1941, a move which finally awarded its members full military status, a step away from the official status of camp follower which until that point had formally described them. In this story of progress and achievement, the decision to form the WRAC as a permanent Corps within the regular army after the war can be seen as a recognition by the government and the War Office of women's worth, proof that women had undertaken an important role within the wartime military and were to be rewarded with the creation of the WRAC. However, the formation of the WRAC can also be seen as testimony to the War Office's success in maintaining separate roles for men and women within the army.

The celebratory discourse which rejoices in women's movement into the armed forces as evidence of women's wider progress in society fits both the military's desire to be seen as a modern organisation where equal opportunities are paramount, and the desire of some who study women's lives to see women's history as progress towards equality. However, although women have undoubtedly made progress within the British army, and individual accounts of service with the army often emphasise the sense of personal growth and of achievement that army life gave to many women, this study, which has focused on the discourses of masculinity and femininity, military and civilian, found within various sites of official policy and public debate, illustrates the enduring nature of the belief that militarism is 'naturally' linked with masculinity.[11] The debate which accompanied the expansion of available occupations for women within the British Army in the 1990s demonstrates the continuity of the idea that the military is fundamentally a masculine space, one which women enter on strictly limited terms. As Christopher Dandeker has argued, militaries have to be

> Janus faced organizations: on the one hand they have to respond to the changing strategic context by building militarily effective organizations and, on the other, they have to establish an organization that is responsive to wider social values and thus to the society that pays for the armed services and without whose support they can do little.[12]

Thus, in order to be militarily effective, armies have to combine an ability to adapt to social change in order to both win consent and encourage recruitment from the civilian societies which they purport to represent and defend, with an awareness of combat effectiveness in the shifting conditions of modern warfare. A certain elasticity has to exist in order for the armed forces to adapt to changing military demands and social values. As in the first half of the twentieth century, this was the case in the Strategic Defence Review, which was responding to both the developing demands of the military for a more highly skilled and technically qualified workforce and to the shifting patterns of gender in British society. However, a nuanced reading of the debate which accompanied the Review demonstrates the endurance of the belief that the military, especially when taking part in warfare, is an essentially male territory. Indeed, combat remains a key means by which femininity and masculinity are defined and distinguished.

The debate which accompanied the expansion of women's roles in the army contrasted a discourse which largely represented this expansion as evidence of the growth of equal opportunities and equal rights in contemporary Britain with one which defended masculinity's links with the military and, essentially, with combat. The decision, as part of the government's Strategic Defence Review of 1997, to open up an expanded range of roles for women in the army was certainly presented as part of a modernising process, described as 'another step towards our promise to modernise the armed forces' in the House of Commons by George Robinson, the Secretary of State for Defence.[13] John Reid, Minister for the Armed Forces, expanded on this in his statement that 'today's armed forces must be seen as somewhere where women can make progress', as an institution where 'ability, rather than gender, social class or ethnic origin must be the criterion according to which recruitment and promotion to leadership takes place'.[14] The new emphasis on technical skill rather than on brute force in the military combined with wider debate about gender roles in society to open up new roles for women in the British army. As in the first half of the twentieth century, however, the demand for an appropriately trained labour force in the military was balanced by a widely shared consensus that women should be excluded from the 'front line' of combat, and although the Strategic Defence Review did increase the percentage of regular army posts open to women from 47 per cent to 70 per cent, women were still excluded from front-line roles in the infantry, the Household Cavalry and the Royal Armoured Corps.[15]

The ongoing exclusion of women from combat roles was largely represented as an issue of 'operational effectiveness', with MPs arguing that the movement of women into fighting roles would impair the troops' 'front-line effectiveness', commenting that 'it would be operationally unsustainable and wholly repugnant if female soldiers were to fix bayonets and close with the enemy'.[16] In a statement which would not have been out of place in the debates of the first half of the century Sir Geoffrey Johnson-Smith MP drew on his own memories of combat in the Second World War to argue that

> I was in a fox-hole and I am damned if I would have found it suitable to have a woman there, exposed as I was to front line infantry from the other side... there are plenty of dangerous jobs that women can do, but there are some that are not appropriate.[17]

In a further echo of earlier debates about women's role in the military, MPs commented on the possibility of sexual relationships between male and female soldiers in the front line, Robert Key's comment that 'many wives will worry about an increase in the number of women in the forces' being trumped by Desmond Swayne's colourful claim that 'to be with a woman and not to have intercourse with her is more difficult than to raise the dead', to which he added 'as one is not capable of the latter, one is certainly not capable of the former'.[18] Although the House did vote in favour of implementing the Strategic Defence Review, front-line combat positions remained closed to women. The Secretary of State for Defence announced that further research would be carried out into the possibility of moving women into front-line combat roles, but in 2002 concluded that 'the case for lifting the current restrictions on women serving in close combat roles had not been made'.[19] The study of women in the armed forces examined women's physiological and psychological aptitude for combat, concluding that only 1 per cent of women 'can equal the performance of the average man' and that 'the capacity for aggression was generally lower for women'.[20] However, the key argument put forward against allowing women into front-line combat positions where they would have to 'close with and kill the enemy face to face' was one of combat effectiveness as 'there is no way of knowing whether mixed gender teams function as well as all male teams in a close combat situation'.[21] The prohibition on women in front-line combat remains in place in the army, and although women serve in front-line positions on Royal Navy ships and can fly combat aircraft in the Royal Air Force, the close combat roles of infantry and tank regiments remain the preserve of men. Despite the huge social, economic and cultural changes which Britain underwent in the first half of the twentieth century, and despite, in some ways' revolutionary movement of women into the armed forces, the maintenance of traditional gender roles within that institution has been remarkably resilient.

It is important not to oversimplify the history of women's work with the military, not to write it as either a straightforward record of progress and achievement, nor as a simple catalogue of the mechanisms by which women's movement towards new opportunities and roles was constrained and controlled. The work of the feminist historian is, to a large degree, about tracing the patterns of change and continuity in women's lives, tracking the subtle and not so subtle shifts in gender roles which occur over time, attempting to account for them and rediscovering the many small battles of women (and sometimes men) in the past for equality. In times of war and in peace debates over women's role in the military reflect wider patterns of gender relationships and gendered identities. The development of a role for women in the military and the concurrent attempts to constrain female armed service demonstrate those patterns of change and continuity which make up the history of gender relationships. Whilst women's movement into the armed forces can be seen as indicative of changes in gender relationships, the continuity of the idea that soldiering is a man's job and a man's job alone demonstrates the military's enduring role as a key site within which masculinity and femininity are defined.

Notes

Preface

1 Employment of Women in the Armed Forces Steering Group, *Women in the Armed Forces*, London: Ministry of Defence, 2002, p. 51.
2 Employment of Women in the Armed Forces Steering Groups, *Women in the Armed Forces: Summary*, London: Ministry of Defence, 2002, p. 6.
3 J. Bourke, 'From Surrey to Basra, abuse is a fact of British army life', *The Guardian*, 26/2/2005.
4 http://www.arrse.co.uk (accessed 7 June 2005).
5 Annual Report and Accounts 2002–2003, http://www.mod.uk/publications/performance/2002/chapter 5 (accessed 8 June 2005).

1 Introduction: gendering war

1 http://news.bbc.co.uk/1/low/scotland (accessed 6 June 2002).
2 K. Thewelweit, *Male Fantasies. Volume One: Women, Floods, Bodies, History*, London: Polity, 1987.
3 J. Braine, *Room at the Top*, London: Penguin, 1957, p. 95.
4 C. Enloe, *The Morning After. Sexual Politics at the End of the Cold War*, Berkeley, CA: University of California Press, 1993 p. 184.
5 M. Botchkareva, *Yashka: My Life as a Peasant and Exile* (as set down by Isaac Don Levine), London: Constable, 1919, p. 91.
6 Ibid., p. 159.
7 L. Bryant, *Six Months in Red Russia*, New York: George H. Doran, 1918, p. 212.
8 F. Sandes, *An Englishwoman Sergeant in the Serbian Army*, London: Hodder & Stoughton, 1918, F. Sandes, *The Autobiography of a Woman Soldier: A Brief Record of Adventure With the Serbian Army 1916–1919*, London: H.F.G. Witherby, 1927.
9 S. N. Hendrix, 'In the Army: Women, Camp Followers and Gender Roles in the British Army in the French and Indian Wars, 1755–1765' in G. De Groot and C. Penniston-Bird (eds) *A Soldier and A Woman: Sexual Integration in the Military*, Harlow: Longman, 2000, pp. 33–48.
10 De Groot, 'Introduction: Arms and the Woman', in *A Soldier and a Woman*, p. 10.
11 M. RWP. Higonnet and P.L.R. Higonnet, 'The Double Helix' in M. Higonnet, J. Jenson, S. Michel and M. Collins Weitz (eds) *Behind the Lines: Gender and the Two World Wars*, New Haven, CT: Yale University Press, 1987, p. 34.
12 Homer, *The Iliad*, trans. R. Fitzgerald, Oxford: Oxford University Press, 1984, Book 6, p. 111, 1488–1491.
13 S. Weil, *The Iliad or the Poem of Force*, trans. M. McCarthy, Wallingord: Pendle Hill Paperbacks, 1956, first published 1940/41.
14 Homer, *The Iliad*, 1984, Book 6, p. 104, 1243–1247.
15 Ibid., Book 6, p. 100, 182–185.

16 U. Rublack, 'Wench and Maiden: Women, War and the Pictorial Function of the Feminine in German Cities in the Early Modern Period', *History Workshop Journal*, Vol. 44, Autumn 1997, p. 3.
17 C. Enloe, *The Morning After*, pp. 239–241.
18 H. von Trietschke, 'Politics', Book one, trans. 1916, quoted in S. Oldfield, *Women Against the Iron Fist: Alternatives to Militarism 1900–1989*, Oxford: Blackwell, 1989, p. 7.
19 H. Newbolt, 'Vitaï Lampada', 1898, quoted in P. Fussell, *The Great War and Modern Memory*, Oxford: Oxford University Press, 1975, p. 25.
20 A. Tennyson, *Poems of Tennyson*, Oxford: Oxford University Press, 1917, p. 420.
21 R. Brooke, *The Collected Poems of Rupert Brooke*, London: Sidgwick & Jackson, 1918, p. 5.
22 F. T. Marinetti, 'The Founding and Manifesto of Futurism', first published 1909, in R.W. Flint (ed.) *Marinetti: Selected Writings*, London: Secker & Warburg, 1971, p. 42.
23 J. Keegan, *A History of Warfare*, London: Hutchinson, 1993, pp. 75–76.
24 J. Laffin, *Women in Battle*, London: Ackland-Schuman, 1967, p. 184.
25 Ibid., p. 185.
26 An exception to this is Joanna Bourke's *An Intimate History of Killing: Face to Face Killing in Twentieth Century Warfare*, London: Granta, 1999.
27 M. Gilbert, *The First World War*, London: Wiedenfield & Nicholson, 1994, *The Second World War*, London: Wiedenfield & Nicholson, 1989.
28 P. Fussell (ed.) *The Bloody Game: An Anthology of Modern War*, London: Scribners, 1991.
29 A. Sinclair (ed.) *The War Decade: An Anthology of the 1940s*, London: Hamilton, 1989.
30 M. Higonnet, 'Not So Quiet in No-Woman's Land', in M. Cooke and A. Wollacott (eds) *Gendering War Talk*, Princeton, NJ: Princeton University Press, 1993.
31 S. Hynes (ed.) *The Soldier's Tale: Bearing Witness to Modern Warfare*, New York: Penguin, 1997, p. 5.
32 K. Muir, *Arms and the Woman*, London: Coronet, 1992, p. 24.
33 *Chicago Tribune*, 11/3/2004.
34 J. Goldstein, *War and Gender: How Gender Shapes the War System and Vice Versa*, Cambridge: Cambridge University Press, 2001, p. 80.
35 D. Izraeli, 'Gendering Military Service in the Israel Defence Force' in G. De Groot and C. Penniston-Bird (eds) *A Soldier and a Woman*, p. 264.
36 Bourke, *An Intimate History of Killing*, p. 341.
37 Goldstein, *War and Gender*, p. 61.
38 Bourke, *An Intimate History of Killing*, p. 338.
39 C. Enloe, *Maneuvers: The International Politics of Militarising Women's Lives*, Berkeley, CA: University of California Press, 2000, p. 283.
40 Goldstein, *War and Gender*, p. 85.
41 B. Alpern Engel, 'The Womanly Face of War: Soviet Women Remember World War II' in N. Dombrowski (ed.) *Women and War in the Twentieth Century: Enlisted with or Without Consent*, New York: Garland Publishing, 1999, p. 150.
42 C. Enloe, *Maneuvers*, p. 251.
43 L. Bryant, *Six Months in Red Russia*, New York: George H. Doran, 1918, p. 213.
44 F. Sandes, *An Englishwoman Sergeant in the Serbian Army*, Introduction, 1918, p. VI.
45 Keegan, *A History of Warfare*, p. 76.
46 See for example, Oldfield, *Women Against the Iron Fist*.
47 M. L. Degan, *The History of the Women's Peace Movement*, New York: Garland Publishing, 1972, p. 40.
48 C. Marshall, 'Women and War', first published 1915, in M. Kamester and J. Vellacott (eds) *Militarism Versus Feminism: Writings on Women and War*, London: Virago, 1987, p. 39.
49 Y. Bennett, 'Vera Brittain and the Peace Pledge Union' in R. Roach Pierson (ed.) *Women and Peace: Theoretical, Historical and Practical Perspectives*, London: Croom Helm, 1987, p. 197.

50 V. Woolf, *Three Guineas*, London: Hogarth Press, 1938, p. 197. Julian Bell had been killed in 1937, whilst working as an ambulance driver in Spain.

51 L. Segal, *Is the Future Female? Troubled Thoughts on Contemporary Feminism*, London: Virago, 1987, p. 163.

52 A. Dworkin, *Pornography: Men Possessing Women*, London: The Women's Press, 1987, p. 51.

53 See for example L. Fenner, 'Either You Need These Women or You Do Not: Informing the Debate on Military Service and Citizenship', *Gender Issues*, Summer 1998, Vol. 16, No. 3, J. Hicks Stiehm, *Arms and the Enlisted Woman*, Philadelphia, PA: Temple University Press, 1989, Major General J. Holm, *Women in the Military: An Unfinished Revolution*, California: Presidio, 1982.

54 In 1981 the United States National Organization for Women called for women to be registered for the draft alongside men. A. Carter, 'Should Women Be Soldiers or Pacifists?' in L. A. Lorentzen and J. Turpin (eds) *The Women and War Reader*, New York: New York University Press, 1998, p. 35.

55 J. Goldstein, *War and Gender*, pp. 94–95, Lucy Noakes, *War and the British: Gender and National Identity 1939–1991*, London: I.B. Tauris, 1998, p. 146.

56 Muir, *Arms and the Woman*, p. 22.

57 A. Marwick, *War and Social Change in the Twentieth Century*, London: Macmillan, 1974.

58 G. Braybon, *Women Workers in the First World War: The British Experience*, London: Croom Helm, 1981, P. Summerfield, *Women Workers in the Second World War: Production and Patriarchy in Conflict*, London: Croom Helm, 1984, G. Braybon and P. Summerfield, *Out of the Cage: Women's Experiences in Two World Wars*, London: Pandora, 1987.

59 P. Summerfield, *Reconstructing Women's Wartime Lives: Discourse and Subjectivity in Oral Histories of the Second World War*, Manchester: Manchester University Press, 1998, pp. 2–3.

60 M. Shaw, *Post-Military Society: Militarization, Demilitarization and War at the End of the Twentieth Century*, Philadelphia, PA: Temple University Press, 1991, p. 188.

61 C. Dandeker, 'Don't Ask, Don't Tell and Don't Pursue: Is a Pragmatic Solution the Way Forward for the Armed Services in Today's Society?', *RUSI Journal*, June 1999, pp. 87–89.

62 This is slowly improving, evidenced by the Royal Navy's work with the gay campaigning group Stonewall to improve working conditions for gay and lesbian members of the force in 2005, and its decision to advertise on the Gay press for recruits.

63 S. Grayzel, *Women's Identities at War: Gender, Motherhood and Politics in Britain and France During the First World War*, Chapel Hill, NC: University of North Carolina Press, 1999, p. 200.

64 See, for example, D. Mitchell, *Women on the Warpath. The Story of the Women of the First World War*, London: Cape, 1966, R. Terry, *Women in Khaki: The Story of the British Woman Soldier*, London: Columbus, 1988.

2 Early days: women and the armed forces before 1914

1 C. Hymowitz and M. Wiseman, *A History of Women in America*, New York: Bantam, 1978, p. 29, cited in C. Enloe, *Maneuvers: The International Politics of Militarizing Women's Lives*, Berkeley, CA: University of California Press, 2000, p. 41.

2 Enloe, *Maneuvers*, p. 40.

3 See J. Wheelwright, *Amazons and Military Maids: Women Who Dressed as Men in the Pursuit of Life, Liberty and Happiness*, London: Pandora, 1989.

4 G. Dawson, *Soldier Heroes: British Adventure, Empire and the Imagining of Masculinity*, London: Routledge, 1994, pp. 233–258.

5 M. Paris, *Warrior Nation: Images of War in British Popular Culture 1850–2000*, London: Reaktion Books, 2000.

6 J. Richards (ed.) *Imperialism and Juvenile Literature*, Manchester: Manchester University Press, 1989, p. 3.

7 Paris, *Warrior Nation*, p. 50.

8 Ibid., p. 57.

9 Cited in J. Mackay and P. Thane 'The Englishwoman' in R. Colls and P. Dodd (eds) *Englishness: Politics and Culture 1880–1920*, Kent: Croom Helm, 1986, p. 193.

10 Mackay and Thane, 'The Englishwoman', p. 196.

11 A. Davin, 'Imperialism and Motherhood', *History Workshop Journal*, Vol. 5, 1978.

12 G. Stanley Hall, *Adolescence: Its Psychology, and its Relations to Physiology, Anthropology, Sociology, Sex, Crime, Religion and Education*, New York: Appleton, 1904.

13 C. Dyhouse, *Girls Growing Up In Victorian and Edwardian England*, London: Routledge & Kegan Paul, 1981.

14 The Hon. Mrs Evelyn Cecil, 'The Needs of South Africa II: Female Emigration', *The Nineteenth Century*, April 1902, cited in P. Thane, 'The British Imperial State and the Construction of National Identities' in B. Melman (ed.) *Borderlines: Genders and Identities in War and Peace 1870–1930*, London: Routledge, 1998, p. 31.

15 E. Ewing, *Women in Uniform Through the Centuries*, London: Batsford, 1975, p. 40.

16 Ibid., pp. 42–44.

17 A. Summers, *Angels and Citizens: British Women as Military Nurses 1854–1914*, London: Routledge & Kegan Paul, 1988 p. 278.

18 Ibid., pp. 278–279.

19 Ibid., p. 279.

20 Dyhouse, *Girls Growing Up*, p. 110.

21 R. Baden-Powell, *Scouting for Boys*, London, 1908, p. 3.

22 E. Wade, *The World Guide Chief, Olave, Lady Baden-Powell*, London: Hutchinson, 1957, p. 68, cited in Dyhouse, *Girls Growing Up*, p. 111.

23 R. Baden-Powell, *Girl Guides: A Suggestion for Character Training for Girls*, London: Bishopgate Press, 1909, p. 4, cited in Mackay and Thane, *The Englishwoman*, p. 216.

24 A. Summers, 'Edwardian Militarism' in R. Samuel (ed.) *Patriotism: The Making and Unmaking of British National Indentity*, Vol. 1, London: Routledge, 1988, p. 237.

25 H. Cunningham, *The Volunteer Force: A Social and Political History 1859–1908*, London: Croom Helm, 1975, p. 129.

26 Summers, 'Edwardian Militarism', pp. 243–244.

27 J. Springhall, 'The Boy Scouts, Class and Militarism in Relation to British Youth Movements', *International Review of Social History*, Vol. 16, No. 2, 1971, p. 135.

28 Paris, *Warrior Nation*, pp. 91–92.

29 Ibid., pp. 100–101.

30 C. E. G. Masterson, *The Heart of the Empire*, 1901, p. viii, cited in A. Davin, 'Imperialism and Motherhood' in R. Samuel (ed.) *Patriotism*, Vol. 1, London: Routledge, 1988, p. 217.

31 See, for example, E. Pankhurst, *My Own Story*, London: Eveleigh Nash, 1914.

32 J. Purvis, 'Deeds, Not Words: Daily Life in the Women's Social and Political Union in Edwardian Britain', in J. Purvis and S. Stanley Holton (eds) *Votes for Women*, London: Routledge, 2000, p. 135.

33 E. S. Pankhurst, *The Suffragette Movement: An Intimate Account of Persons and Ideals*, London: Longman, Green, 1931, p. 265–266.

34 Summers, *Angels and Citizens*, pp. 204–208.

35 Cited in R. Terry, *Women in Khaki: The Story of the British Woman Soldier*, London: Columbus, 1988, p. 25, no further reference given.

36 *Women and War*, June 1910.

37 'A Foreword by the C.O.', *Women and War*, June 1910.

38 'Why Private Muldoon Changed His Mind', *Women and War*, June 1910.

39 *Daily Graphic*, 25/2/1908, cited in I. Ward, *F.A.N.Y. Invicta*, London: Hutchinson, 1955, pp. 23–24.

40 K. Robert, 'Gender, Class and Patriotism in Britain: Women's Paramilitary Units in First World War Britain', *The International History Review*, XIX, February 1997, pp. 52–65.

41 Poem from undated edition of *Women and War*, cited in H. Popham, *The Story of the Women's Transport Service FANY 1907–1984*, London: Leo Cooper, 1984, p. 16.

42 Ibid., p. 22.
43 Ibid., p. 30.
44 P. Beauchamp, *Fanny Went to War*, London: Routledge & Kegan Paul, 1940, p. 1.
45 Ward, *F.A.N.Y. Invicta*, p. 27.
46 Cited in Popham, *The Story of the Women's Transport Service*, p. 4. No further reference given.
47 Cited in Terry, *Women in Khaki*, p. 27. No further reference given.
48 Cited in Ward, *F.A.N.Y. Invicta*, pp. 34–35. No further reference given.
49 Popham, *The Story of the Women's Transport Service*, p. 5.
50 Ward, *F.A.N.Y. Invicta*, p. 36.
51 *London Budget*, 2/11/1913.
52 *Nursing Mirror*, 20/3/9, cited in Summers, *Angels and Citizens*, p. 208.
53 Summers, *Angels and Citizens*, p. 217.
54 Mrs Robinson in Ward, *F.A.N.Y. Invicta*, p. 31.
55 *First Aid*, April 1907, cited in Summers, *Angels and Citizens*, p. 212.
56 British Red Cross Devonshire Branch, JSC Davis, County Director, *Devonshire VAD-A Handbook for Workers*, Exeter, 1910, p. 8, cited in Summers, *Angels and Citizens*, p. 223.
57 Summers, *Angels and Citizens*, p. 220.
58 *First Aid*, January 1913, cited in Summers, *Angels and Citizens*, p. 229.
59 *First Aid*, December 1913, cited in Summers, *Angels and Citizens*, p. 229.
60 Summers, *Angels and Citizens*, p. 231.
61 Terry, *Women in Khaki*, p. 27, Ward, *F.A.N.Y. Invicta*, p. 26.

3 'The Women Were Marvellous': the First World War and the female volunteer

1 G. De Groot, *Blighty: British Society in the Era of the Great War*, London: Longman, 1996, p. 46.
2 V. Brittain, *Chronicle of Youth: War Diary 1913–1917*, A. Bishop and T. Smart (eds) London: Victor Gollancz, 1981, p. 84.
3 E. Miles, *Untold Tales of Wartime London*, London: Cecil Palmer, 1930, p. 13.
4 Brooke cited in A. Marwick, *The Deluge: British Society and the First World War*, London: Macmillan, 1965, this edition, 1991, p. 76.
5 A. Gregory, 'British "War Enthusiasm" in 1914: A Reassessment' in G. Braybon (ed.) *Evidence, History and the Great War: Historians and the Impact of 1914–1918*, Oxford: Berghahn Books, 2003, p. 80.
6 Ibid., p. 77.
7 *The Times*, 1/8/1914.
8 See, for example, the propagandist text, W. Le Queux, *German Atrocities: A Record of Shameless Deeds*, London: n.p., 1914. Posters were also produced which played on ideas of British civilisation and German barbarity, urging men to join up in order to protect the rights of small nations and of civilians, such as the 1914 poster entitled 'Remember Belgium: Your Country Needs You' which showed a British soldier standing guard while a woman and young children fled from a burning homestead. Imperial War Museum (IWM), Department of Art, Catalogues and Posters, PRC 19, PST 5901.
9 See, for example, descriptions of the demonstrations in the *Daily Chronicle* and the *Globe*, 5/8/1914, both cited in Gregory 'British "War Enthusiasm" ', p. 78.
10 M. Pugh, *Women and the Women's Movement in Britain*, Basingstoke: Macmillan, this edition 2000 (first published 1992), p. 7.
11 Marwick, *The Deluge*, p. 75. For example, Edward Brittain, brother of Vera, first tried to enlist on 5 August, appeared before the Officer Training Corps panel on 11 September, and was finally 'gazetted' on 21 November. Brittain's father was opposed to his joining the Army. Brittain, *Chronicle of Youth* 1981, pp. 88–126.
12 Mrs Alec Tweedie, *Women and Soldiers*, London: Bodley Head, 1918, p. 2.

13 D. Thom, *Nice Girls and Rude Girls: Women Workers in World War One*, London: I.B. Tauris, 1998, p. 29.

14 M. Pugh, *Women and the Women's Movement in Britain 1914–1999*, 1992, p. 18.

15 *Daily Telegraph*, 10/8/1914.

16 Brittain, *Chronicle of Youth*, p. 89.

17 *Daily Call*, 19/11/1914.

18 M. Frances Billington, *The Roll Call of Serving Women: A Record of Women's Work for Combatants and Sufferers in the Great War*, London: The Religious Tract Society, 1915, p. 27.

19 IWM, Department of Art, Catalogues and Posters, PRC 75/ PST/0313.

20 Lady Frances Balfour, 'Women as Standard Bearers', *Gentlewoman*, 21/11/1914. Belgium was routinely referred to as female in contemporary writing about the German invasion. For further discussion see S. Grayzel, *Women's Identities at War: Gender, Motherhood and Politics in Britain and France During the First World War*, Chapel Hill, NC: University of North Carolina Press, 1999, Chapter 2; R. Harris, 'The Child of the Barbarian: Rape, Race and Nationalism in France During the First World War', *Past And Present*, Vol. 141, October 1993.

21 IWM, Department of Art, Catalogues and Posters, PRC 69/POS/247.

22 M. Garrett Fawcett, 'Women's Work in Wartime', *Contemporary Review*, December 1914, Vol. CV1, p. 782.

23 *Evening Standard*, 26/8/1914.

24 Ibid.

25 IWM, Department of Art, Catalogues and Posters, PRC 55/PST/4884.

26 *The Times*, 29/8/1914.

27 Cited in C. Haste, *Keep the Home Fires Burning: Propaganda in the First World War*, London: Allen Lane, 1977, p. 56.

28 'To the Women of Britain', Parliamentary Recruiting Committee poster, IWM, Department of Art, Catalogues and Poster, PRC 69/PST 4904.

29 For more on this campaign, see N. Gullace, 'White Feathers and Wounded Men: Female Patriotism and the Memory of the Great War', *Journal of British Studies*, Vol. 36, No. 2, April 1997.

30 Haste, *Keep the Home Fires Burning*, p. 56.

31 *The Times*, 13/8/1914.

32 *Westminster Gazette*, 26/8/1914.

33 Margaret Llewelyn Davies, *Maternity: Letters from Working Women*, London: Virago, 1978, first published 1915.

34 *Daily Mail*, 18/8/1914, *Sunday Pictorial*, 21/3/19.

35 'Glaxo' advert, *The Woman Worker*, August 1917.

36 For a discussion of the 'war babies' panic see Grayzel, *Women's Identities at War*, pp. 91–103, S. Kingsley Kent, *Making Peace: The Reconstruction of Gender in Post-War Britain*, Princeton, NJ: Princeton University Press, 1993, pp. 28–30, A. Woollacott, '"Khaki Fever" and its Control: Gender, Class, Age and Sexual Morality on the British Homefront in the First World War', *Journal of Contemporary History*, Vol. 29, 1994.

37 Billington, *The Roll Call of Serving Women*, p. 96.

38 *Daily Express*, 3/11/1914.

39 *The Herald*, 19/12/1914.

40 C. Nina Boyle, 'The Prime Minister and a scrap of paper: the C.D. Acts re-established in a new forum', *The Vote*, December 1914.

41 *The Herald*, 19/12/1914.

42 Mrs Alec Tweedie, 'Martial Law and Women', *English Review*, 3/2/1917.

43 Tweedie, *Women and Soldiers*, p. 85. For a discussion of the construction of sexually active women as 'internal enemies' in the Second World War, see S. Gubar, 'This is My Rifle, This is My Gun: World War Two and the Blitz on Women' in M. R. Higonnet, J. Jenson, S. Michel and M. Collins Weitz (eds) *Behind the Lines: Gender and the Two World Wars*, New Haven, CT: Yale University Press, 1987, pp. 227–259.

44 For a description of these see Billington, *The Roll Call of Serving Women*, pp. 84–85. In response to concerns about 'the alleged prevalence of drinking among women', which was believed to be undermining national efficiency as well as moral behaviour, the Home Office set up a Women's Advisory Committee under the leadership of Mrs L. Creighton to investigate levels of drinking by women in working class districts. The Women's Advisory Committee Report concluded in February 1916 that although drink and 'immorality' were often connected, sustained increased alcohol consumption was only found amongst women who had drunk to excess before the war. The National Archives (TNA), Home Office (HO) 185/258, *Women's Advisory Committee, Reports and Correspondence, Report of the Women's Advisory Committee*, February 1916, Appendix, p. 21.

45 The Report of the Women's Advisory Committee recommended the formation of women police patrols, TNA, HO 185/258, p. 9. See D. May, 'Women Police: The Early Years', *Police Review*, No. 9, 9/3/1979, pp. 358–365 for more on the early history of women police officers.

46 *The Times*, 31/8/1914.

47 Ibid., 11/8/1914.

48 *News of the World*, 16/8/1914.

49 *Nation*, 19/1/1918.

50 C. Hamilton, *William – An Englishman*, London: Persephone, 1999, first published London: Skeffington & Son, 1919, p. 29.

51 The suffrage movement was not the only oppositional force in British society which suspended its actions on the outbreak of war. Both the Home Rule movement and the anti-independence forces in Ireland, such as the Ulster Volunteer Force, suspended their campaigns temporarily in 1914.

52 J. Purvis, *Emmeline Pankhurst: A Biography*, London: Routledge, 2002, p. 271.

53 Ibid., p. 269.

54 M. Potter-Daggett, *Women Wanted: The Story Written in Blood Red Letters on the Horizon of the Great World War*, London: Hodder & Stoughton, 1918, p. 225.

55 Purvis, *Emmeline Pankhurst: A Biography*, p. 277.

56 *The Times*, 7/7/1915, *The Daily Chronicle*, 19/7/1915.

57 M. Potter-Daggett, *Women Wanted*, p. 78.

58 *The Times*, 7/7/1915.

59 *Hansard, House of Commons*, 5th Series, Vol. 81, 1916, col. 1193. Martin Pugh comments that, in the alliance between the Pankhursts and Lloyd George, at this point Minister for Munitions and later to become Prime Minister, 'the Pankhursts shrewdly attached themselves to the one politician whose star was rising, and effected a satisfying transition from public enemies to arch-patriots.' Pugh, *Women and the Women's Movement in Britain*, p. 9.

60 Pugh, *Women and the Women's Movement in Britain*, p. 9.

61 *Evening News*, 4/6/1915.

62 *Kentish Independent*, 8/3/1918.

63 *Daily Telegraph*, 2/6/1915.

64 *Common Cause*, 23/10/1914.

65 Ibid., 7/8/1914. For more on the shifting ideology of the feminist movement in wartime, see S. Kingsley Kent, *Making Peace*.

66 Women's International League for Peace and Freedom, *Monthly Newsheet*, November 1917.

67 *Gentlewoman*, 17/7/1915, figures from M. Pugh, *Women and the Women's Movement in Britain*, 2000, p. 10.

68 *Millgate Monthly*, July 1915, p. 593.

69 *The Times*, 8/8/1914.

70 IWM, WWC, Volunteer Corps, Women's Emergency Corps, 2/1.

71 *Liverpool Daily Post*, 28/9/1915.

72 H. Popham, *The Story of the Women's Transport Service*, London: Leo Cooper, 1984, pp. 15–26.

73 Dr Inglis went on to organise the Scottish Women's Hospitals, which served in France, Serbia, Romania and Russia. Similarly, Louisa Garrett Anderson and Flora Murray, both active in the pre-war feminist movement, ran a women's hospital at Wimereux, near Boulogne and Endell Street Hospital in London.
74 Tweedie, *Women and Soldiers*, p. 9.
75 E. Robins, 'War Service at Home', *Nineteenth Century and After*, Vol. 126, November 1914, p. 1113.
76 Ibid., p. 1115.
77 *Daily Citizen*, 24/2/1915.
78 Women's Emergency Corps, First Annual Report, 1915, IWM, WWC, Volunteer Corps, WEC, 2/3, p. 4.
79 Prior to this, women could register on the War Service Register, but by June 1915, of 87,241 women who had registered, only 2,332 had been placed in war-related employment. *Hansard*, Vol. 71, col. 1919.
80 *Hansard*, Vol. 73, col. 141.
81 Ibid., cols 94 and 439.
82 *Millgate Monthly*, July 1915, p. 593.
83 K. Robert, 'Gender, Class and Patriotism: Women's Paramilitary Units in First World War Britain', *The International History Review*, Vol. XIX, No. 1, February 1997, pp. 52–65, identifies seven uniformed, voluntary, paramilitary Units for women in existence by 1916. This number excludes other uniformed, volunteer organisations such as the 'Green Cross', the Women's Reserve Ambulance Corps which met soldiers returning from the front.
84 *Common Cause*, January 1915.
85 Ibid.
86 Recruiting Pamphlet, IWM, Women's Work Collection, Voluntary Corps, 2/27.
87 *Women's Volunteer Reserve Magazine*, Vol. 1, No. 1, January 1916, p. 5.
88 *The London Opinion*, 20/1/1915.
89 Report of London Battalion, IWM, Women's Work Collection, Voluntary Corps 2/25, J. Watson, 'Khaki Girls, VADs and Tommy's Sisters: Gender and Class in First World War Britain', *The International History Review*, Vol. XIX, No. 1, February 1997, p. 38. Additionally, the foundation of the WAAC in 1917 meant that women could be paid for undertaking many of the duties that the WVR had carried out voluntarily.
90 *Women's Volunteer Reserve Magazine*, Vol. 1, No. 1, January 1916, p. 5.
91 Recruiting Pamphlet, IWM, Women's Work Collection, Voluntary Corps, 2/27.
92 For more on this, see Grayzel, *Women's Identities at War*, pp. 192–196.
93 Letter to *The Morning Post*, 16/8/1915.
94 *Bournemouth Echo*, 22/4/1915.
95 See, for example, the 1914 recruitment poster 'Remember Scarborough', where potential recruits were told that 'The Germans who brag of their "Culture" have shown what it is made of by murdering defenceless women and children at Scarborough. But this only strengthens Great Britain's resolve to crush the German Barbarian. Enlist Now!' In terms of wartime gender roles, this poster is also interesting for its use of a fiercely militaristic Britannia, urging men to war in front of the burning town. The poster used an original painting by Edith Kemp-Welch and was widely reproduced. For example, it was used as the frontispiece to a special edition of *The Windsor Magazine*, 'Recruiting By Poster: A Remarkable Campaign', No. 246, 1915. IWM, Department of Art, Catalogues and Posters, PRC 29/PST/8685.
96 *Yorkshire Evening Post*, 17/12/14.
97 *Ladies Pictorial*, 26/12/1914.
98 Letter to *The Ladies Pictorial*, 21/8/1915.
99 Letter: 'The King's Uniform', to *The Morning Post*, 26/7/1915.
100 Letter to the *Newcastle Chronicle*, 19/3/1915. It should be noted that both of these letters provoked a large response from readers, both supporting and opposing the appearance and activities of the WVR.

101 *Evening News*, 9/8/1916 and 13/9/1916.

102 *Evening Standard*, 21/8/1915.

103 *Midland Country Express*, 30/4/1915.

104 *Northern Mail*, 12/3/1915.

105 WVR Recruitment pamphlet, IWM, WWC, Volunteer Corps, WVR 2/27.

106 For a definitive discussion of the influence of eugenics on women's lives during this period, see A. Davin, 'Imperialism and Motherhood', *History Workshop Journal*, Vol. 5, 1978.

107 'Sacrament of the Dust',*Women's Volunteer Reserve Magazine*, Vol. 1, No. 12, December 1916, p. 240.

108 *Women's Volunteer Reserve Magazine*, Vol. 2, No. 17, March 1917, p. 45.

109 'Ats off to the Women', *Women's Volunteer Reserve Magazine*, Vol. 1, No. 1, January 1916, p. 13.

110 *Birmingham Daily Mail*, 15/10/15, *Daily Mail*, 7/8/1915.

111 *Morning Post*, 6/7/1915.

112 *Rugby Advertiser*, 6/11/1915.

113 *Northern Mail*, 9/6/1915.

114 *The Ladies Pictorial*, 20/2/1915.

115 *Daily Express*, 24/8/1915.

116 Marchioness of Londonderry, *Retrospect*, London: Frederick Muller, 1938, p. 112.

117 *Daily Graphic*, 22/7/1916.

118 *Evening Standard*, 13/1/1916.

119 Women's Emergency Corps First Annual Report, 1915, IWM, WWC, Volunteer Corps, WEC 2/3, p. 6.

120 Lady Londonderry, cited in Col. J. Cowper, *A Short History of QMAAC*, Aldershot: WRAC Association, 1957, p. 10.

121 J. Cowper, *A Short History of the QMAAC*, 1957, p. 11.

122 *Bayswater Chronicle*, 12/12/1914.

123 *Ladies Pictorial*, 14/11/14.

124 *The Observer*, 13/8/1916, *The Hendon Advertiser*, 3/5/1918.

125 Susan Kingsley Kent argues that the bombardment of the east coast towns of Scarborough, Whitby and Hartlepool in December 1914, by blurring the distinction between home front and war front, led to a shift in feminist discourse away from the reassertion of separate spheres seen at the beginning of the war and towards arguments that women had a wider, public, duty to fill in wartime. S. Kingsley Kent, *Making Peace*, p. 31.

126 *Hansard: House of Lords*, 5th Series, Vol. 27, November 1917–January 1918, col. 91.

127 Ibid., col. 472.

128 Ibid., col. 416.

129 There are many examples of articles directly linking female suffrage with women's work in wartime. See, for example, 'Women's Work in Wartime', *The Sphere*, Vol. LXXIII, No. 954, 4/5/1918, and *The Hendon Advertiser*, 3/5/1918, which reported on a speech by the Hon. Mrs John Fortesque where she claimed that women's 'quiet work during this great crisis gained the confidence of the nation and won them the vote.' In this view, she was echoing that of the Prime Minister, Lloyd George, who told the House of Commons during the earlier debate on Franchise and Electoral Reform that 'women's work in the war has been a vital contribution to our success . . . the women's question has become very largely a war question'. *Hansard: House of Commons*, Vol. 92, col. 493.

130 *Evening News*, 9/8/1916, *Pall Mall Gazette*, 6/3/1916. Forteseque's comment regarding 'women's quiet work' in *n*.94 could be seen as an oblique criticism of this phenomenon, and a direct exclusion of their work from the belief that women's war service earned them the vote.

131 *Daily Mail*, 10/6/1916. The same newspaper contrasted 'necessary' with 'unnecessary' work, adopting a well-known recruiting poster to argue that more women were needed in munitions work, asking male readers 'is your best girl in an overall?' *Daily Mail*, 12/6/1916.

4 'Eve in Khaki': the Women's Army Auxiliary Corps

1 G. De Groot, *Blighty: British Society in the Era of the Great War*, London: Longman, 1996, p. 93.
2 Imperial War Museum (IWM), Department of Art, Catalogues and Posters, PRC 136/PST/5061.
3 De Groot, *Blighty*, p. 93.
4 'Ashamed of her Country', *Evening Standard*, 26/8/1914.
5 *Bystander*, 21/6/1916, *Daily Graphic*, 6/11/1916.
6 The National Archives (TNA), War Office (WO) 162/31 *'Conference on the Organization of Women Employed by the Army (in Connection with Military Service)*, 5/1/1917. Adjutant-General Leith-Wood expected 'compulsion for women aged 20–40 in about four months from now'.
7 *The Times*, 13/6/1916.
8 *The Globe*, 19/9/1917.
9 See, for example, 'Are Women Losing Men's Respect?' Max Pemberton, *Parson's Weekly*, 29/9/1917, which attacked both types of women. Pemberton criticised both women in 'the uniform of a well-known corps', a 'bevy of finely-built girls who called each other "old chappie"' and, conversely, girls of leisure who 'flit hither and thither but always of they can to those centres where men congregate'.
10 TNA, HO185/258, *Women's Service Committee, Violet Markham, Notes on Organization of Women Power*, 1/12/1916.
11 See, for example *The Times*, 16/9/1917, *Daily Express*, 15/9/1917, 19/9/1917.
12 *Pall Mall Gazette*, 8/3/1917.
13 IWM, Department of Art, Catalogues and Posters, PRC 49, PST/5102.
14 TNA, WO162/30 *Sir George Newman: Report of the Women's Services Committee*, 14/12/1916, p. 6.
15 Ibid., p. 6.
16 TNA, HO185/258, Markham.
17 Ibid., *Memorandum to Women's Services Committee by Mrs Furse*, 24/11/1916.
18 TNA, WO 162/30, p. 6.
19 By the end of the first day of Battle on the Somme, there were approximately 60,000 British casualties. T. Ashworth, *Trench Warfare 1914–1918. The Live and Let Live System*, London: Macmillan, 1980, p. 55. When the Somme offensive finally ended on 19 November 1916 there were 419,654 British casualties. J. Keegan, *The First World War*, London: Pimlico, 1999, p. 321.
20 IWM, Women's Work Collection (WWC), Lieutenant General H. M. Lawson, *The Number and Physical Catalogue of Men Employed out of the Fighting Area in France and an Economy of Manpower in the Fighting Areas in France*, Army 3/3, January 1917, p. 11.
21 TNA, WO162/30, TNA CAB17/156 Montagu, *'Notes on 3rd Report of Man-Power Distribution Board'*, 18/11/1916.
22 G. D. H. Cole, *Workshop Organization*, Oxford: Clarendon Press, 1923, p. 48, cited in D. Thom, *Nice Girls and Rude Girls: Women Workers in World War One*, London: I.B. Tauris, 1998, p. 55.
23 TNA, WO32/5093, *Letter from Haig to War Office Secretary*, 25/2/1917.
24 Ibid.
25 IWM, WWC, 'Army' 3/4/7, *Letter from Field-Marshal Haig to the Secretary, War Office*, 11/3/1917.
26 TNA, WO32/5093.
27 IWM, WWC, 'Army', 3/4/7, *Letter from Field-Marshal Haig to Lord Derby, Secretary of State for War, War Office*, 28/1/1917.
28 Ibid.
29 TNA, WO32/5093.
30 IWM, WWC, 'Army', 3/4/7.

31 IWM, WWC, 'Army', 3/6/3, *Adjutant General Neville Macready to Lord Derby, Secretary of State for War, War Office*, 24/1/1917.
32 Ibid., Macready, 24/1/1917.
33 Ibid., Derby, 25/1/1917.
34 J. Gould, 'Women's Military Service in First World War Britain' in M. R. Higonnet, J. Jenson, S. Michel and M. Collins Weitz, *Behind the Lines: Gender and the Two World Wars*, New Haven, CT: Yale University Press, 1987, p. 124.
35 TNA, WO162/31, *Conference on the Organization of Women Employed by the Army (in Connection with Compulsory Service)*, 5/1/1917.
36 Ibid., *Mrs Ellis, Women's Legion, Conference*, 15/1/1917.
37 Ibid., 15/1/1917.
38 TNA, WO32/5253 *Women's Army Auxiliary Corps-Status Of*, May 1917.
39 C. Enloe, *Maneuvers: The International Politics of Militarising Women's Lives*, Berkeley, CA: University of California Press, 2000, p. 37.
40 TNA, WO32/5250, *Employment of Women with the Armies at Home and Abroad: Conditions of Service etc.*, February 1917.
41 TNA, WO32/5251, *Women's Service in the Army*, 18/12/1916.
42 TNA, WO32/5530, *Organization of WAAC*, 1917.
43 Ibid.
44 For more discussion of attitudes towards female patriotism, see K. Roberts, 'Gender, Class and Patriotism: Women's Paramilitary Units in First World War Britain', *International History Review*, Vol. XIX, No. 1, February 1997, pp. 52–65.
45 TNA, WO162/6, *History of the Development and Work of the Directorate of Organization August 1914–December 1918*, p. 576.
46 TNA, HO185/258, *Memorandum by Katherine Furse*, 24/11/1916.
47 *Daily Chronicle*, 1/10/1917.
48 This argument is made by Helen Gwynne-Vaughan in her autobiography, where she comments on the civilian titles 'which, I suspect, were given to keep us in our place'. H. Gwynne-Vaughan, *Service With the Army*, London: Hutchinson, 1942, p. 16.
49 S. Grayzel, *Women's Identities at War: Gender, Motherhood and Politics in Britain and France During the First World War*, Chapel Hill, NC: University of North Carolina Press, 1999, p. 198.
50 *Evening Standard*, 26/5/1917.
51 *East Kent Times*, 16/5/1917, also see *Western Mail*, 21/6/1917, which asked its readers 'how many fit men in this huge army are replaceable by women?'
52 WO32/5253.
53 National Army Museum (NAM), WRAC Collection, *Army Council Instruction 1069 of 1917*, 9401-247-433, p. 2.
54 NAM WRAC, 9401-247-433, p. 3.
55 F. Tennyson Jesse, *The Sword of Deborah: First Hand Impressions of the British Women's Army in France*, London: Richard Clay & Sons 1918, p. 59.
56 *Daily Telegraph*, 24/11/1917.
57 *Answers*, 26/1/1918.
58 *Daily Express*, 18/5/1917, *Evening Standard*, 26/5/1917.
59 *The Times*, 28/8/1917, *Weekly Dispatch*, 2/9/1917.
60 Tennyson Jesse, *Sword of Deborah*, p. 27.
61 IWM, Women's Work Collection (WWC), Army 3/3, Lieutenant-General H. M. Lawson, *The Number and Physical Catalogue of Men Employed out of the Fighting Area in France and an Economy of Manpower in the Fighting Areas in France*, January 1917.
62 IWM, WWC, Army, 3/7/5, *Minutes of Conference at War Office*, 11/4/1917.
63 IWM, WWC, Army, 3/8/4, Draft General Rules, WAAC.
64 NAM, WRAC Collection, 9401-252-12, *Dame Helen Gwynne-Vaughan Papers, Letters*, 25/5/1917.

65 TNA, WO32/5252, *Women's Army Auxiliary Corps: Uniform of Officers*.

66 Ibid.

67 NAM, WRAC, 9401-253, *Dame Helen Gwynne-Vaughan Papers, WAAC Routine Orders 1917 (Draft)*.

68 S. Grayzel, ' "The Outward and Visible Sign of Her Patriotism": Women, Uniforms and National Service During the First World War', *Twentieth Century British History*, Vol. 8, No. 2, 1997, p. 157.

69 The image of the 'mannish' lesbian in military uniform was used by Radclyffe Hall in her 1928 novel *The Well of Loneliness*, London: Virago, 1982, first published 1928. Lillian Fayderman claims that 'openly expressed love between women for the most part ceased to be possible after World War 1. Women's changed status and the new medical knowledge cast such affection in a new light'. L. Fayderman, *Surpassing the Love of Men: Romantic Friendship and Love Between Women from the Renaissance to the Present*, New York: Morrow, 1981, p. 20.

70 *The Globe*, 19/9/1917.

71 *National News*, 7/10/1917.

72 *The Spectator*, 9/2/1918.

73 M. H. Mason, 'Tyranny of Fashion in Wartime', *Nineteenth Century and After*, Vol. 31, March 1917, p. 676.

74 Ibid., p. 671.

75 E. Barton and M. Cody, *Eve in Khaki*, London: Nelson, 1918, p. 50.

76 *Punch*, 22/3/1916.

77 Mrs Alec Tweedie, *Women and Soldiers*, London: Bodley Head, 1918, p. 61.

78 *The Times*, 23/3/1917.

79 Ibid., 19/2/1917.

80 *Punch*, Almanack for 1915, Vol. CXLVII.

81 Barton and Cody, *Eve in Khaki*, p. 50. For similar calls, see Tweedie, *Women and Soldiers*, who suggested putting 'every female clerk, munition workers or wage earner of any kind into a cheap simple uniform', p. 58, and letters to *The Times*, 24/1/1917.

82 Doron Lamm provides an alternative explanation for the slowdown in recruitment to the WAAC seen between September 1917 and March 1918, attributing it to wider changes in the demand for women's work. Lamm argues that the flood of applicants to the WAAC in March 1918 had its origins in the contraction of other, more lucrative, employment opportunities such as munitions work. D. Lamm, 'Emily Goes to War: Explaining the Recruitment to the Women's Army Auxiliary Corps in World War One' in B. Melman (ed.) *Borderlines: Genders and Identities in War and Peace*, New York: Routledge, 1998, pp. 377–395.

83 NAM, WRAC Collection, 9401-253-20,*Gwynne-Vaughan papers, letter from Chalmers-Watson to Gwynne-Vaughan, undated*.

84 IWM, DD, 83/17/1, *Papers of Miss O.M. Taylor*.

85 For more on this, see Janet S. K. Watson, 'Khaki Girls, VADs and Tommy's Sisters: Gender and Class in First World War Britain', *The International History Review*, Vol. XIX, No. 1, February 1997, pp. 32–51.

86 S. Kingsley Kent, *Making Peace: The Reconstruction of Gender in Interwar Britain*, Princeton, NJ: Princeton University Press, 1993, pp. 65–73.

87 M. Potter Daggett, *Women Wanted: The Story Written in Blood Red Letters on the Horizon of the Great World War*, London: Hodder & Stoughton, 1918, p. 221.

88 P. Fussell, *The Great War and Modern Memory*, Oxford: Oxford University Press, 1975, p. 86.

89 Col. J. Cowper, *A Short History of the Queen Mary's Army Auxiliary Corps*, Aldershot: WRAC Association, 1957, p. 11.

90 IWM, Documents Department (DD), *Diary of Private Robert Cude*, 15/7/1918.

91 IWM, DD, Misc. 221 3180,*Diary of a Visit to the Western Front by an Anonymous Entertainer*, entries for 25/7/1917 and 27/7/1917.

92 IWM. DD, 82/29/1 *Papers of Captain Paul Sulman*, letter dated 28/11/1917.

93   IWM. DD, Misc. 221 3180, entry for 11/7/1917.
94   'Moral and Social Hygiene: Protest Against Double Standard', *The Vote*, 8/3/1918.
95   Some contemporary commentaries on the role of women in France saw the women as actual or potential victims of a military system which condoned prostitution, and a war in which the ever-present possibility of violent death for the men in the trenches was believed to heighten their sexual appetites. See 'The Cayeux Scandal', *Daily News*, 14/3/1918 in which the Vice President of the YWCA urged that women should not be sent to France until the Maisons Tolerees had been closed down. See also Anon. *WAAC: The Woman's Story of the War*, London: T. Werner Laurie, 1930, where the author, about to leave for France as a VAD recalls her father telling her 'War changes some men's natures completely, makes some of us beasts', p. 12.
96   Tweedie, *Women and Soldiers*, p. 87.
97   *The Times*, 12/7/1917.
98   IWM, DD, Con. Shelf, *Letters of the Honourable D. F. Pickford, Officer with WAAC*, letter dated 30/1/1918.
99   NAM, WRAC, 9401-248-1-3, *Papers of Maud Lillian Emsley*, letter dated 18/9/1917.
100 IWM, DD, 83/17/1, *Papers of Miss O. M. Taylor*.
101 TNA, WO162/42, *Minutes of Weekly Conferences of the Women's Services Held at the Ministry of Labour*, 5/11/1917.
102 Cited in Cowper, *A Short History of the Queen Mary's Army Auxiliary Corps*, p. 44. No further reference given.
103 *Weekly Dispatch*, 13/1/1918, *Daily Sketch*, 24/1/1918.
104 *Daily Sketch*, 24/1/1918.
105 IWM, DD, *Pickford*, 14/3/1918.
106 TNA, WO162/53.
107 TNA, WO162/55, *Notes on Recruitment*, 10/8/1917.
108 *The Times*, 12/2/1918.
109 *Sussex Daily News*, 31/3/1918.
110 *Western Daily News*, 14/2/1918, *Daily Telegraph*, 16/4/1918. W. H. Mainwaring, a socialist leader from South Wales, was also charged and fined £50.00. See *The Vigilance Record*, May 1918.
111 *Manchester Dispatch*, 26/2/1918.
112 *Report of the Commission of Enquiry into the Women's Army Auxiliary Corps in France*, Ministry of Labour, 1918, p. 3, para. 3.
113 *Report of the Commission of Enquiry*, Ministry of Labour, 1918, p. 6, para 11. The Commissioners also suggested that there had been an initial antagonism towards the WAAC amongst the French public – 'a race with domestic customs wholly different from our own', p. 5, para. 10.
114 Figures from N. Goldman and R. Stites, 'Great Britain and the World Wars' in N. Goldman (ed.) *Female Soldiers – Combatants or Non-Combatants? Historical and Contemporary Perspectives*, West Port, CT: Greenwood Press, 1982, p. 26, *Report of the Commission of Enquiry*, Ministry of Labour, 1918, p. 7, para. 13.
115 *Report of the Commission of Enquiry*, Ministry of Labour, 1918, p. 8, para. 17. This suggestion fits into the discourse suggested earlier, in which proximity to the battlefield was closely associated with sex. See Anon., *WAAC*, p. 51 and p. 210 for descriptions of this impulse in both men and women.
116 *Report of the Commission of Enquiry*, Ministry of Labour, 1918, p. 4, para. 7.
117 Ibid., p. 4, para. 7.
118 Ibid., p. 7, para. 15a.
119 See R. Terry, *Women in Khaki: The Story of the British Woman Soldier*, London: Columbus, 1988, p. 73, Cowper, *A Short History of the Queen Mary Army Auxiliary Corps*, 1957, p. 44.
120 *Times*, 1/6/1918. The German offensive also bought to the fore another fear about women in military zones, namely the risk of capture, and potential rape, by the enemy. See Daily Telegraph, 15/4/1918, and also L. Noakes, *War and the British: Gender and National*

Identity 1939–1991, London: I.B. Tauris, 1998, p. 149 for a discussion of similar fears during the 1991 Gulf War.

121 Cited in Terry, *Women in Khaki*, p. 7. Confusingly, the corps was still widely referred to as the WAAC.

122 See, for example, Daily Sketch, 2/4/1918, *Daily Express*, 25/4/1918, *York Herald*, 22/4/1918. Sir William Bull, M. P. drafted a parliamentary Bill to enable female conscription.

123 *Daily Express*, 20/9/1918, *Evening News*, 24/9/1918.

124 See WAAC diaries for this. For example, NAM, WRAC 9401-248-10, papers of Maud Lillian Emsley and IWM, DD 93/30/1, papers of Miss P. Dalgliesh, both of whom record numerous air raids over camps they worked in as WAACs in the spring of 1918.

5 Between the wars: women's military organisations 1919–1938

1 Imperial War Museum (IWM), Department of Documents (DD), Private R. Cude, Diary, Conservation Shelf.

2 IWM, DD, Dorothy Pickford, Letters, Conservation Shelf.

3 Cited in M. Brown, *The Imperial War Museum Book of 1918: Year of Victory*, London: Sidgwick & Jackson, 1998, p. 298.

4 V. Brittain, *Testament of Youth: An Autobiographical Study of the Years 1900–1925*, London: Virago, 1978, first published London: Victor Gollancz, 1935, pp. 460–463.

5 Cited in Brown, *The Imperial War Museum Book of 1918*, p. 299.

6 Figures cited in K. Jeffrey, 'The Post-War Army' in I. Beckett and K. Simpson (eds). *A Nation in Arms: A Social Study of the British Army in the First World War*, Manchester: Manchester University Press, 1985, p. 212, and The National Archive (TNA), War Office (WO) 162/6, *History of the Development and Work of the Directorate of Organization August 1914–December 1918*, p. 591.

7 *Daily Herald*, 7/12/1918.

8 *Daily Express*, 30/12/1918.

9 M. Izzard, *A Heroine in Her Time: A Life of Dame Helen Gwynne-Vaughan 1879–1967*, London: Macmillan, 1969, p. 205. Demonstrations also took place in London, Brighton and Dover.

10 Jeffrey, 'The Post-War Army', p. 213.

11 *Daily Chronicle*, 10/1/1919.

12 IWM, Women's Work Collection, (WWC), Army 3/31/3, *Report of the Women War Workers' Resettlement Committee*, 18/11/1918, p. 4, col. 14.

13 IWM, WWC, Army 3/31/3, 18/11/1918, p. 4, col. 15.

14 For a description of this, see National Army Museum (NAM), Women's Royal Army Corps (WRAC) Archive, 9801-26-2, *Article for 'Tea and Talk'*.

15 'Tommywaacs', *Everyweek*, 28/8/1918.

16 *The Mentor: England Under War Conditions*, Vol. 7, No. 1, 15/2/1919, frontispiece.

17 *Sheffield Daily Telegraph*, 12/6/1919.

18 *The Times*, 28/8/1919. Also see *Liverpool Daily Post*, 31/3/1919 and the *Manchester Dispatch*, 4/4/1919 for similar comment.

19 G. De Groot, *Blighty: British Society in the Era of the Great War*, London: Longman, 1996, p. 262.

20 Irene Clapham, *Towards Sex Freedom*, London: John Lane, 1935, p. 201.

21 *Pall Mall Gazette*, 28/6/1916, *Edinburgh Evening News*, cited in M. Pugh, *Women and the Women's Movement in Britain 1914–1999*, Basingstoke: Macmillan, 1992, p. 81.

22 *Woman Worker*, February 1919, cited in G. Braybon, *Women Workers in the First World War: The British Experience*, London: Croom Helm, 1981, p. 183.

23 *Manchester Evening Chronicle*, 9/1/1919, *Evening Standard*, 9/1/1919, *Truth*, 1/1/1919.

24 *Daily Telegraph*, 22/1/1919.

25 *Daily Express*, 3/1/1919.